Healthful Living

Ellen G. White

CONTENTS

CHAPTER I. - OUR BODIES, TEMPLES OF THE HOLY GHOST.

GOD'S WORKMANSHIP

1. God is the owner of the whole man. Soul, body, and spirit are his.God gave his only begotten Son for the body as well as the soul, and our entire life belongs to God, to be consecrated to his service, that through the exercise of every faculty he has given, we may glorify him.— *The Youth's Instructor*, September 7, 1893.

2. From the first dawn of reason the human mind should become intelligent in regard to the physical structure of the body. Here Jehovah has given a specimen of himself; for man was made in the image of God.—*Unpublished Testimonies*, January 11, 1897.

3. The living organism is God's property. It belongs to him by creationand by redemption; and by a misuse of any of our powers we rob God of the honor due him.—*Unpublished Testimonies*, August 30, 1896.

4. We are God's workmanship, and his word declares that we are "fearfully and wonderfully made." He has prepared this living habitation for the mind; it is "curiously wrought," a temple which the Lord himself has fitted up for the indwelling of the Holy Spirit.—*Special Testimonies On Education*, 33.

5. The very flesh in which the soul tabernacles, and through which itworks, is the Lord's—*Unpublished Testimonies*, October 12, 1896.

CREATION'S CROWN

6. Man was the crowning act of the creation of God, made in the imageof God, and designed to be a counterpart of God…. Man is very dear to God, because he was formed in his own image. This fact should impress us with the importance of teaching by precept and example the sin of defiling, by the indulgence of appetite or by any other sinful practise, the body which is designed to represent God to the world.— *The Review and Herald*, June 18, 1895.

7. The wonderful mechanism of the human body does not receive halfthe care that is often given to a mere lifeless machine.—*Gospel Workers*, 175.

PERSONAL RIGHTS

8. Have I not the right to do as I please with my own body?—No,you have no moral right, because you are violating the laws of life and health which God has given you. You are the Lord's property,—his by creation and his by redemption. Every human being is under obligation to preserve the living machinery that is so fearfully and wonderfully made.—*Unpublished Testimonies*, May 19, 1897.

9. The physical organism should have special care, that the powersof the body may not be dwarfed, but developed to their full extent.—*The Youth's Instructor*, July 27, 1893.

10. The health should be as sacredly guarded as the character.—*Christian Temperance and Bible Hygiene*, 83.

11. Jesus did not ignore the claims of the body, He had respect for thephysical condition of man, and went about healing the sick, and restoring their
faculties to those suffering from their loss. How incumbent, then, is it upon us to preserve the natural health with which God has endowed us, and to avoid dwarfing or weakening our powers.—*The Health Reformer*, November 1, 1877.

MIND SUPREME

12. As they more fully understand the human body, the wonderful workof God's hand, formed in the image of the divine, they will seek to bring their bodies into subjection to the noble powers of the mind. The body will be regarded by them as a wonderful structure, formed by the Infinite Designer, and given into their charge to be kept in harmonious action.—*The Health Reformer*, September 1, 1871.

13. The obligation we owe to God in presenting to him clean, pure,healthy bodies is not comprehended.—*Unpublished Testimonies*, May 19, 1897.

CHRIST IN MAN

14. Christ is to live in his human agents, and work through their faculties, and act through their capabilities.—*Thoughts from the Mount of Blessing*, 128.

15. When human agents choose the will of God, and are conformed to the character of Christ, Jesus acts through their organs and faculties.—*Special Testimonies to Ministers and Workers* 3:49.

16. The Spirit of Christ is to take possession of the organs of speech, ofthe mental powers, of the physical and moral powers.—*Special Testimonies for Ministers and Workers* 6:53.

SERVICE

17. Our very bodies are not our own, to treat as we please, to crippleby habits that lead to decay, making it impossible to render to God perfect service. Our lives and all our faculties belong to him. He is caring for us every moment; he keeps the living machinery in action; if we were left to run it for
one moment, we should die. We are absolutely dependent upon God.—*Unpublished Testimonies*, October 12, 1896.

18. It was a wonderful thing for God to create man, to make mind. Hecreated him that every faculty might be the faculty of the divine mind. The glory of God is to be revealed in the creating of man in God's image, and in his redemption. One soul is of more value than a world. The Lord Jesus is the author of our being, and he is also the author of our redemption; and every one who will enter the kingdom of God must develop a character that is the counterpart of the character of God. None can dwell with God in a holy heaven but those who bear his likeness. Those who are redeemed will be overcomers; they will be elevated, pure, one with Christ.—*The Signs of the Times*, May 31, 1896.

CHAPTER II. - DUTY TO STUDY THE LAWS OF LIFE.

19. It is our duty to study the laws that govern our being, and conform tothem. Ignorance in these things is sin.—*Unpublished Testimonies*, August 25, 1897.

20. From the first dawn of reason, the human mind should becomeintelligent in regard to the physical structure. We may behold and admire the work of God in the natural world, but the human habitation is the most wonderful.—*Unpublished Testimonies*, January 11, 1897.

PHYSIOLOGY AS A STUDY

21. A practical knowledge of the science of human life is necessary inorder to glorify God in our bodies. It is therefore of the highest importance that among studies selected for childhood, physiology should occupy the first place.—The Health Reformer, August 1, 1866.

22. It is well that physiology is introduced into the common schools asa branch of education. All children should study it. It should be regarded as the basis of all educational effort. And then parents should see to it that practical hygiene be added. This will make their knowledge of physiology of practical benefit.—The Health Reformer, November 1, 1871.

IGNORANCE OF PHYSICAL LAWS

23. We have special duties resting upon us. We should be acquainted with our physical structure and the laws controlling natural life. While

Greek and Latin, which are seldom of any advantage, are made

a study by many, physiology and hygiene are barely touched upon. The study to which to give thought is that which concerns natural life, a knowledge of oneself.... It is the house in which we live that we need to preserve, that we may do honor to God who has redeemed us. We need to know how to preserve the living machinery, that our soul, body, and spirit may be consecrated to his service. As rational beings we are deplorably ignorant of the body and its requirements. While the schools we have established have taken up the study of physiology, they have not taken hold with the decided energy they should. They have not practised intelligently that which they have received in knowledge, and do not realize that unless it is practised, the body will decay.... This living machinery should be understood. Every part of its wonderful mechanism should be carefully studied.—*Unpublished Testimonies*, May 19, 1897.

24. Physical life cannot be treated in a haphazard manner. Awaken toyour responsibilities.—*Unpublished Testimonies*, August 25, 1897.

25. Ignorance of physiology and neglect to observe the laws of healthhave brought many to the grave who might have lived to labor and study intelligently.—*Special Testimonies On Education*, 98.

26. To become acquainted with the wonderful human organism,—thebones, muscles, stomach, liver, bowels, heart, and pores of the skin,—and to understand the dependence of one organ upon another for the healthful action of all, is a study in
which most mothers take no interest.—*Testimonies for the Church* 3:136.

27. Study that marvelous organism, the human system, and the laws bywhich it is governed.—*Christian Temperance and Bible Hygiene*, 120.

HOW TO REDUCE MORTALITY

28. If people would reason from cause to effect, and would follow the light which shines upon them, they would pursue a course which would insure health, and the mortality would be far less.... All who possess common capabilities should understand the wants of their own system.—*How to Live*, 51.

LEARN IN YOUTH

29. It is of the highest importance that men and women be instructed inthe science of human life, and in the best means of preserving and acquiring physical health. Especially is youth the time

to lay up a stock of knowledge to be put in daily practise through life.—
The Health Reformer, November 1, 1877.

30. Those who have occupied positions of influence have not appreciated the work which has been so long neglected.... They consider it far more important to become learners upon subjects of less consequence to the human agent. Thousands upon thousands know nothing of the body, and how to care for it. David declared, "I am fearfully and wonderfully made." And when God has given us such a habitation, why should not every apartment be critically examined?— *Unpublished Testimonies*, January 11, 1897.

31. It is best for those who claim to be sons and daughters of God toavail themselves, while they can, of the opportunities now presented to gain a knowledge of the human system, and how it may be
preserved in health.... The Lord will not work a miracle to preserve any one in health who will not make an effort to obtain knowledge within his reach concerning this wonderful habitation that God has given. By the study of the human organism we are to learn to correct what may be wrong in our habits, and which, if left uncorrected, will bring the sure result, disease and suffering, that make life a burden.... Let the mind become intelligent, and the will be placed on the Lord's side, and there will be a wonderful improvement in the physical health. But this can never be accomplished in mere human strength.—The Medical Missionary, December 1, 1892.

DUTY OF MINISTERS

32. The ministers in our land need to become acquainted with the science of physiology. Then they will be intelligent in regard to the laws that govern physical life, and their bearings upon the health of mind and soul. Then they will be able to speak correctly upon this subject. In their obedience to physical laws they are to hold forth the word of life to the people, and lead up higher and still higher in the work of reform.—*Unpublished Testimonies*, January 11, 1897.

33. In order to be fitted for translation, the people of God must knowthemselves. They must understand in regard to their own physical frames, that they may be able with the psalmist to exclaim, "I will praise thee, for I am fearfully and wonderfully made."—*Testimonies for the Church* 1:486.

CHAPTER III. - THE GREAT DECALOGUE.

CHARACTER OF GOD

34. He who hungers and thirsts after God will seek for an understandingof the laws which the God of wisdom has impressed upon creation. These laws are a transcript of his character. They must control all who enter the heavenly and better country.—*Unpublished Testimonies*, August 30, 1896.

35. God's law is written by his own finger upon every nerve, everymuscle, every faculty which has been entrusted to man.—*Unpublished Testimonies*, August 30, 1896.

OBEDIENCE TO LAW

36. God in his wisdom has established natural laws for the proper control of our dress, our appetites, and our passions, and he requires of us obedience in every particular.—The Review and Herald, October 16, 1883.

PHYSICAL SIN

37. The transgression of physical law is transgression of God's law. Our Creator is Jesus Christ. He is the author of our being. He is the author of the physical law as he is the author of the moral law. And the human being who is careless and reckless of the habits and practises that concern his physical life and health, sins against God. God is not reverenced, respected, or recognized. This is shown by the injury done to the body in violation of physical law.—*Unpublished Testimonies*, May 19, 1897.

BLESSINGS FOLLOW OBEDIENCE

38. God loves his creatures with a love that is both tender and strong.

He has established the laws of nature; but his laws are not arbitrary exactions. Every "Thou shalt not," whether in physical or moral law, contains or implies a promise. If it is obeyed, blessings will attend our steps; if it is disobeyed, the result is danger and unhappiness.—*Testimonies For The Church ?:5.444.*

39. Health, strength, and happiness depend upon immutable laws; but these laws cannot be obeyed where there is no anxiety to become acquainted with them.—The Health Reformer, September 1, 1871.

40. A knowledge of the laws by which health is secured and preservedis of pre-eminent importance.—Signs of the Times, August 26, 1886.

41. Indifference and ignorance in regard to the laws which govern ourbeing are sins so common that we have learned to look upon them with undue tolerance.—The Health Reformer, February 1, 1877.

42. We have no right wantonly to violate a single principle of the lawsof health.—*The Review and Herald*, July 29, 1884.

43. God is greatly dishonored by the way in which man treats his organism, and he will not work a miracle to counteract a perverse violation of the laws of life and health.—*Unpublished Testimonies*, August 30, 1896.

44. The Lord has made it a part of his plan that man's reaping shall beaccording to his sowing.—*Unpublished Testimonies*, May 19, 1897.

HEREDITY

45. Wherever the habits of the parents are contrary to physical law, the injury done to themselves will be repeated in future generations.—*Unpublished Testimonies*, January 11, 1897.

46. You should move out from principle, in harmony with natural law,irrespective of feeling.—*Testimonies for the Church* 3:76.

47. To make plain natural law, and urge the obedience of it, is thework that accompanies the third angel's message to prepare a people for the coming of the Lord.—*Testimonies for the Church* 3:161.

48. A flower of the field must have its root in the soil; it must haveair, dew, showers, and sunshine. It will flourish only as it receives these advantages, and all are from God. So with man.—*Special Instruction Relating to the Review and Herald Office*, and The Work in Battle Creek, 36.

49. God calls for reformers to stand in defense of the laws he has established to govern the human system, and to maintain an elevated standard in the training of the mind and culture of the heart.—*Special Testimonies to Ministers and Workers* 3:22.

KNOWLEDGE A DUTY

50. It is the duty of every human being, for his own sake and for the sakeof humanity, to inform himself or herself in regard to the laws of organic life, and conscientiously to obey them.... It is the duty of every person to become intelligent in regard to disease and its causes. You must study your Bible, in order to understand the value that the Lord places on the men whom Christ has purchased at such an infinite price. Then we should become acquainted with the laws of life, that every action of the human agent may be in perfect harmony with the laws of God. When there is so great peril in ignorance, is it not best to be wise in regard to the human habitation fitted up by our Creator, and over which he desires that we shall be faithful stewards?—*Unpublished Testimonies*, December 4, 1896.

CHAPTER IV. - NATURAL LAW PART OF THE LAW OF GOD.

51. The same law obtains in the spiritual as in the natural world.—*Thoughts from the Mount of Blessing*, 126.

52. The transgression of the physical law is transgression of God's law.
Our Creator is Jesus Christ.—*Unpublished Testimonies*, May 19, 1897.

NATURAL LAW DIVINE

53. Every law governing the human machinery is to be considered justas truly divine in origin, in character, and in importance as the word of God. Every careless action, any abuse put upon the wonderful

mechanism, by disregarding his specified laws of the human habitation, is a violation of God's law. This law embraces the treatment of the entire being. *Unpublished Testimonies*, January 11, 1897.

54. God's law is written by his own finger upon every nerve, everymuscle, every faculty which has been entrusted to man.— *Unpublished Testimonies*, August 30, 1896.

ITS PENALTY

55. God has formed laws to govern every part of our constitutions,and these laws which he has placed in our being are divine, and for every transgression there is a fixed penalty, which sooner or later must be realized.—The Health Reformer, October 1, 1866.

56. Our first duty, one which we owe to God, to ourselves, and toour fellow men, is to obey the laws of God, which include the laws of health.—*Testimonies for the Church* 3:164.

57. The laws governing the physical nature are as truly divine in theirorigin and character as the law of the ten commandments. Man is fearfully and wonderfully made; for Jehovah has inscribed his law by his own mighty hand on every part of the human body.—*Unpublished Testimonies*, August 5, 1896.

PHYSICAL SIN

58. It is just as much sin to violate the laws of our being as to break oneof the ten commandments, for we cannot do either without breaking God's law.—*Testimonies for the Church* 2:70.

59. The human being who is careless and reckless of the habits and practises that concern his physical life and health, sins against God.— *Unpublished Testimonies*, May 19, 1897.

60. A violation of these laws is a violation of the immutable law of God, and the penalty will surely follow.—*The Review and Herald*, October 16, 1883.

CHAPTER V. - BLESSINGS FROM OBEYING NATURAL LAW.

61. Those who understand something of the wisdom and beneficenceof his laws, and perceive the evidences of God's love and the blessings that result from obedience, will come to regard their duties and obligations from an altogether different point of view. Instead of looking upon the observance of the laws of health as a matter of sacrifice and self-denial, they will regard it, as it really is, an inestimable blessing.—*Christian Temperance and Bible Hygiene*, 120.

62. All our enjoyment or suffering may be traced to obedience or transgression of natural law.—*Testimonies for the Church* 3:161.

CO-OPERATION

63. God, the Creator of our bodies, has arranged every fiber and nerveand sinew and muscle, and has pledged himself to keep the machinery in order if the human agent will co-operate with him and refuse to work contrary to the laws which govern the human system.—*Unpublished Testimonies*, August 30, 1896.

64. A careful conformity to the laws which God has implanted in ourbeing will insure health, and there will not be a breaking down of the constitution.—The Health Reformer, August 1, 1866.

65. God has pledged himself to keep this machinery in healthful action if the human agent will obey his laws, and co-operate with him.—*Unpublished Testimonies*, January 11, 1897.

66. Every "Thou shall not," whether in physical or moral law, contains or implies a promise. If it is obeyed, blessings will attend our steps.—*Testimonies for the Church* 5:444.

67. He requires us to obey natural law, to preserve physical health.—*Testimonies for the Church* 3:63.

68. If Christians will keep the body in subjection, and bring all theirappetites and passions under the control of enlightened conscience, feeling it a duty that they owe to God and to their neighbors to obey the laws which govern health and life, they will have the blessing of physical and mental vigor. They will have moral power to engage in the warfare against Satan; and in the name of him who conquered

appetite in their behalf, they may be more than conquerors on their own account.—*Testimonies for the Church* 4:36.

ADHERENCE TO PRINCIPLE

69. If laborers who are now in the field had intelligently used their physical and mental powers according to the laws of hygiene, they would not only have been able to become proficient in common branches of education, but would have been versed in different languages, and thus would have been qualified to become missionaries in foreign countries.—*The Youth's Instructor*, May 31, 1894.

70. The souls and bodies of people have been fast becoming a corrupted mass of disease. This would not have been the case if those who claimed to believe the truth had lived out its sacred principles in their lives.—*Unpublished Testimonies*, January 11, 1897.

71. If man had obeyed the laws of Jehovah in his natural laws, theimage of God would have been revealed in him.—*Ibid*.

CHAPTER VI. - THE CONSEQUENCE OF VIOLATING

Natural Law.

72. Proportionately as nature's laws are transgressed, mind and soulbecome enfeebled.... Physical suffering of every type is seen.... Suffering must follow this course of action. The vital force of the system cannot bear up under the tax placed upon it, and it finally breaks down.—*Unpublished Testimonies*, August 30, 1896.

CAUSE OF SICKNESS

73. Every misuse of any part of our organism is a violation of the law which God designs shall govern us in these matters; and by violating this law, human beings corrupt themselves. Sickness, disease of every kind, ruined constitutions, premature decay, untimely deaths,—these are a result of a violation of nature's laws.—*Unpublished Testimonies*, August 30, 1896.

74. Sickness is caused by violating the laws of health; it is the result of violating nature's laws.—*Testimonies for the Church* 3:164.

75. The gloom and despondency supposed to be the result of obedience to God's moral law are often attributable to disregard of physical laws.—*The Signs of the Times*, June 15, 1882.

DISEASED SOULS

76. Everything that conflicts with natural law creates a diseased condition of the soul.—*The Review and Herald*, January 25, 1881.

77. The moral powers are weakened because men and women will not live in obedience to the laws of health, and make this great subject a personal duty.—*Testimonies for the Church* 3:140.

WE REAP WHAT WE SOW

78. The Lord has made it a part of his plan that man's reaping shall be according to his sowing. And this is the explanation of the misery and suffering in our world, which is charged back upon God. The man who serves himself, and makes a god of his stomach, will reap that which is the sure result of the violation of nature's laws. He who abuses any organ of the body to gratify lustful appetites and debased passions will bear testimony to the same in his countenance. He has sown to fleshly lusts, and he will just as surely realize the consequence. He is like a hunted being; he is a slave to passion, the chains of which he is unwilling to break. And at last he is left of God, without conviction, without mercy, without hope, to destroy himself. He is left to the natural processes of corrupting practises which degrade him beneath the brute creation. His sinfulness has ruined the mechanism of the living machinery, and nature's laws, transgressed, become his tormentors.—*Unpublished Testimonies*, May 19, 1897.

CONTROL OF WILL

79. Satan knows that he cannot overcome man unless he can control his will. He can do this by deceiving men so they will co-operate with him in transgressing the laws of nature, which is transgression of the law of God.—*Unpublished Testimonies*, January 11, 1897.

SATAN TAUNTING GOD

80. The results which Satan has, through his specious temptations, brought about, he uses to taunt God with. He presents before God the appearance of
the human being whom Christ has purchased as his property. And what an unsightly representation of his Maker! God is dishonored, because man has corrupted his ways before the Lord.—*Unpublished Testimonies*, January 11, 1897.

81. One human being becomes Satan's copartner to tempt, allure, anddeceive his fellow men to vicious practises; and the sure result is diseased bodies, because of the violation of moral law. "Because iniquity shall abound, the love of many shall wax cold." It is Satan's determined purpose to deceive the human family so that he can bring them as a mass on his side, to work with him in making void the law of God. Thus he finds agencies which multiply his efficiency. And as they do this, he rules them with a rod of iron. And not only the human race, but the brute creation also are made to suffer through Satan's attributes wrought out through the human agent.—*Unpublished Testimonies*, January 11, 1897.

CHAPTER VII. - NATURAL LAW; HOW VIOLATED.

GENERAL STATEMENTS

82. Needlessly to transgress the laws of our being is a violation of thelaw of God.—*Testimonies for the Church* 2:538.

83. If we unnecessarily injure our constitutions, we dishonor God, forwe transgress the laws of our being.—The Health Reformer, October 1, 1871.

84. If appetite, which should be strictly guarded and controlled, is indulged to the injury of the body, the penalty of transgression will surely result.—*Unpublished Testimonies*, August 30, 1896.

85. Every careless action, any abuse put upon the Lord's mechanism,by disregarding his specified laws in the human habitation, is a violation of God's law.—*Unpublished Testimonies*, January 11, 1897.

86. Intemperance of any kind is a violation of the laws of our being.—The Health Reformer, March 1, 1878 par. 2.

INDULGENCE OF APPETITE

87. The laws of our being cannot be more successfully violated than bycrowding upon the stomach unhealthful food just because it is craved by a morbid appetite.—*How to Live*, 52.

88. Eating merely to please the appetite is a transgression of nature'slaws.—*Unpublished Testimonies*, August 30, 1896.

89. Any course of action in eating, drinking, or dressing that is unhealthful injures the fine works of the human machinery, and interferes with God's order. Obstructions are created in bone, brain, and muscle, which destroy this wonderful machinery that God has organized to be kept in order. Any misuse of the delicate workmanship results in suffering.—*Unpublished Testimonies*, May 19, 1897.

90. God has not changed, neither does he propose to change, our physical organism, in order that we may violate a single law without feeling the effects of its violation.... By indulging their inclinations and appetites, men violate the laws of life and health; and if they obey conscience, they must be controlled by principle in their eating and

dressing, rather than be led by inclination, fashion, and appetite.—The Health Reformer, September 1, 1871.

LACK OF EXERCISE

91. Neglecting to exercise the entire body, or a portion of it, will bring on morbid conditions. Inaction of any of the organs of the body will be followed by a decrease in size and strength of the muscles, and will cause the blood to flow sluggishly through the blood-vessels.— *Testimonies for the Church* 3:76

CHAPTER VIII. - HEALTH.

GENERAL STATEMENTS

92. Health is a great treasure. It is the richest possession that mortalscan have. Wealth, honor, or learning is dearly purchased, if it be at the loss of the vigor of health. None of these attainments can secure happiness if health is wanting.—*Christian Education*, 16.

93. The health should be as sacredly guarded as the character.— *Christian Temperance and Bible Hygiene*, 83.

94. Our physical, mental, and moral powers are not our own, but lentus of God to be used in his service.—The Health Reformer, November 1, 1877.

95. The more perfect our health, the more perfect will be our labor.—*Testimonies for the Church* 3:13.

96. The importance of the health of the body is to be taught as a Biblerequirement.—*Unpublished Testimonies*, August 30, 1896.

97. All who profess to be followers of Jesus should feel that a duty restsupon them to preserve their bodies in the best condition of health, that their minds may be clear to comprehend heavenly things.— *Testimonies for the Church* 2:522.

98. That time is well spent which is directed to the establishment andpreservation of sound physical and mental health.... It is easy to lose health, but it is difficult to regain it.—*The Review and Herald*, September 23, 1884.

CIRCULATION

99. Perfect health depends upon perfect circulation.—*Testimonies for the Church* 2:531.

100. The health of the entire system depends upon the healthy action ofthe respiratory organs.—*How to Live*, 57.

101. If we would have health, we must live for it.—The Health Reformer, December 1, 1870.

102. We can ill afford to dwarf or cripple a single function of mind orbody by overwork, or by abuse of any part of the living machinery.—*The Review and Herald*, September 23, 1884.

103. A sound body is required for a sound intellect.—*Christian Education*, 17.

FAITH AND PRACTISE

104. When we do all we can on our part to have health, then may weexpect that the blessed results will follow, and we can ask God in faith to bless our efforts for the preservation of health. He will then answer our prayer, if his name can be glorified thereby; but let all understand that they have a work to do. God will not work in a miraculous manner to preserve the health of persons who are taking a sure course to make themselves sick.—*How to Live*, 64.

105. A careful conformity to the laws God has implanted in our being will insure health, and there will not be a breaking down of the constitution.—The Health Reformer, August 1, 1866.

HOW TO PRESERVE HEALTH

106. Many have inquired of me, What course shall I take best to preserve my health? My answer is, Cease to transgress the laws of your being; cease to gratify a depraved appetite, eat simple food, dress healthfully, which will require modest simplicity,
work healthfully, and you will not be sick.... Many are suffering in consequence of the transgression of their parents. They cannot be censured for their parents' sins, but it is nevertheless their duty to ascertain wherein their parents violated the laws of their being; and wherein their parents' habits were wrong, they should change their own

course, and place themselves, by correct habits, in a better relation to health.—The Health Reformer, August 1, 1866.

107. The harmonious, healthy action of all the powers of body andmind results in happiness; the more elevated and refined the powers, the more pure and unalloyed the happiness. An aimless life is a living death. The mind should dwell upon themes relating to our eternal interests. This will be conducive to health of body and mind.— *The Review and Herald*, July 29, 1884.

108. God has pledged himself to keep this living machinery in healthful action if the human agent will obey his laws and co-operate with God.—*Unpublished Testimonies*, January 11, 1897.

CHAPTER IX. - HEALTH REFORM.

LIGHT GIVEN

109. The Lord has given his people a message in regard to health reform. This light has been shining upon their pathway for thirty years, and the Lord cannot sustain his servants in a course which will counteract it.... Can he be pleased when half the workers laboring in a place teach that the principles of health reform are as closely allied to the third angel's message as the arm is to the body, to have their co-workers, by their practise, teach principles that are entirely opposite? ... The light which God has given upon health reform cannot be trifled with without injury to those who attempt it; and no man can hope to succeed in the work of God while, by precept and example, he acts in opposition to the light which God has sent.—*Special Testimonies for Ministers and Workers* 7:40.

110. No man, woman, or child who fails to use all the powers Godhas given him can retain his health. He cannot conscientiously keep the commandments of God. He cannot love God supremely and his neighbor as himself.—*Unpublished Testimonies*, September 17, 1897.

111. We begin to comprehend better the light given years ago,—thathealth reform principles would be as an entering wedge to be followed by a religious influence.—*Unpublished Testimonies*, November 19, 1895.

112. Your interest and effort are to be given, not to the health questionalone, but to making known the truths for these last times, truths that are deciding the destiny of souls.—*Unpublished Testimonies*, May 29, 1896.

COMMON SENSE IN HEALTH REFORM

113. There is real common sense in health reform.—*Christian Temperance and Bible Hygiene*, 57.

114. The principles of health reform have the highest authority, anddeserve a wider sphere than has yet been given them by many who profess present truth.—*Unpublished Testimonies*, November 8, 1896.

115. God's way is to make man something he is not; God's plan is to setman to work in reformatory lines; then he will learn by experience how long he has pampered fleshly appetites, and ministered to his own temperament, bringing weakness upon himself.—*Unpublished Testimonies*, October 12, 1896.

116. There are those who have stood directly in the way of the advanceof health reform. They have held the people back by their indifferent or depreciatory remarks, and their supposed pleasantries and jokes.... Had all walked unitedly in the light, from the time it was first given on the subject, there would have been an army of sensible arguments employed to vindicate the work of God. But it has only been by the most aggressive movements that any advance has been made....

DUTY OF MINISTERS

The ministers of our land should become intelligent upon health reform. They need to become acquainted with the science of physiology. Then they will be intelligent in regard to the laws that govern physical life and their bearings upon the health of mind and soul, and will be able to speak correctly upon this subject. In their obedience to

physical laws they are to hold forth the word of life to the people, and lead up higher and still higher in the work of reform.—*Unpublished Testimonies*, January 11, 1897.

117. Blindness mingles with the want of moral courage to deny yourappetite, to lift the cross, which means to take up the very duties

that cut across the natural appetites and passions.—*Unpublished Testimonies*, November 5, 1896.

118. Many have misinterpreted health reform, and have received perverted ideas of what constitutes right living.—*The Youth's Instructor*, May 31, 1894.

119. Nature's path is the road God marks out, and it is broad enoughfor any Christian.—*Testimonies for the Church* 3:63.

AVOID EXTREMES

120. Health reformers, above all others, should be careful to shun extremes.—*Testimonies for the Church* 2:538.

121. All are bound by the most sacred obligations to God to heed the sound philosophy and genuine experience which he is now giving them in reference to health reform. He designs that the great subject of health reform shall be agitated, and the public mind deeply stirred to investigate.—*Testimonies for the Church* 3:162.

122. Do not catch hold of isolated ideas, and make them a test, criticising others whose practise may not agree with your opinion; but study the subject broadly and deeply.—*Christian Temperance and Bible Hygiene*, 119, 120.

123. The lack of stability in regard to the principles of health reform isa true index of their character and their spiritual strength.—*Testimonies for the Church* 2:481.

124. When we adopt the health reform, we should adopt it from a sense of duty, not because somebody else has adopted it.—*Testimonies for the Church* 2:371.

THE EDUCATIONAL PROCESS

125. In reforms we would better come one step short of the mark than go one step beyond it. And if there is error at all, let it be on the side next to the people.... We must go no faster than we can take those with us whose consciences and intellects are convinced of the truths we advocate. We must meet the people where they are.... But we should be very cautious not to advance too fast, lest we be obliged to retrace our steps.... If we come to persons who have not been enlightened in regard to health reform, and present our strongest positions at first, there is

danger of their becoming discouraged as they see how much they have to give up, so that they will make no effort to reform. We must lead the people along patiently and gradually, remembering the hole of the pit from which we were digged.—*Testimonies for the Church* 3:20, 21.

126. The greatest objection to health reform is that this people do notlive it out.—*Testimonies for the Church* 2:486.

127. Guilt rests upon us who as a people have had much light, becausewe have not appreciated or improved the light given upon health reform.... This is not a matter to be trifled with, to be passed off with a jest.—*The Medical Missionary*, 216.

Relation of Health Reform to the Present Closing Work.

An Entering Wedge.

128. This work we begin to comprehend better,—the light given yearsago,—that health reform principles would be as an entering wedge to be followed by a religious influence. To voice the words of John, "Behold the Lamb of God, which taketh away the sin of the world,"— *Unpublished Testimonies*, November 19, 1895.

129. In the time of confusion and trouble such as never was since therewas a nation, the uplifted Saviour will be presented to the people in all lands and in all places, that all who look may live.—*Special Testimonies Relating to Various Matters in Battle Creek*, 7.

130. The need of healthful habits is a part of the gospel which must be presented to the people by those who hold forth the word of life. Every minister should carefully consider what effect eating and drinking have upon the health of the soul. By precept and example, by a life of obedience to nature's laws, he can present the truth in a forcible manner.—*Unpublished Testimonies*, August 30, 1896.

131. Take the living principles of health reform into communities thatto a large degree are ignorant of what they should do.—*Special Testimonies for Ministers and Workers* 5:5.

PREPARATION FOR LOUD CRY

132. We as a people must make an advance move in this great work.Ministers and people must act in concert. God's people are not prepared for the loud cry of the third angel; they have a work to do for themselves which they should not leave for God to do for them. It is an

individual work; one cannot do it for another.—*Testimonies for the Church* 1:486.

133. You have stumbled at the health reform. It appears to you to be a needless appendix to the truth. It is not so; it is a part of the truth.—*Testimonies for the Church* 1:546.

134. Its place is among those subjects which set forth the preparatorywork to meet the events brought to view by the message; among them it is prominent.—*Testimonies for the Church* 1:559.

135. The presentation of health principles must be united with this message, but must not be independent of it or in any way take the place of it.—*Unpublished Testimonies*, May 27, 1896.

136. This branch of the Lord's work has not received due attention, andthrough this neglect much has been lost.—*Christian Temperance and Bible Hygiene*, 121.

PREJUDICE REMOVED

137. Much of the prejudice that prevents the truth of the third angel's message from reaching the hearts of the people, might be removed if more attention were given to health reform. When people become interested in this subject, the way is often prepared for the entrance of other truths.—*Christian Temperance and Bible Hygiene*, 121.

138. Those who proclaim the message should teach health reform also.... Satan and his angels are seeking to hinder this work of reform, and will do all they can to perplex and burden those who heartily engage in it.—*Christian Temperance and Bible Hygiene*, 122.

139. To make plain natural law, and urge the obedience of it, is thework that accompanies the third angel's message, to prepare a people for the coming of the Lord.—*Testimonies for the Church* 3:161.

OBJECT OF HEALTH REFORM

140. Let it ever be kept before the mind that the great object of hygienicreform is to secure the highest possible development of mind and soul and body.—*Christian Temperance and Bible Hygiene*, 120.

141. He who cherishes the light which God has given him upon healthreform has an important aid in the work of becoming sanctified

through the truth, and fitted for immortality.—*Christian Temperance and Bible Hygiene*, 10.

142. God requires all who believe the truth to make special perseveringefforts to place themselves in the best possible condition of bodily health, for a solemn and important work is before us. Health of body and mind is required for this work; it is as essential to a healthy religious experience, to advancement in the Christian life, and progress in holiness, as is the hand or foot to the human body.—*Testimonies for the Church* 1:619 Relation of Health Reform to Spirituality.

Control of the Will.

143. Satan knows that he cannot overcome man unless he can controlhis will. He can do this by deceiving man so that he will co-operate with him in transgressing the laws of nature.—*Unpublished Testimonies*, January 11, 1897.

144. Anything that lessens the physical power enfeebles the mind andmakes it less clear to discriminate between good and evil, between right and wrong.—*Special Testimonies On Education*, 35.

145. The principles of health reform, ... which are adopted by him whogives the word of God to others, will have a molding influence upon his work, and upon those with whom he labors. If his principles are wrong, he can and will misrepresent the truth to others; if he accepts the truth which appeals to reason rather than to perverted appetite, his influence for the right will be decided.—*Special Testimonies for Ministers and Workers* 7:41.

LIGHT UNHEEDED

146. One reason why we do not enjoy more of the blessing of the Lordis, we do not heed the light which he has been pleased to give us in regard to the laws of life and health.—The Review and Herald, May 8, 1883.

147. The lack of stability in regard to the principles of health reform isa true index of their character and their spiritual strength.—*Testimonies for the Church* 2:487.

148. It is not possible for us to glorify God while living in violation ofthe laws of life.—The Health Reformer, March 1, 1878.

149. All who profess to be followers of Jesus should feel that a dutyrests upon them to preserve their bodies in the best condition of health, that their minds may be clear to comprehend heavenly things.—*Testimonies for the Church* 2:522.

THE INFLUENCE OF HABIT

150. If our physical habits are not right, our mental and moral powerscannot be strong; for great sympathy exists between the physical and the moral.... Habits which lower the standard of physical health, enfeeble the mental and moral strength.—*Testimonies for the Church* 3:50, 51.

151. If you pursue a wrong course, and indulge in wrong habits ofeating, and thereby weaken the intellectual powers, you will not place that high estimate upon salvation and eternal life which will inspire you to conform your life to the life of Christ; you will not make those earnest, self-sacrificing
efforts for entire conformity to the will of God which his word requires, and which are necessary to give you a moral fitness for the finishing touch of immortality.—*Testimonies for the Church* 2:66.

152. In order to live a perfect life, we must live in harmony with thosenatural laws which govern our being.—*Testimonies for the Church* 3:163.

EFFECTS UPON THE MIND

153. That which darkens the skin and makes it dingy, also clouds the spirits, and destroys the cheerfulness and peace of mind.... Every wrong habit which injures the health of the body, reacts in effect upon the mind.—The Health Reformer, February 1, 1877.

154. Those things which fret and derange the stomach will have a benumbing influence upon the finer feelings of the heart.—*Testimonies for the Church* 2:537.

155. The gloom and despondency supposed to be the result of obedience to God's moral law is often attributable to disregard of physical law. Those whose moral faculties are beclouded by disease are not the ones rightly to represent the Christian life, and show forth the joys of salvation or the beauties of holiness. They are too often in the

fire of fanaticism, or the waters of cold indifference or stolid gloom.—
Signs of the Times, June 15, 1882.

156. Unless they practise true temperance, they will not, they cannot, be susceptible to the sanctifying influence of the truth.—*Christian Temperance and Bible Hygiene*, 117.

157. Eating, drinking, and dressing all have a direct bearing upon ourspiritual advancement.—*The Youth's Instructor*, May 31, 1894.

158. By indulging in a wrong course of action in eating and drinking,thousands upon thousands are
ruining their health, and not only is their health ruined, but their morals are corrupted, because diseased blood flows through their veins.—*Unpublished Testimonies*, August 30, 1896. Morals Corrupted.

159. Overeating prevents the free flow of thought and words, and thatintensity of feeling which is so necessary in order to impress the truth upon the heart of the hearer.—*Testimonies for the Church* 3:310.

160. Excessive eating of even the best of food will produce a morbidcondition of the moral feelings.... Wrong habits of eating and drinking lead to errors in thought and action. Indulgence of appetite strengthens the animal propensities, giving them the ascendency over the mental and spiritual powers.... Everything that conflicts with natural law creates a diseased condition of the soul.—*The Review and Herald*, January 25, 1881.

161. Irregularity in eating and drinking, and improper dressing, depravethe mind and corrupt the heart, and bring the noble attributes of the soul in slavery to the animal passions.—The Health Reformer, October 1, 1871.

162. If those who profess to be Christians desire to solve the questionsso perplexing to them,—why their minds are so dull, why their religious aspirations are so feeble,—they need not, in many instances, go farther than the table; here is cause enough, if there were no other.—*Christian Temperance and Bible Hygiene*, 83.

163. A religious life can be more successfully gained and maintainedif flesh meats are discarded; for a meat diet stimulates into intense activity lustful propensities, and enfeebles the spiritual and moral nature.—*Unpublished Testimonies*, November 5, 1896.

164. Children reared in a healthful way are much more easily controlledthan those who are indulged in eating everything their appetite craves, and at all times. They are usually cheerful, contented,

and healthy. Even the most stubborn, passionate, and wayward have become submissive, patient, and possessed of self-control by persistently following up this order of diet, united with a firm but kind management in regard to other matters.—The Health Reformer, May 1, 1877.

A LIVING SACRIFICE

165. The Lord requires a *living* sacrifice of mind, soul, body, and strength. All that we have and are is to be given him, that we may answer the purpose of our creation.—*Unpublished Testimonies*, August 25, 1897.

166. True sanctification is not merely a theory, an emotion, or a formof words, but a living, active principle, entering into the every-day life. It requires that our habits of eating, drinking, and dressing be such as to secure the preservation of physical, mental, and moral health, that we may present to the Lord our bodies, not an offering corrupted by wrong habits, but a "living sacrifice, holy, acceptable unto God."—*The Review and Herald*, January 25, 1881.

167. It should ever be kept prominent that the great object to be attained through this channel is not only health, but perfection and the spirit of holiness, which cannot be attained with diseased bodies and minds. This object cannot be secured by working merely from the worldling's standpoint.—*Testimonies for the Church* 1:554.

168. A diseased body causes a disordered brain, and hinders the workof sanctifying grace upon the mind and heart.—The Health Reformer, September 1, 1871.

169. If man will cherish the light that God in mercy gives him upon health reform, he may be sanctified through the truth, and fitted for immortality.—*Testimonies for the Church* 3:162.

170. If Christians ... obey the laws which govern health and life, theywill have the blessing of physical and mental vigor. They will have moral power to engage in the warfare against Satan; and in the name of him who conquered appetite in their behalf, they may be more than conquerors on their own account.—*Testimonies for the Church* 4:35, 36.

171. The character and efficiency of the work depend largely on thephysical condition of the workers.... Many a sermon has received a dark shadow from the minister's indigestion. Health is an inestimable

blessing, and one which is more closely allied to conscience and religion than many realize.—*Gospel Workers*, 175.

172. In order to render to God perfect service, we must have a clearconception of his will. This will require us to use only healthful food, prepared in a simple manner, that the fine nerves of the brain be not injured, making it impossible for us to discern the value of the atonement, and the priceless worth of the cleansing blood of Christ.— *The Review and Herald*, March 18, 1880.

God's Plan. The Kingdom Within.

173. God's way is to give man something that he has not, to makehim something that he is not. Man's way is to get an easy place, and indulge appetite and selfish ambition. God's plan is to set man at work in reformatory lines, then he will learn by experience how long he has tampered with fleshly appetites, and
ministered to his own temperament, bringing weakness upon himself. God's way is to work in power. He gives grace if the sick man realizes that he needs it. God proposes to purify and refine the defiled soul, then he will implant in the heart his own righteousness and peace and health, and man will become complete in him. This is the kingdom of God within you. Day by day men are revealing whether the kingdom of God is within them. If Christ rules in their hearts, they are gaining strength of principle, with power and ability to stand as faithful sentinels, true reformers. Then, like Daniel, they make impressions upon other hearts that will never be effaced, and their influence will be carried to all parts of the world.—*Unpublished Testimonies*, October 12, 1896.

OUR DUTY TO OTHERS

174. It is the duty of those who have received light upon this importantsubject to manifest a greater interest for those who are still suffering for want of knowledge. Those who are looking for the soon appearing of their Saviour should be the last to manifest a lack of interest in this great work of reform.... This (2 Corinthians 7:1) is our work as Christians, to cleanse our robes of character from every spot. The spirit must be in harmony with the Spirit of Christ; the habits must be in conformity to his will, in obedience to his requirements.—*The Review and Herald*, July 29, 1884.

CHAPTER X. - VITAL VIGOR AND ENERGY.

General Statements.

175. God has provided us with constitutional force, which will be needed at different periods of our life. If we recklessly exhaust this force by continual overtaxation, we shall sometime be losers. Our usefulness will be lessened, if not life itself destroyed.—*Christian Temperance and Bible Hygiene*, 65.

176. God endowed man with so great vital force that he has withstoodthe accumulation of disease upon the race in consequence of perverted habits, and has continued for six thousand years....

If Adam, at his creation, had not been endowed with twenty times as much vital force as men now have, the race, with their present habits of living in violation of natural law, would have become extinct.—*Testimonies for the Church* 3:138, 139.

177. The tree of life possessed the power to perpetuate life, and aslong as they [Adam and Eve] ate of it, they could not die. The lives of the antediluvians were protracted because of the life-giving power of this tree, which was transmitted to them from Adam and Eve.—*The Review and Herald*, January 26, 1897.

The Bible

CONDITIONS CONDUCIVE TO HEALTH AND VIGOR

178. The Bible is a leaf from the tree of life, and by eating it, by receiving it into our minds, we
shall grow strong to do the will of God.—*The Review and Herald*, May 4, 1897.

Exercise

179. Neither are they willing to wait the slow process of nature to buildup the overtaxed energies of the system.—*How to Live*, 60.

180. Useful employment would bring into exercise the enfeebled muscles, enliven the stagnant blood, and the entire system would be

invigorated to overcome bad conditions.—The Health Reformer, January 1, 1871.

181. If physical exercise were combined with mental exertion, the blood would be quickened in its circulation, the action of the heart would be more perfect, impure matter would be thrown off, and new life and vigor would be experienced in every part of the body.—*Testimonies for the Church* 3:490.

182. If invalids would recover health, they should not discontinue physical exercise.... There will be increased vitality, which is so necessary to health.—*Testimonies for the Church* 2:529.

Pure Air

183. They are deprived in a great measure of air, which will invigoratethem and give them energy and vitality.—*Testimonies for the Church* 2:533.

184. Fresh air is the free blessing of Heaven, calculated to electrify thewhole system.—*Testimonies for the Church* 1:701.

Sleep

185. Nature will restore their vigor and strength in their sleeping hours,if her laws are not violated.—*A Solemn Appeal*, 62.

Bathing

186. Bathing helps the bowels, stomach, and liver, giving energy andnew life to each.—*Testimonies for the Church* 3:70.

Influence of the Mind

187. The latter class do not exercise the mind; their muscles are exercised while their brains are robbed of intellectual strength; just as the minds of thinking men are worked while their bodies are robbed of strength and vigor by their neglect to exercise the muscles. Those who are content to devote their lives to physical labor, and leave others to do the thinking for them, while they simply carry out what other brains have planned, will have strength of muscle, but feeble intellects. This class fall more readily if attacked by disease, because the system is not vitalized by the electrical force of the brain to resist disease.—*Testimonies for the Church* 3:157.

188. Bring to your aid the power of the will, which will resist cold, andwill give energy to the nervous system.—*Testimonies for the Church* 2:533.

Irregular Habits

CONDITIONS UNFAVORABLE TO STRENGTH AND VIGOR

189. Misuse of the body shortens that period of time which God designsshall be used in his service. By allowing ourselves to form wrong habits, by keeping late hours, by gratifying appetite at the expense of health, we lay the foundation for feebleness. By neglecting to take physical exercise, by overworking mind or body, we unbalance the nervous system. Those who thus shorten their lives by disregarding nature's laws, are guilty of robbery before God.—*The Review and Herald*, December 1, 1896.

Overwork

190. Those who make great exertions to accomplish just so much workin a given time, and continue to labor when their judgment tells them they should rest, are never gainers. They are living on borrowed capital. They are expending the vital force which they will need at a future time. And when the energy they have so recklessly used, is demanded, they fail for want of it. If all the hours of the day are well improved, the work extended into the evening is so much extra, and the overtaxed system will suffer from the burden imposed upon it. I have been shown that those who do this often lose much more than they gain, for their energies are exhausted, and they labor on nervous excitement. They may not realize any immediate injury, but they are surely undermining their constitution.—*Christian Temperance and Bible Hygiene*, 65.

Impure Air

191. The effects produced by living in close, ill-ventilated rooms arethese: The system becomes weakened, the circulation is depressed, the blood moves sluggishly through the system, because it is not

purified and vitalized by the pure, invigorating air of heaven. The mind becomes depressed and gloomy, while the whole system is enervated.— *Testimonies for the Church* 1:702, 703.

A Disturbed Mind

192. Doubt, perplexity, and excessive grief often sap the vital forces and induce nervous diseases of a most debilitating and distressing character.—The Review and Herald, October 16, 1883.

Errors in Diet

193. Unhealthful habits of eating are injuring thousands and tens of thousands. Food should be thoroughly cooked, neatly prepared, and appetizing.—*Unpublished Testimonies*, November 5, 1896.

Cold Food

194. I do not approve of eating much cold food, for the reason that thevitality must be drawn from
the system to warm the food until it becomes of the same temperature as the stomach, before the work of digestion can be carried on.— *Testimonies for the Church* 2:603.

195. They eat improperly, and this calls their nervous energies to the stomach, and they have no vitality to expend in other directions.— *Testimonies for the Church* 2:365.

Children

196. Children are permitted to indulge their tastes freely, to eat at all hours.... The digestive organs, like a mill which is continually kept running, become enfeebled, vital force is called from the brain to aid the stomach in its overwork, and thus the mental powers are weakened. The unnatural stimulation and wear of the vital forces make the children nervous, impatient of restraint, self-willed, and irritable.—The Health Reformer, May 1, 1877.

Students

197. They closely apply their minds to books, and eat the allowanceof the laboring man. Under such habits some grow corpulent, because the

system is clogged. Others become lean, feeble, and weak, because their vital powers are exhausted in throwing off the excess of food.—*Testimonies for the Church* 3:490.

198. This is the way you treat the stomach. It is thoroughly exhausted,but instead of letting it rest, you give it more food, and then call the vitality from other parts of the system to the stomach to assist in the work of digestion.—*Testimonies for the Church* 2:363.

Overworked Stomachs

199. The poor tired stomach may complain of weariness in vain. Morefood is forced upon it, which sets the digestive organs in motion, again to perform the same round of labor through the sleeping hours. In the morning there is a sense of languor and loss of appetite; a lack of energy is felt through the entire system.—*How to Live*, 55.

200. And what influence does overeating have upon the stomach?— Itbecomes debilitated, the digestive organs are weakened, and disease, with all its train of evils, is brought on as the result. If persons were diseased before, they thus increase the difficulties upon them, and lessen their vitality every day they live. They call their vital powers into unnecessary action to take care of the food that they place in their stomachs.—*Testimonies for the Church* 2:364.

201. Those who are excited, anxious, or in a great hurry would do wellnot to eat until they have found rest or relief, for the vital powers, already severely taxed, cannot supply the necessary gastric juice.—*The Review and Herald*, July 29, 1884.

Improper Clothing

202. She should not call vitality unnecessarily to the surface to supplythe want of sufficient clothing.—*Testimonies for the Church* 2:382.

Rearing Children

203. Everywhere you may look you will see pale, sickly, care-worn, broken-down, dispirited, discouraged women. They are generally overworked, and their vital energies exhausted by frequent child-bearing.—*How to Live*, 31.

204. Children who are robbed of that vitality which they should haveinherited from their parents should have the utmost care.—*How to Live*, 59.

Vice

205. Secret indulgence is, in many cases, the only real cause of thenumerous complaints of the young. This vice is laying waste the vital forces, and debilitating the system—*A Solemn Appeal*, 57, 58.

Drugs

206. Sick people who take these drug poisons do appear to get well.With some there is sufficient life force for nature to draw upon, so far to expel the poison from the system that the sick, having a period of rest, recover.—*How to Live*, 50.

Unsocial Surroundings

207. Some preserve a cold, chilling reserve, an iron dignity, that repelsthose who are brought within their influence. This spirit is contagious, ... it chokes the natural current of human sympathy, cordiality, and love; and under its influence people become constrained, and their social and generous attributes are destroyed for want of exercise. Not only is the spiritual health affected, but the physical health suffers by this unnatural depression.—*Testimonies for the Church* 4:64.

208. The burden of sin, with its unrest and unsatisfied desires, lies at the very foundation of a large share of the maladies the sinner suffers.—*Testimonies for the Church* 4:579.

CHAPTER XI. - DISEASE AND PROVIDENCE.

209. The violation of physical law, and the consequence, human suffering, have so long prevailed that men and women look upon the present state of sickness, suffering, debility, and premature death as the appointed lot of humanity.—*Testimonies for the Church* 3:139.

DISEASE THE RESULT OF NATURAL CAUSES

210. Many persons complain of Providence because of the discomfortand inconvenience which they suffer, when this is the sure result of their own course. They seem to feel that they are ill-treated of God, when they themselves are alone responsible for the ills which they endure.—The Review and Herald, October 16, 1883.

211. Are these ills visited upon the race through God's providence?—No; they exist because the people have gone contrary to his providence, and still continue rashly to disregard his laws.—*The Review and Herald*, July 29, 1884.

212. The souls and bodies of people are fast becoming corrupted, a mass of disease. This would not have been the case if those who had claimed to believe the truth had lived out its sacred principles.—*Unpublished Testimonies*, January 11, 1897.

213. There is a divinely appointed connection between sin and disease. Sin and disease bear to each other the relationship of cause and effect.—*Testimonies For The Church ?:200.*

214. The course professed Christians generally pursue in following fashion, irrespective of health and life, brings upon them a train of evils which they charge back upon Providence, and place arguments in the mouths of infidels wherewith to assail Christianity.—The Health Reformer, November 1, 1870.

215. God is not responsible for the suffering which follows the non-conformity to natural law and moral obligations to him.—The Health Reformer, October 1, 1871.

216. Sickness and premature death do not come without a cause.—*How to Live*, 61.

217. When standing by the graves of their children, the afflicted parentslook upon their bereavement as a special dispensation of Providence, when by inexcusable ignorance their own course has destroyed the lives of their children. To then charge their death to Providence is blasphemy.—*Testimonies for the Church* 3:136.

218. They should not charge the result of their own sinful course uponour gracious and merciful Heavenly Father. He doth not willingly afflict or grieve the children of men.—The Health Reformer, January 1, 1873.

219. Mothers are slow to learn that the suffering and death of theirchildren is the result of their own course. They do not become intelligent upon the subject of how to live to prevent disease and premature death. What a thought! Mothers are the murderers of their own children, and are mourning over their death, and are trying hard to be reconciled to Providence, which they think has bereaved them.— The Health Reformer, January 1, 1873.

CHAPTER XII. - THE INFLUENCE OF DISEASE UPON THE MIND AND MORALS.

Mental Depression.

220. A diseased body affects the brain. With the mind we serve theLord.—*Facts of Faith*, 146.

221. All should guard the senses, lest Satan gain victory over them; forthese are the avenues to the soul.—*Testimonies for the Church* 3:507.

222. The brain nerves which communicate to the entire system are theonly medium through which Heaven can communicate to man, and affect his inmost life. Whatever disturbs the circulation of the electric currents in the nervous system, lessens the strength of the vital powers, and the result is a deadening of the sensibilities of the mind.— *Testimonies for the Church* 2:347.

MORAL INSENSIBILITY

223. In consequence of the brain's being congested, its nerves lose theirhealthy action, and take on morbid conditions, making it almost impossible to arouse the moral sensibilities.—The Health Reformer, October 1, 1871.

224. It should ever be kept prominent that the great object to be attained through this channel is not only health, but perfection and the spirit of holiness, which cannot be attained with diseased bodies and minds.—*Testimonies for the Church* 1:554.

225. Mental and moral power is dependent upon the physical health.—The Health Reformer, November 1, 1871.

226. Physical and moral health are closely united.—*How to Live*, 32.

GOD MISREPRESENTED

227. The children of God cannot glorify him with sickly bodies ordwarfed minds. Those who indulge in any species of intemperance, either in eating or drinking, waste their physical energies and weaken moral power.—*Christian Temperance and Bible Hygiene*, 53.

228. Those whose moral faculties are beclouded by disease, are notthe ones rightly to represent the Christian life, to show forth the joys of salvation or the beauties of holiness. They are too often in the fire of fanaticism or the water of cold indifference or stolid gloom.—*The Signs of the Times*, June 15, 1885.

229. While men and women professing godliness are diseased fromthe crown of their head to the soles of their feet, while their physical, mental and moral energies are enfeebled through gratification of depraved appetite and excessive labor, how can they weigh the evidences of truth, and comprehend the requirements of God? If their moral and intellectual faculties are beclouded, they cannot appreciate the value of the atonement or the exalted character of the work of God, nor delight in the study of his word. How can a nervous dyspeptic be ready always to give an answer to every man that asketh him for a reason of the hope that is in him, with meekness and fear?—*Testimonies for the Church* 1:488.

230. Perfection and the spirit of holiness cannot be attained with diseased bodies and minds.—*Testimonies for the Church* 1:554.

CHAPTER XIII. - HEREDITY.

Habits Repeated.

231. The physical and mental condition of parents is perpetuated intheir offspring. This is a matter that is not duly considered. Wherever the habits of the parents are contrary to physical law, the injury done to themselves will be repeated in future generations. Satan knows this very well, and he is perpetuating his work through transmission.... Those who will indulge the animal passions and gratify lust will surely stamp upon their offspring the debasing practices, the grossness, of their own physical and moral defilement. By physical, mental, and moral culture all may become co-workers with Christ. Very much depends upon the parents. It lies with them whether they will bring into the world children who will prove a blessing or a curse.—*Unpublished Testimonies*, January, 1897.

232. In past generations if mothers had informed themselves in regard to the laws of their being, they would have understood that their constitutional strength, as well as the tone of their morals and their mental faculties, would in a great measure be represented in their offspring.—*How to Live*, 37.

233. He should not have committed so great a crime as to bring intobeing children that reason
must teach him would be diseased, because they must receive a miserable legacy from their parents.—*Testimonies for the Church* 2:379.

TRANSMISSION OF DISEASE

234. As a rule every intemperate man who rears children transmitshis inclinations and evil tendencies to his offspring; he gives them disease from his own inflamed and corrupted blood. Licentiousness, disease, and imbecility are transmitted as an inheritance of woe from father to son, and from generation to generation, and this brings anguish and suffering into the world.—*Testimonies for the Church* 4:30.

235. Thousands are devoid of principle. These very ones are transmitting to their offspring their own miserable, corrupt passions. What a legacy! Thousands drag out their unprincipled lives, tainting their associates, and perpetuating their debased passions by transmitting them to their children.—*Testimonies for the Church* 2:351.

236. You have transmitted to your children a miserable legacy; a depraved nature rendered still more depraved by your gross habits of eating and drinking.—*Testimonies for the Church* 2:62.

PARENTS SIN AGAINST CHILDREN

237. Parents sin not only against themselves in swallowing drug poisons, but they sin against their children. The vitiated state of the blood, the poison distributed throughout the system, the broken constitution, and various diseases, as the result of drug poisons, are transmitted to their offspring, and left to them a wretched inheritance, which is another great cause of the degeneracy of the race.—*How to Live*, 50.

MENTAL AND MORAL EFFECTS OF HEREDITY

238. Tobacco and liquor stupefy and defile the user. But the evil doesnot stop here. He transmits irritable tempers, polluted blood, enfeebled intellects, and weak morals to his children.—*Testimonies for the Church* 4:31.

239. Those who have indulged the appetite for these stimulants have transmitted their depraved appetites and passions to their children and greater moral power is required to resist intemperance in all its forms.—*Testimonies for the Church* 3:488.

240. As a rule, every intemperate man who rears children transmitshis inclinations and evil tendencies to his offspring.—*Testimonies for the Church* 4:30.

241. Parents who freely use wine and liquor leave to their childrenthe legacy of a feeble constitution, mental and moral debility, unnatural appetites, irritable temper, and an inclination to vice.... The child of the drunkard or the tobacco inebriate usually has the depraved appetites and passions of the father intensified, and at the same time inherits less

of his self-control and strength of mind.—The Health Reformer, August 1, 1878.

PHYSICAL EFFECTS OF HEREDITY

242. Parents leave maladies as a legacy to their children.—*Testimonies for the Church* 4:30.

243. Many women never should have become mothers. Their blood wasfilled with scrofula, transmitted to them from their parents, and increased by their gross manner of living.—*How to Live*, 37.

244. Very many children are born with their blood tainted with scrofulathrough the wrong habits of the mother in her eating and dressing.... These fashionably dressed women cannot transmit good constitutions to their children.... Wasp waists may have been transmitted to them from their mothers, as the result of their sinful practise of tight lacing, and in consequence of imperfect breathing. Poor children born of these miserable slaves of fashion have diminished vitality, and are predisposed to disease.... The impurities retained in the system in consequence of improper breathing are transmitted to their offspring.—The Health Reformer, November 1, 1871.

245. If the mother is deprived of an abundance of wholesome, nutritiousfood, she will lack in the quantity and quality of blood. Her circulation will be poor, and her child will lack in the very same things.—*Testimonies for the Church* 2:382.

246. Her children were born with feeble digestive powers and impoverished blood. From the food the mother was compelled to receive, she could not furnish a good quality of blood, and therefore gave birth to children filled with humors.—*Testimonies for the Church* 2:378.

247. Disease has been transmitted to your offspring, and the free use offlesh meats has increased the difficulty. The eating of pork has aroused and strengthened a most deadly humor that was in the system. Your offspring are robbed of vitality before they are born.—*Testimonies for the Church* 2:94.

CHAPTER XIV. - CAUSES OF DISEASE.

Predisposing Causes.

248. Satan is the originator of disease.... There is a divinely appointedconnection between sin and disease.... Sin and disease bear to each other the relationship of cause and effect.—*Testimonies for the Church* 5:443.

249. Disease never comes without a cause. The way is first prepared,and disease invited by disregarding the laws of health.—*How to Live*, 70.

250. Sickness is caused by violating the laws of health.—*Testimonies for the Church* 3:164.

251. The majority of diseases which the human family have been and are still suffering under, have been created by ignorance of their own organic law.—The Health Reformer, October 1, 1866.

Heredity

252. Through disease transmitted to them from their parents, and anerroneous education in youth, they have imbibed wrong habits, injuring the constitution, affecting the brain, causing the moral organs to become diseased, and making it impossible for them to think and act rationally upon all points.—The Review and Herald, March 11, 1880.

253. Many are suffering in consequence of the transgressions of theirparents; they cannot be
censured for their parents' sins, but it is nevertheless their duty to ascertain wherein their parents violated the laws of their being; and wherein their parents' habits were wrong, they should change their course, and place themselves, by correct habits, in a better relation to health.—The Health Reformer, August 1, 1866.

Impure Air

254. The effects produced by living in close, ill-ventilated rooms are these: The system becomes weak and unhealthy, the circulation is depressed, the blood moves sluggishly through the system because it is not purified and vitalized by the pure, invigorating air of heaven. The

mind becomes depressed and gloomy, while the whole system is enervated; and fevers and other acute diseases are liable to be generated.... The system is peculiarly sensitive to the influence of cold. A slight exposure produces serious diseases.—*Testimonies for the Church* 1:702.

Imperfect Breathing

255. Stomach, liver, lungs, and brain are suffering for want of deep, fullinspirations of air.—*Testimonies for the Church* 2:67.

Indoor Life

256. Close confinement indoors makes women pale and feeble, andresults in premature death.—The Health Reformer, April 1, 1871.

Improper Diet

257. Indulging in eating too frequently, and in too large quantities,overtaxes the digestive organs, and produces a feverish state of the system. The blood becomes impure, and then diseases of various kinds occur.—*Facts of Faith*, 133.

258. The time women devote to studying how to prepare food in amanner to suit the perverted appetite is worse than lost; ... for they are only learning the most successful way to tear down and debase the physical, mental, and moral faculties
by gluttony. Then, as a natural result, comes sickness.—The Health Reformer, October 1, 1866.

259. It is the wrong habit of indulgence of appetite, and the careless,reckless inattention to the proper care of the body, that tells upon the people. Habits of cleanliness, and care in regard to that which is introduced into the mouth, should be observed.—*Unpublished Testimonies*, July 10, 1896.

Overeating

260. What influence does overeating have upon the stomach?—It becomes debilitated, the digestive organs are weakened, and disease, with all its train of evils, is brought on as the result.—*Testimonies for the Church* 2:364.

261. And the dyspeptic—what has made him dyspeptic is taking thiscourse. Instead of observing regularity, he has let appetite control him, and has eaten between meals.—*Testimonies for the Church* 2:374.

262. They closely apply their minds to books, and eat the allowanceof laboring men.... The liver becomes burdened, and unable to throw off the impurities of the blood, and sickness is the result.—*Testimonies for the Church* 3:490.

263. Scanty, impoverished, ill-cooked food is constantly depraving theblood, by weakening the bloodmaking organs.—*Testimonies for the Church* 1:682.

264. The free use of sugar in any form tends to clog the system, andis not unfrequently a cause of disease.—*Christian Temperance and Bible Hygiene*, 57.

265. A great amount of milk and sugar ... clog the system, irritate thedigestive organs, and affect the brain.—*Testimonies for the Church* 2:370.

Flesh Foods

266. The liability to take disease is increased tenfold by meat eating.—*Testimonies for the Church* 2:64.

267. The eating of flesh meats has made a poor quality of blood andflesh. Your systems are in a state of inflammation, prepared to take on disease. You are liable to acute attacks of disease, and to sudden death, because you do not possess the strength of constitution to rally and resist disease.—*Testimonies for the Church* 2:61.

268. When we feed on flesh, the juices of what we eat pass into the circulation. A feverish condition is created, because the animals are diseased, and by partaking of their flesh, we plant the seeds of disease in our own tissue and blood. Then, when exposed to the changes in a malarious atmosphere, to prevailing epidemics and contagious diseases, these are more sensibly felt, for the system is not in a condition to resist disease.—*Unpublished Testimonies*, November 5, 1896.

269. Flesh meats constitute the principal article of food upon the tables of some families, until their blood is filled with cancerous and scrofulous humors. Their bodies are composed of what they eat. But when suffering and disease come upon them, it is considered an affliction of Providence.—*Testimonies for the Church* 3:563.

270. Rich and complicated mixtures of food are health destroying. Highly seasoned meats and rich pastry are wearing out the digestive organs of children.—*Unpublished Testimonies*, November 5, 1896.

271. Simple grains, fruits, and vegetables have all the nutrient properties necessary to make good blood. This a flesh diet cannot do.—*Unpublished Testimonies*, November 5, 1896.

Stimulants

272. It is these hurtful stimulants that are surely undermining the constitution and preparing the
system for acute diseases, by impairing nature's fine machinery, and battering down her fortifications erected against disease and premature decay.—*Testimonies for the Church* 1:548.

273. A tendency to disease of various kinds, as dropsy, liver complaint, trembling nerves, and a determination of the blood to the head, results from a habitual use of sour cider. By its use, many bring upon themselves permanent disease. Some die of consumption, or fall under the power of apoplexy from this cause alone. Some suffer from dyspepsia. Every vital function refuses to act, and the physicians tell them that they have liver complaint.—*The Review and Herald*, March 25, 1884.

Improper Clothing

274. The fashionable style of woman's dress is one of the greatest causes of all these terrible diseases.—The Health Reformer, April 1, 1872.

275. More die as the result of following fashion than from all other causes.—The Health Reformer, November 1, 1870.

276. Women especially are the victims of various maladies which might be lessened, if not entirely prevented, by right habits of life. Half their sufferings may be attributed to their manner of dress, and the insane desire to conform to the fashions of the world.—The Health Reformer, February 1, 1877.

277. In order to follow the fashions, mothers dress their children with limbs nearly naked; and the blood is chilled back from its natural course and thrown upon the internal organs, breaking up the circulation and producing disease.—*Testimonies for the Church* 2:531.

278. The chief, if not the only, reason why many become invalids isthat the blood does not circulate freely, and the changes in the vital fluid, which are necessary to life and health, do not take place.—*Testimonies for the Church* 2:525.

Exposure to Cold

279. When we overtax our strength, and become exhausted, we areliable to take cold, and at such times there is danger of disease assuming a dangerous form.—*Testimonies for the Church* 3:13.

Damp Rooms

280. Rooms that are not exposed to light and air become damp.... Various diseases have been brought on by sleeping in these fashionable health-destroying apartments.—*How to Live*, 62.

281. Choice, closed rooms, deprived of the health-giving rays of thesun, seem like damp cellars.... The air in unoccupied rooms may be cold; but this is no evidence that it is pure.—The Health Reformer, April 1, 1871.

Drugs

282. Drugging should be forever abandoned; for while it does not cure any malady, it enfeebles the system, making it more susceptible to disease.—*Testimonies for the Church* 5:311.

The Condition of the Mind

283. There is another class whose highest aim in life is physical labor.This class do not exercise the mind. Their muscles are exercised, while their brains are robbed of intellectual strength.... This class fall more rapidly if attacked by disease, because the system is not vitalized by the electrical force of the brain to resist disease.—*Testimonies for the Church* 3:157.

284. That which brings sickness of body and mind to nearly all, is dissatisfied feelings and discontented repinings.—*Testimonies for the Church* 1:566.

285. Nothing is so fruitful a cause of disease as depression, gloominess,and sadness.—*Testimonies for the Church* 1:702.

Secret Vice

286. This vice is laying waste the constitution of very many, and preparing them for diseases of almost every description.—*A Solemn Appeal*, 53.

287. Some of nature's fine machinery gives way, leaving a heavier taskfor the remainder to perform, which disorders nature's fine arrangement, and there is often a sudden breaking down of the constitution; and death is the result.—*A Solemn Appeal*, 64.

EXCITING CAUSES

Unhygienic Surroundings.

288. Filth is a breeder of disease.—*The Review and Herald*, February 4, 1896.

289. A neglect of cleanliness will induce disease.... Stubborn feversand violent diseases have prevailed in neighborhoods and towns that had formerly been considered healthy, and some have died, while others have been left with broken constitutions to be crippled with disease for life. In many instances their own yards contained the agent of destruction, which sent forth deadly poisons into the atmosphere, to be inhaled by the family and the neighborhood.—*How to Live*, 61.

290. Many suffer decayed vegetable matter to remain about their premises. They are not awake to the influence of these things. There is constantly arising from these decaying substances effluvium that is poisoning the air. By inhaling the impure air, the blood is poisoned, the lungs become affected, and the whole system is diseased. Disease of almost every description will be caused by inhaling the atmosphere affected by these decaying substances.—*Ibid*.

291. If a house be built where water settles around it, remaining for atime and then drying away, a poisonous miasma arises, and fever and ague, sore throat, lung diseases, and fevers will be the result.—*How to Live*, 64.

Flesh Diet

292. The mortality caused by eating meat is not discerned.... Animalsare diseased, and by partaking of their flesh we plant the seeds

of disease in our own tissues and blood.—*Unpublished Testimonies*, November 5, 1896.

293. The prevalence of cancers and tumors is largely due to gross livingon dead flesh.—*Unpublished Testimonies*, November 5, 1896.

294. The practice of eating largely of meat is causing diseases of allkinds,—cancers, tumors, scrofula, tuberculosis, and numbers of other like affections.—*Unpublished Testimonies*, January 11, 1897.

295. The meat is served reeking with fat, because it suits the pervertedtaste. Both the blood and the fat of animals is consumed as a luxury. But the Lord has given special directions that these should not be eaten. Why?—Because their use would make a diseased current of blood in the human system. Disregard of the Lord's special directions has brought a variety of difficulties and diseases upon human beings.... If they introduce into their system that which cannot make good flesh and blood, they must endure the results of the disregard of God's word.—*Unpublished Testimonies*, March, 1896.

296. The eating of pork has aroused and strengthened a most deadlyhumor which was in the system.—*Testimonies for the Church* 2:94.

CHAPTER XV. - RESISTANCE AGAINST DISEASE.

General Statements.

297. The object of the health reform and the Health Institute is not... to quiet the pains of today. No, indeed! Its great object is to teach the people how to live so as to give nature a chance to remove and resist disease.—*Testimonies for the Church* 1:643.

298. The power of the human system to resist the abuses put upon it, iswonderful.—*The Review and Herald*, January 25, 1881.

299. A careful conformity to the laws which God has implanted in ourbeing would insure health, and there would not be a breaking down of the constitution.—The Health Reformer, August 1, 1866.

300. A great amount of suffering might be saved if all would labor toprevent disease, by strictly obeying the laws of health.—*How to Live*, 60.

THE POWER OF THE WILL

301. The power of the will is a mighty soother of the nerves, and can resist much disease, simply by not yielding to ailments and settling down into a state of inactivity.—*Facts of Faith*, 145.

TEMPERANCE

302. In order to preserve health, temperance in all things is necessary,—temperance in labor, temperance in eating and drinking.—*How to Live*, 57.

NOURISHMENT

303. The body must have sufficient nourishment. The God who gives his beloved sleep has furnished

them also suitable food to sustain the physical system in a healthy condition.—*Christian Temperance and Bible Hygiene*, 50.

SLEEP

304. Nature will restore their vigor and strength in their sleeping hours, if her laws are not violated.—*A Solemn Appeal*, 62.

EXERCISE

305. Each faculty of the mind and each muscle has its distinctive office, and all require to be exercised in order to become properly developed and retain healthful vigor. Each organ and muscle has its work to do in the living organism. Every wheel in the machinery must be a living, active, working wheel. Nature's fine and wonderful works need to be kept in active motion in order to accomplish the object for which they were designed. Each faculty has a bearing upon the others, and all need to be exercised in order, to be properly developed.—*Testimonies for the Church* 3:77.

BATHING

306. Bathing frees the skin from the accumulation of impurities which are constantly collecting, and keeps the skin moist and supple, thereby increasing and equalizing the circulation. Persons in health should on no account neglect bathing. They should by all means bathe as often as twice a week.—*Testimonies for the Church* 3:70.

CLOTHING

307. In order to maintain equal circulation, there should be an equal distribution of clothing, which will bring equal warmth to all parts of the body.—The Health Reformer, May 1, 1872.

UNSELFISH WORK

308. There is a much greater work upon us than we as yet have any ideaof, if we would insure health by placing ourselves in the right relation to life.... The peculiar people whom God is purifying unto himself, to be translated to heaven without seeing death, should not be behind others in good works. In their efforts to cleanse themselves from all filthiness of the flesh and spirit, perfecting holiness in the fear of God, they should be as far ahead of any other class of people on the earth as their profession is more exalted than that of others.—*Testimonies for the Church* 1:487.

309. Those who, so far as possible, engage in the work of doing goodto others by giving practical demonstration of their interest in them, are not only relieving the ills of human life in helping them bear their burdens, but are at the same time contributing largely to their own health of soul and body. Doing good is a work that benefits both giver and receiver. If you forget self in your interest for others, you gain a victory over your infirmities.... The pleasure of doing good animates the mind and vibrates through the whole body.—*Testimonies for the Church* 2:534.

CHAPTER XVI. - VENTILATION.

General Statements.

310. Air is the free blessing of heaven, calculated to electrify the wholesystem.—*Testimonies for the Church* 1:701.

311. Air must be in constant circulation to be kept pure.—*Testimonies for the Church* 1:702.

VENTILATION OF THE SLEEPING-ROOM

312. Sleeping-rooms especially should be well ventilated, and the atmosphere made healthy by light and air. Blinds should be left open several hours each day, the curtains put aside, and the room thoroughly aired.—*How to Live*, 62.

313. Sleeping apartments should be large, and so arranged as to havea circulation of air through them day and night. Those who have excluded the air from their sleeping-rooms should commence to change their course immediately. They should let in air by degrees, and increase its circulation until they can bear it winter and summer, with no danger of taking cold. The lungs, in order to be healthy, must have pure air.—*How to Live*, 63.

VENTILATION IN THE SICK-ROOM

314. The sick-room, if possible, should have a draught of air throughit day and night, The draught should not come directly upon the invalid. While burning fevers are raging, there is but little danger of taking cold.... The sick must have pure, invigorating air. If no other way can be devised, the sick, if possible, should be removed to another room, and another bed, while the sick-room, the bed, and bedding are being purified by ventilation.—*How to Live*, 60.

315. Every breath of vital air in the sick-room is of the greatest value,although many of the sick are very ignorant on this point. They feel much depressed, and do not know what the matter is. A draught of pure air through their room would have a happy, invigorating influence upon them.—*How to Live*, 59.

BENEFITS OF PURE AIR

316. Air, air, the precious boon of heaven, which all may have, will bless you with its invigorating influence if you will not refuse it entrance. Welcome it, cultivate a love for it, and it will prove a precious soother of the nerves.... The influence of pure, fresh air is to cause the blood to circulate healthfully through the system. It refreshes the body, and tends to render it strong and healthy, while at the same time its influence is decidedly felt upon the mind, imparting a degree of composure and serenity. It excites the appetite, and renders the digestion of food more perfect, and induces sound, sweet sleep.— *Testimonies for the Church* 1:702.

HARMFUL EFFECTS OF IMPURE AIR

317. The harmful effects of living in close, ill-ventilated rooms are these: The system becomes weak and unhealthy; the circulation is depressed; the blood moves sluggishly through the system, because it is not purified and vitalized by the pure, invigorating air of heaven; the mind becomes depressed and gloomy, while the whole system is enervated, and fevers and other acute diseases are liable to be generated.—*Testimonies for the Church* 1:702.

318. Many young children have passed five hours each day in schoolrooms not properly ventilated, nor sufficiently large for the healthful accommodation of the scholars. The air of such rooms soon becomes poison to the lungs that inhale it.—*Testimonies for the Church* 3:135.

319. Many families suffer with sore throat, lung diseases, and livercomplaint, brought upon them by their own course of action. Their sleeping-rooms are small, unfit to sleep in for one night, but they occupy the small apartments for weeks, and months, and years.... They breathe the same air over and over, until it becomes impregnated with the poisonous impurities and waste matter thrown off from their bodies through the lungs and the pores of the skin.... Those who thus abuse their health must suffer with disease.—*How to Live*, 63.

CHAPTER XVII. - APPETITE.

320. Many are made sick by the indulgence of their appetite. They eat what suits their perverted taste, thus weakening the digestive organs, and injuring their power to assimilate the food that is to sustain life.... Thus the delicate machinery is worn out by the suicidal practises of those who ought to know better. Sin indeed lies at the door. The door is the mouth.—*Unpublished Testimonies*, August 25, 1897.

321. The declension in virtue and the degeneracy of the race are chieflyattributable to the indulgence of perverted appetite.—*Testimonies for the Church* 3:486.

322. If the appetite is allowed to rule, the mind will be brought underits control.—*Unpublished Testimonies*, January 11, 1897.

323. One of the strongest temptations that man has to meet is upon thepoint of appetite.—*Testimonies for the Church* 3:485.

324. As our first parents lost Eden through the indulgence of appetite,our only hope of regaining Eden is through the firm denial of appetite and passion.... The controlling power of appetite will prove the ruin of thousands, when, if they had conquered on this point, then they would have had the moral power to gain the victory over every other temptation of Satan. But those who are slaves to appetite will fail in perfecting Christian character.

... As we near the close of time, Satan's temptation to indulge appetite will be more powerful and more difficult to overcome.—*Testimonies for the Church* 3:491.

325. Satan sees that he cannot have such a controlling power over us ashe could if appetite were indulged.—*Testimonies for the Church* 3:569.

326. Our habits of eating and drinking show whether we are of theworld or among the number that the Lord by his mighty cleaver of truth has separated from the world.—*Unpublished Testimonies*, August 25, 1897.

327. Christ began this work of redemption by reforming the physicalhabits of man.—*Testimonies for the Church* 3:486.

328. In order for us to enjoy the natural appetite, which will preservehealth and prolong life, God restricts the appetite. He says, Beware; restrain, deny unnatural appetite.—*Testimonies for the Church* 3:63.

329. In its natural state, the taste might indicate, in a great degree, thefood best adapted to the wants of the system.... This [the taste] might be correct if the appetite had never been perverted. There is a natural, and there is a depraved appetite.—The Health Reformer, December 1, 1870.

CHAPTER XVIII. - DIET.

General Statements.

330. The diet question deserves careful study.—*The Youth's Instructor*, May 31, 1894.

331. A reform in eating would be a saving of expense and labor.— *Facts of Faith*, 132.

332. The diet affects both physical and moral health.—*Christian Temperance and Bible Hygiene*, 79.

333. Learn for yourselves what you should eat, what kinds of food bestnourish the body, and then follow the dictates of reason and conscience. This is not a matter of trifling importance.—*Gospel Workers*, 174.

334. Those who will not eat and drink from principle, will not be governed by principle in other things.—The Health Reformer, August 1, 1866.

COOKING

335. The many dishes usually prepared for dessert should be dispensedwith.—*Unpublished Testimonies*, August 30, 1896.

336. The large amount of cooking usually done is not at all necessary.Neither should the diet be poor, either in quality or quantity.—*Unpublished Testimonies*, November 5, 1896.

337. The proper cooking of food is a most essential requirement, especially where meat is not made an article of diet. Something must be prepared to take the place of meat, and these foods must be well prepared, so that meat will not be desired.—*Unpublished Testimonies*, December 20, 1896.

338. We need persons who will educate themselves to cook healthfully.Many know how to cook meats and vegetables in different

forms, yet do not understand how to prepare simple and appetizing dishes.—*The Youth's Instructor*, May 31, 1894.

339. There is religion in good cooking, and I question the religion of that class who are too ignorant and too careless to learn to cook.—*Testimonies for the Church* 2:537.

340. It is the positive duty of physicians to educate, educate, educate,by pen and voice, all who have the responsibility of preparing food for the table.—*Unpublished Testimonies*, August 30, 1896.

341. You profess to be health reformers, and for this very reason you should become good cooks. Those who can avail themselves of the advantages of properly conducted hygienic cooking-schools, will find it a great benefit, both in their own practise and in teaching others.... One reason why many have become discouraged in practising health reform is that they have not learned how to cook so that proper food, simply prepared, would supply the place of the diet to which they have been accustomed.—*Christian Temperance and Bible Hygiene*, 119.

342. This [cooking] can be done in a simple, healthful, and easy manner, without the use of lard, butter, or flesh meats.... Skill must be united with simplicity. To do this, women must read, and then patiently reduce what they have read to practise. Many are suffering because they will not take the
trouble to do this.... It is a religious duty for those who cook to learn how to prepare healthful food in different ways, so that it may be eaten with enjoyment.... What branch of the education of a young lady can be so important as this?—*Testimonies for the Church* 1:681, 682.

PROPER FOOD

343. Is my diet such as will bring me in a position where I can accomplish the greatest amount of good?—*The Review and Herald*, June 17, 1880.

344. People cannot all eat the same things. Some articles of food thatare wholesome and palatable to one person may be hurtful to another. So it is impossible to make an unvarying rule by which to regulate every one's dietetic habits.—*Christian Temperance and Bible Hygiene*, 157.

345. The Lord intends to bring his people back to live upon simplefruits, vegetables, and grains.... God provided fruit in its natural state for our first parents.—*Unpublished Testimonies*, November 5, 1896.

346. All the elements of nutrition are contained in the fruits, vegetables,and grains.—The Review and Herald, May 8, 1883.

347. Grains and fruits prepared free from grease, and in as natural acondition as possible, should be the food for the tables of all who claim to be preparing for translation to heaven.—*Testimonies for the Church* 2:352.

348. Fruits, grains, and vegetables, prepared in a simple way, free from spice and grease of all kinds, make, with milk and cream, the most healthful diet. They impart nourishment to the body, and give a power of endurance and vigor of intellect that are not produced by a stimulating diet.—*Christian Temperance and Bible Hygiene*, 47.

349. Meat eating is doing its work, for the meat is diseased. We maynot long be able to use even milk.—*Unpublished Testimonies*, August 30, 1896.

350. Good, ripe, undecayed fruit is a thing for which we should thank the Lord, for it is beneficial to health.—*Unpublished Testimonies*, November 5, 1896.

351. Dry food which requires mastication is far preferable to porridges.The health food preparations are a blessing in this respect.—*Unpublished Testimonies*, January 11, 1897.

352. My sisters, do not place upon your tables food that is exciting andirritating, but that which is plain, wholesome, and nutritious.—*The Review and Herald*, July 29, 1884.

353. Good brown bread and rolls, prepared in a simple manner, yetwith painstaking effort, are healthful.—*Unpublished Testimonies*, January 11, 1897.

PREPARATION OF FOOD

354. In the preparation of food, the golden rays of light are to be kept shining, teaching those who sit at the table how to live.—*Unpublished Testimonies*, August 12, 1896.

355. Food should be thoroughly cooked, nicely prepared, and appetizing.—*Unpublished Testimonies*, November 5, 1896.

Palatability

356. The food should have been prepared in a simple form, and free from grease; but pains should have been taken to have it nutritious, healthful, and inviting.—*Testimonies for the Church* 2:485.

357. Food should be prepared with simplicity, and yet with a nicety thatwill invite the appetite.—*Testimonies for the Church* 2:63.

358. Great care should be taken when the change is made from a flesh meat to a vegetarian diet, to supply the table with wisely prepared, well-cooked articles of food.—*Unpublished Testimonies*, January 11, 1897.

359. It is important that the food should be prepared with care, that theappetite, when not perverted, may relish it.—*Testimonies for the Church* 2:367.

360. Unless the food is prepared in a wholesome, palatable manner, it cannot be converted into good blood, to build up the wasting tissues.—*Testimonies for the Church* 2:538.

361. Many do not feel that this is a matter of duty, and hence they do nottry to prepare food properly. This can be done in a simple, healthful, and easy manner, without the use of lard, butter, or flesh meats.—*Testimonies for the Church* 1:681.

362. In every line of cooking the question which should be considered,is, How can the food be prepared in the most natural and inexpensive manner? And there should be careful study that the fragments of food left over from the table be not wasted.—*Unpublished Testimonies*, January 11, 1897.

Bread

363. Hot raised bread of any kind is difficult of digestion.—The Reviewand Herald, May 8, 1883.

364. Bread should never have the slightest taint of sourness. It shouldbe cooked until it is most thoroughly done. Thus all softness and stickiness will be avoided.... Milk should not be used in place of water in bread making. All this is extra expense, and is not wholesome. If the bread thus made is allowed to stand over in warm weather, and is then broken open, there will frequently be seen
long strings like cobwebs. Such bread soon causes fermentation to take place in the stomach.... Every housekeeper should feel it her duty to educate herself to make good sweet bread in the most inexpensive

manner, and the family should refuse to have upon the table bread that is heavy and sour, for it is injurious.—*Unpublished Testimonies*, January 11, 1897.

365. Hot biscuit raised with soda or baking-powder should never appearupon our tables. Such compounds are unfit to enter the stomach.—The Review and Herald, May 8, 1883.

366. Saleratus in any form should not be introduced into the stomach;for the effect is fearful. It eats the coatings of the stomach, causes inflammation, and frequently poisons the entire system. Some plead, "I cannot make good bread and gems unless I use soda or saleratus." You surely can if you will learn. Is not the health of your family of sufficient value to inspire you with ambition to learn how to cook and how to eat?—*Testimonies for the Church* 2:537 Variety.

367. There should not be many kinds at any one meal, but all meals should not be composed of the same kinds of food without variation.—*Testimonies for the Church* 2:63.

368. When fruit and bread, together with a variety of other foods thatdo not agree, are crowded into the stomach at one meal, what can we expect but that a disturbance will be created?—*Unpublished Testimonies*, June 11, 1897.

369. If your work is sedentary, take exercise every day, and at each mealeat only two or three kinds of simple food, taking no more of these than will satisfy the demands of hunger.—*Unpublished Testimonies*, August 30, 1896.

370. It would be better to eat only two or three different kinds of foodat each meal than to load the stomach with many varieties.—*Unpublished Testimonies*, August 30, 1896.

371. Do not have too great a variety at a meal; three or four dishes area plenty. At the next meal you can have a change. The cook should tax her inventive powers to vary the dishes she prepares for the table, and the stomach should not be compelled to take the same kinds of food meal after meal.—*The Review and Herald*, July 29, 1884.

372. Some think that they must eat only just such an amount, and justsuch a quality, and confine themselves to two or three kinds of food. But in eating too small an amount, and that not of the best quality, they do not receive sufficient nourishment.—*Christian Temperance and Bible Hygiene*, 57.

Food Combinations

373. Mixed and complicated dishes are injurious to the health of humanbeings.—*Unpublished Testimonies*, November 5, 1896.

374. It is not well to take a great variety of food at one meal. When avariety of foods that do not agree are crowded into the stomach at one meal, what can we expect but that a disturbance will be created?—*Unpublished Testimonies*, January 11, 1897.

375. I advise the people to give up sweet puddings or custards madewith eggs and milk and sugar, and to eat the best home-made bread, both graham and white, with dried or green fruits, and let that be the only course for one meal; then let the next meal be of nicely prepared vegetables.—*Unpublished Testimonies*, October 29, 1894.

376. If we would preserve the best health, we should avoid eating vegetables and fruit at the same meal. If the stomach is feeble, there will be distress, and the brain will be confused, and unable to put forth mental effort. Have fruit at one meal and vegetables at the next.—*The Youth's Instructor*, May 31, 1894.

377. We advise you to change your habits of living; but while youdo this, we caution you to move understandingly. I am acquainted with families who have changed from a meat diet to one that is impoverished. Their food is so poorly prepared that the stomach loathes it.... Here is one reason why some have not been successful in their efforts to simplify their food.—*Testimonies for the Church* 2:63.

378. Large quantities of milk and sugar eaten together are injurious.—*Testimonies for the Church* 2:369.

379. Some use milk and a large amount of sugar on mush, thinkingthat they are carrying out health reform. But the sugar and the milk combined are liable to cause fermentation in the stomach, and are thus harmful. The free use of sugar in any form tends to clog the system, and is not unfrequently a cause of disease.—*Christian Temperance and Bible Hygiene*, 57.

380. Rich and complicated mixtures of food are health destroying.—*Unpublished Testimonies*, November 5, 1896.

Number of Meals

381. The stomach must have careful attention.... After it has done itswork for one meal, do not crowd more work upon it before it has had

a chance to rest, and before a sufficient supply of gastric juice is provided. Five hours at least should be given between each meal, and always bear in mind that if you would give it a trial, you would find two meals better than three.—*Unpublished Testimonies*, August 30, 1896.

382. A second meal should never be eaten until the stomach has hadtime to rest from the labor of digesting the preceding meal.—*How to Live*, 55.

383. It is quite a common custom with the people of the world to eatthree times a day, besides eating at irregular intervals between meals; and the last meal is generally the most hearty, and is often taken just before retiring. This is reversing the natural order; a hearty meal should never be taken so late in the day. Should these persons change their practise, and eat but two meals a day, and nothing between meals, not even an apple, a nut, or any kind of fruit, the result would be seen in a good appetite and greatly improved health.—*The Review and Herald*, July 29, 1884.

384. Most people enjoy better health while eating two meals a day thanthree; others, under their existing circumstances, may require something to eat at supper time; but this meal should be very light. Let no one think himself a criterion for all, that every one must do exactly as he does.—*Christian Temperance and Bible Hygiene*, 58.

385. If the third meal be eaten at all, it should be light, and severalhours before going to bed.—*How to Live*, 55.

386. The stomach, when we lie down to rest, should have its work alldone, that it may enjoy rest, as well as other portions of the body. The work of digestion should not be carried on through any period of the sleeping hours.—*How to Live*, 56.

387. If you feel that you must eat at night, take a drink of cold water, andin the morning you will feel much better for not having eaten.—*Testimonies for the Church* 4:502.

388. The stomach may be educated to desire food eight times a day,and feel faint if it is not supplied. But this is no argument in favor of so frequent eating.—The Review and Herald, May 8, 1883.

ERRORS IN DIET

Condition of the Mind at Meals.

389. At meal-time cast off care and taxing thought. Do not be hurried,but eat slowly and with cheerfulness, your heart filled with gratitude to God for all his blessings.—*Gospel Workers*, 174.

390. If you are in constant fear that your food will hurt you, it mostassuredly will.—*Testimonies for the Church* 2:530.

391. Some health reformers are constantly worrying for fear their food,however simple and healthful, will hurt them. To these let me say, Do not think that your food is going to hurt you; but when you have eaten according to your best judgment, and have asked the Lord to bless the food, believe that he has heard your prayer, and be at rest.—*Christian Temperance and Bible Hygiene*, 59.

Eating between Meals

392. You should never let a morsel pass your lips between your regularmeals. Eat what you ought, but eat it at one meal, and then wait until the next.—*Testimonies for the Church* 2:373.

393. Three meals a day and nothing between meals—not even an apple—should be the utmost limit of indulgence. Those who go further violate nature's laws and will suffer the penalty.—The Review and Herald, May 8, 1883.

394. When traveling, some are almost constantly nibbling, if there isanything within their reach. This is a most pernicious practise. Animals that do not have reason, and that know nothing of mental taxation, may do this without injury, but they are no criterion for rational beings, who have mental powers that should be used for God and humanity.—*The Review and Herald*, July 29, 1884.

395. Food taken into the stomach at untimely seasons leaves an influence on every fiber of the system.—The Health Reformer, June 1, 1878.

Hasty Eating

396. In order to have healthy digestion, food should be eaten slowly.Those who wish to avoid dyspepsia, and those who realize the obligation to keep all their powers in a condition which will enable them to render the best service to God, will do well to remember this. If your time to eat is limited, do not bolt your food, but eat less, and eat slowly.—*The Review and Herald*, July 29, 1884.

397. Do not be hurried, but eat slowly and with cheerfulness, your heartfilled with gratitude to God for all his blessings.—*Gospel Workers*, 174.

398. Eat slowly, and allow the saliva to mingle with the food. The moreliquid there is taken into the stomach with the meals, the more difficult it is for the food to digest.... The benefit you derive from your food does not depend so much on the quantity eaten, as on its thorough digestion, nor the gratification of the taste so much on the amount of food swallowed as on the length of time it remains in the mouth.—*The Review and Herald*, July 29, 1884.

Overeating

399. If more food is eaten than can be digested and appropriated, adecaying mass accumulates in the stomach, causing an offensive breath, and a bad taste in the mouth. The vital powers are exhausted in an effort to throw off the excess, and the brain is robbed of nerve force.—*Special Testimonies On Education*, 32.

400. Nearly all the members of the human family eat more than thesystem requires.... Even so-called health reform needs reforming on this point.... If more food, even of a simple quality, is placed in the stomach than the living machinery requires, this surplus becomes a burden, the system makes a desperate effort to dispose of it, and this extra work causes a weakly feeling. Some who are continually overeating call this all-gone feeling hunger, but it is caused by the overworked condition of the abused digestive organs.—*Unpublished Testimonies*, August 30, 1896.

401. Some of you feel as though you would like to have somebodytell you how much to eat. This is not the way it should be. We are to act from a moral and religious standpoint.. We are to be temperate in all things, because an incorruptible crown, a heavenly treasure, is before us. And now I wish to say to my brethren and sisters, I would have moral courage to take my position and govern myself. You eat too much, and then you are sorry, and so you keep thinking upon what you eat and drink. Just eat that which is for the best, and go right away, feeling clear in the sight of Heaven, and not having remorse of conscience.—*Testimonies for the Church* 2:374.

402. There is evil in overeating of even healthful food.... If we overeat,the brain power is taxed to take care of a large quantity of food

that the system does not demand, the mind is clouded, and the perceptions enfeebled.—*Unpublished Testimonies*, April 6, 1896.

403. When the brain is constantly taxed, and there is a lack of physicalexercise, they should eat sparingly, even of plain food.—*Testimonies for the Church* 4:515.

404. They closely apply their minds to books, and eat the allowanceof a laboring man. Under such habits some grow corpulent, because the system is clogged. Others become lean, feeble, and weak, because their vital powers are exhausted in throwing off the excess of food; the liver becomes burdened, and unable to throw off the impurities in the blood, and sickness is the result.—*Testimonies for the Church* 3:490.

405. Overeating, even of the simplest food, benumbs the sensitive nerves of the brain, and weakens its vitality. Overeating has a worse effect upon the system than overworking; the energies of the soul are more effectually prostrated by intemperate eating than by intemperate working. The digestive organs should never be burdened with the quantity or quality of food which it will tax the system to appropriate. All that is taken into the stomach, above what the system can use to convert into good blood, clogs the machinery; for it cannot be made into either flesh or blood, and its presence burdens the liver, and produces a morbid condition of the system.—*Testimonies for the Church* 2:412.

406. Overeating is intemperance just as surely as is liquor drinking.—*Unpublished Testimonies*, August 30, 1896.

407. And what influence does overeating have upon the stomach?—Itbecomes debilitated, the digestive organs are weakened, and disease, with all its train of evils, is brought on as the result. If persons were diseased before, they thus increase the difficulties upon them, and lessen their vitality every day they live. They call their vital powers into unnecessary action to take care of the food that they place in their stomachs. What a terrible condition is this to be in!—*Testimonies for the Church* 2:364.

408. Eating merely to please the appetite is a transgression of nature'slaws; often this intemperance is felt at once in the form of indigestion, headache, and colic. A load has been placed upon the stomach that it cannot care for, and a feeling of oppression comes. The head is confused, the stomach is in rebellion. But these results do not always follow overeating. In some cases the stomach is paralyzed. No

sensation of pain is felt, but the digestive organs lose their vital force. The foundation of the human machinery is gradually undermined, and life is rendered very unpleasant.—*Unpublished Testimonies*, August 30, 1896.

Drinking at Meals

409. Taken with meals, water diminishes the flow of the salivary glands;and the colder the water the greater the injury to the stomach. Ice water or iced lemonade, drunk with meals, will arrest digestion until the system has imparted sufficient warmth
to the stomach to enable it to take up its work again.—*The Review and Herald*, July 29, 1884.

410. Food should not be washed down; no drink is needed with meals.Eat slowly, and allow the saliva to mingle with the food. The more liquid there is taken into the stomach with the meals, the more difficult it is for the food to digest; for the liquid must be first absorbed.... Hot drinks are debilitating; and besides, those who indulge in their use become slaves to the habit.... Do not eat largely of salt; give up bottled pickles; keep fiery spiced food out of your stomach; eat fruit with your meals, and the irritation which calls for so much drink will cease to exist. But if anything is needed to quench thirst, pure water, drunk some little time before or after a meal, is all that nature requires.... Water is the best liquid possible to cleanse the tissues.—*The Review and Herald*, July 29, 1884.

Liquid Foods

411. I am advising the people wherever I go to give up liquid food asmuch as possible.—*Unpublished Testimonies*, October 29, 1894.

412. Taken in a liquid state, your food would not give healthful vigoror tone to the system. But when you change this habit, and eat more solids and less liquids, your stomach will feel disturbed. Notwithstanding this, you should not yield the point, you should educate your stomach to bear a more solid diet.—*Testimonies for the Church* 3:74.

413. Dry food that requires mastication is far preferable to porridges.The health food preparations are a blessing in this respect.... For those who can use them, good vegetables, prepared in a

healthful manner, are better than soft mushes and porridge. Fruits, used with thoroughly cooked bread two or three days old, which is more healthful than fresh bread, slowly and thoroughly masticated, will furnish all that the system requires.—*Unpublished Testimonies*, January 11, 1897.

Very Hot Foods

414. Very hot food ought not to be taken into the stomach. Soups, puddings, and other articles of the kind, are often eaten too hot, and as a consequence the stomach is debilitated. Let them become partly cooled before they are eaten.—*The Review and Herald*, July 29, 1884.

Cold Food

415. I do not approve of eating much cold food, for the reason that the vitality must be drawn from the system to warm the food until it becomes of the same temperature as the stomach before the work of digestion can be carried on.—*Testimonies for the Church* 2:603.

Rich Diet

416. Rich and complicated mixtures of food are health destroying. Highly seasoned meats and rich pastry are wearing out the digestive organs of children.—*Unpublished Testimonies*, November 5, 1896.

417. At too many tables, when the stomach has received all that it requires to carry on the work of nourishing the system, another course, consisting of pies, puddings, and highly flavored sauces, is placed upon the table.... Many, though they have already eaten enough, will overstep the bounds, and eat the tempting dessert, which, however, proves anything but good to them.... If the extras which are provided for dessert were dispensed with altogether, it would be a blessing.—*Unpublished Testimonies*, August 30, 1896.

418. Many understand how to make different kinds of cakes, but cake is not the best food to be placed upon the table. Sweet cakes, sweet puddings, and custards will disorder the digestive organs; and why should we tempt those who surround the table by placing such articles before them?—*The Youth's Instructor*, May 31, 1894.

419. Cook meat with spices, and eat it with rich cakes and pies, and youhave a bad quality of blood. The system is too heavily taxed in disposing of this kind of food. The mince pies and pickles, which should never find a place in any human stomach, will give a miserable quality of blood.... Flesh meat and rich food and an impoverished diet will produce the same results.—*Testimonies for the Church* 2:368.

Condiments

420. Condiments and spices, used in the preparation of food for thetable, aid digestion in the same way that tea, coffee, and liquor are supposed to help the laboring man to perform his task. After the immediate effects are gone, those who use them drop as far below par as they were elevated above par by these stimulating substances. The system is weakened, the blood contaminated, and inflammation is the sure result. The less frequently condiments and desserts are placed on our tables, the better it will be for all who partake of the food.— *Unpublished Testimonies*, November 5, 1896.

421. Our tables should bear only the most wholesome food, free fromevery irritating substance. The appetite for liquor is encouraged by the preparation of food with condiments and spices. These cause a feverish state of the system, and drink is demanded to allay the irritation. On my frequent journeys across the continent, I do not patronize restaurants, dining-cars, or hotels, for the simple reason that I cannot eat the food there provided. The dishes are highly seasoned with salt and pepper, creating an almost intolerable thirst.... They irritate and inflame the delicate coating of the stomach.... Such is the food that is commonly served upon fashionable tables, and given to the children. Its effect is to cause nervousness, and to create thirst which water does not quench.... Food should be prepared in as simple a manner as possible, free from condiments and spices, and even from an undue amount of salt.—The Review and Herald, November 6, 1883.

Spices

422. Spices at first irritate the tender coating of the stomach, but finallydestroy the natural sensitiveness of this delicate membrane. The blood becomes fevered, the animal propensities are aroused, while the moral and intellectual powers are weakened, and become servants to the baser passions.—*Christian Temperance and Bible Hygiene*, 47.

423. Persons who have indulged their appetite to eat freely of meat,highly seasoned gravies, and various kinds of rich cakes and preserves, cannot immediately relish a plain, wholesome, nutritious diet. Their taste is so perverted they have no appetite for a wholesome diet of fruits, plain bread, and vegetables. They need not expect to relish at first food so different from that in which they have been indulging. If they cannot at first enjoy plain food, they should fast until they can. That fast will prove to them of greater benefit than medicine, for the abused stomach will find the rest which it has
long needed, and real hunger can be satisfied with a plain diet. It will take time for the taste to recover from the abuses it has received, and to gain its natural tone. But perseverance in a self-denying course of eating and drinking will soon make plain, wholesome food palatable, and it will be eaten with greater satisfaction than the epicure enjoys over his rich dainties.—*Facts of Faith*, 130.

Cheese

424. The effect of cheese is deleterious.—*Christian Temperance and Bible Hygiene*, 47.

425. Cheese should never be introduced into the stomach.—*Testimonies for the Church* 2:68.

Grease, fats, etc

426. Meat is served reeking with fat, because it suits the perverted taste.Both the blood and the fat of animals is consumed as a luxury. But the Lord has given special directions that these should not be eaten. Why?—Because their use would make a diseased current of blood in the human system. Disregard of the Lord's special directions has brought many diseases upon human beings.—*Unpublished Testimonies*, March, 1896.

427. Jesus, speaking of the cloudy pillar, gave special direction to the children of Israel, saying: "It shall be a perpetual statute for your generations throughout all your dwellings, that ye eat neither fat nor blood." "And the Lord spake unto Moses, saying, Speak unto the children of Israel, saying, Ye shall eat no manner of fat, of ox, of sheep, or of goat." "For whosoever eateth the fat of the beasts, of which men offer an offering made by fire unto the Lord, even the soul that eateth it shall

be cut off from among his people."—*Unpublished Testimonies*, March, 1896.

428. You should keep grease out of your food. It defiles any preparationof food you may make.—*Testimonies for the Church* 2:63.

429. Grease cooked in the food renders it difficult of digestion.—*Christian Temperance and Bible Hygiene*, 47.

430. Some fall into the error that because they discard meat, they haveno need to supply its place with the best fruits and vegetables, prepared in their most natural state, free from grease and spices.—*Testimonies for the Church* 2:486.

431. Butter and meat stimulate. They have injured the stomach andperverted the taste.—*Testimonies for the Church* 2:486.

432. You place upon your tables butter, eggs, and meat, and your children partake of them. They are fed with the very things that will excite their animal passions, and then you come to meeting and ask God to bless and save your children.—*Testimonies for the Church* 2:362.

Saleratus and Soda

433. Saleratus in any form should not be introduced into the stomach;for the effect is fearful. It eats the coatings of the stomach, causes inflammation, and frequently poisons the entire system.—*Testimonies for the Church* 2:537.

434. Hot soda biscuit are often spread with butter, and eaten as a choicediet; but the feeble digestive organs cannot but feel the abuse placed upon them.—*Unpublished Testimonies*, November 5, 1896.

CHAPTER XIX. - FLESH FOODS.

General Statements.

435. Meat is not essential for health or strength, else the Lord madea mistake when he provided food for Adam and Eve before their fall. All the elements of nutrition are contained in the fruits, vegetables, and grains.—The Review and Herald, May 8, 1883.

The Ideal Diet

436. The Lord intends to bring his people back to live upon simplefruits, vegetables, and grains. He led the children of Israel into the wilderness where they could not get a flesh diet; and he gave them the bread of heaven. "Man did eat angels' food." But they craved the flesh-pots of Egypt, and mourned and cried for flesh, notwithstanding the promise of the Lord that if they would submit to his will, he would carry them into the land of Canaan, and establish them there, a pure, holy, happy people, and that there should not be a feeble one in all their tribes; for he would take away all sickness from among them.... The Lord would have given them flesh had it been essential for their health, but he who had created and redeemed them led them through that long journey in the wilderness to educate, discipline, and train them in correct habits. The Lord understood what influence flesh eating has upon the human system. He would have a people that would, in their physical appearance,
bear the divine credentials, notwithstanding their long journey.—*Unpublished Testimonies*, November 5, 1896.

437. Let no meat be found at our restaurants or dining tents, but letits place be supplied with fruits, grains, and vegetables. We must practise what we preach. When sitting at a table where meat is provided, we should not make a raid on those who use it, but should let it alone ourselves; and when asked the reason for doing this, we should kindly explain why we do not use it.—*Unpublished Testimonies*, March, 1896

438. The diet of animals is vegetables and grains. Must the vegetablesbe animalized, must they be incorporated into the system of an animal, before we get them? Must we obtain our vegetable diet by eating the flesh of dead creatures? God provided food in its natural state

for our first parents. He gave Adam charge of the garden, to dress it and to care for it, saying, "To you it shall be for meat." One animal was not to destroy another animal for food.—*Unpublished Testimonies*, November 5, 1896.

439. Those who have lived upon a meat diet all their lives do not see the evil of continuing the practise, and they must be treated tenderly.—*Unpublished Testimonies*, June 19, 1895.

Substitutes for Meat

440. Something must be prepared to take the place of meat, and these foods must be well prepared, so that meat will not be desired.—*Unpublished Testimonies*, December 20, 1896.

441. I know that with care and skill, dishes could be prepared to takethe place of meat. But if the main dependence of the cook is meat, she will encourage meat eating, and the depraved appetite will frame every excuse for this kind of diet.—*Unpublished Testimonies*, February 14, 1884.

442. Meat is the most expensive diet that can be had.—*Unpublished Testimonies*, February 17, 1884.

EFFECTS OF MEAT EATING

Physical Effects.

443. We do not hesitate to say that flesh meat is not necessary for healthor strength.—*Testimonies for the Church* 2:63.

444. One of the great errors that many insist upon is that muscularstrength is dependent upon animal food. But the simple grains, fruits of the trees, and vegetables have all the nutritive properties necessary to make good blood. This a flesh diet cannot do.—*Unpublished Testimonies*, November 5, 1896.

445. Speaking in support of this diet, they said that without it they wereweak in physical strength. But the words of our Teacher to us were, "As a man thinketh, so is he." The flesh of dead animals was not the original food for man. Man was permitted to eat it after the flood, because all vegetation had been destroyed.... Since the flood the human race has been shortening the period of its existence. Physical, mental,

and moral degeneracy is rapidly increasing in these last days.—
Unpublished Testimonies, January 11, 1897.

446. The weakness experienced on leaving off meat is one of the strongest arguments that I could present as a reason why you should discontinue its use. Those who eat meat feel stimulated after eating this food, and they suppose that they are made stronger. After they discontinue the use of meat, they may for a time feel weak, but when the system is cleansed

from the effect of this diet, they no longer feel the weakness, and will cease to wish for that for which they have pleaded as essential to strength.—*Unpublished Testimonies*, August 30, 1896.

447. You may think that you cannot work without meat; I thought soonce, but I know that in his original plan God did not provide for the use of the flesh of dead animals as a diet for man. It is a gross, perverted taste that will accept such food. To think of dead flesh rotting in the stomach is revolting.—*Unpublished Testimonies*, February 17, 1884.

448. The eating of flesh meats has made a poor quality of blood andflesh. Your systems are in a state of inflammation, prepared to take on disease. You are liable to acute attacks of disease, and to sudden death, because you do not possess the strength of constitution to rally and resist disease.—*Testimonies for the Church* 2:61.

449. The physical powers are depreciated by the habitual use of fleshmeat. Meat eating deranges the system.—*Testimonies for the Church* 2:64.

450. The use of the flesh of animals tends to cause a grossness of thebody.—*Testimonies for the Church* 2:63.

451. Their meat diet, which was supposed to be essential, was not necessary, and as they were composed of what they ate, brain, bone, and muscle were in an unwholesome condition because they lived on the flesh of dead animals. Their blood was being corrupted by this improper diet. The flesh which they ate was diseased, and their entire system was becoming gross and corrupted.—*Unpublished Testimonies*, August 30, 1896.

452. When we feed on flesh, the juices of what we eat pass into the circulation. A feverish condition is created, because the animals are diseased, and by partaking of their flesh we plant the seeds of disease in our own tissue and blood. Then, when exposed to the changes of a malarious atmosphere, to prevailing epidemics and contagious

diseases, these are more sensibly felt, for the system is not in a condition to resist disease.—*Unpublished Testimonies*, November 5, 1896.

453. Because those who partake of animal food do not immediately feelits effects, is no evidence that it does not injure them. It may be doing its work surely upon the system, and yet the persons for the time being realize nothing of it.—*How to Live*, 59.

454. The liability to take disease is increased tenfold by meat eating.—*Testimonies for the Church* 2:64.

455. The practise of eating largely of meat is causing diseases of all kinds,—cancers, tumors, scrofula, tuberculosis, and other like affections.—*Unpublished Testimonies*, January 11, 1897.

456. The mortality caused by meat eating is not discerned. If it were,we should hear no arguments and excuses in favor of the indulgence of the appetite for dead flesh.—*Unpublished Testimonies*, November 5, 1896.

457. Her system is full of scrofulous humors from the eating of fleshmeats. The use of swine's flesh in your family has imparted a bad quality of blood.—*Testimonies for the Church* 2:62.

458. Cancers, tumors, and various other inflammatory diseases are largely caused by meat eating.
From the light which God has given me, the prevalence of cancers and tumors is largely due to gross living on dead flesh.—*Unpublished Testimonies*, November 5, 1896.

459. Cancers, tumors, diseases of the lungs, the liver, and the kidneys,all exist in the animals that are used for food.—*Unpublished Testimonies*, March, 1896

460. When a limb is broken, physicians, recommend their patients not to eat meat, as there would be danger of inflammation's setting in.—*Unpublished Testimonies*, November 5, 1896.

Mental and Moral Effects

461. If we subsist largely upon the flesh of dead animals, we shallpartake of their nature.—*Testimonies for the Church* 2:61.

462. A meat diet changes the disposition, and strengthens animalism....To educate your children to subsist on a meat diet would be harmful to them.—*Unpublished Testimonies*, November 5, 1896.

463. Its use excites the animal propensities to increased activity, and strengthens the animal passions. When the animal propensities are increased, the intellectual and moral powers are decreased. The use of the flesh of animals ... benumbs the fine sensibilities of the mind.—*Testimonies for the Church* 2:63.

464. It is impossible for those who make free use of flesh meats to havean unclouded brain and an active intellect.—*Testimonies for the Church* 2:62.

465. Eating much flesh will diminish intellectual activity. Studentswould accomplish much more in their studies if they never tasted meat. When the animal part of the human nature is strengthened by meat eating, the intellectual powers diminish proportionately.—*Unpublished Testimonies*, November 5, 1896.

466. Meat eating deranges the system, beclouds the intellect, and bluntsthe moral sensibilities.—*Testimonies for the Church* 2:64.

467. Such a diet contaminates the blood and stimulates the lower passions. It prevents vigor of thought and enfeebles the perceptions, so that God and the truth are not understood.—*Unpublished Testimonies*, January 11, 1897.

Spiritual Effects

468. O, if every one could discern these matters as they have beenpresented to me, those who are so careless, so indifferent in regard to their character building, those who plead for indulgence in a fleshmeat diet, would never open their lips in justification of an appetite for the flesh of dead animals.—*Unpublished Testimonies*, January 11, 1897.

469. A religious life can be more successfully attained and maintainedif meat is discarded; for this diet stimulates into intense activity the lustful propensities, and enfeebles the moral and spiritual nature.—*Unpublished Testimonies*, November 5, 1896.

Diseased Meats

470. The meat diet is a serious question. Shall human beings live on the flesh of dead animals? The answer, from the light that God has given, is, No, decidedly no. Our health institutions should educate on this question.... They should point out the increase of disease in the

animal kingdom. The testimony of examiners is that very few animals are free from disease.—*Unpublished Testimonies*, January 11, 1897.

471. Disease of every type is afflicting the human family, and it is largely the result of subsisting on the diseased flesh of dead animals.—*Unpublished Testimonies*, March, 1896

472. Those who subsist largely upon flesh cannot avoid eating the meatof animals which are to a greater or less degree diseased. The process of fitting the animals for market produces in them disease; and fitted in as healthful a manner as they can be, they become heated and diseased by driving before they reach the market. The fluids and flesh of these diseased animals are received directly into the blood, and pass into the circulation of the human body, becoming fluids and flesh of the same. Thus humors are introduced into the system. And if the person already has impure blood, it is greatly aggravated by eating of the flesh of these animals.—*Testimonies for the Church* 2:64.

473. The very animals whose flesh you eat are frequently so diseasedthat, if left alone, they would die of themselves; but while the breath of life is in them, they are killed and brought to market. You take directly into your system humors and poisons of the worst kind, and yet you realize it not.—*Testimonies for the Church* 2:405.

474. There are but few animals that are free from disease. Many havebeen made to suffer greatly for the want of light, pure air, and wholesome food. When they are fattened, they are often confined in close stables, and are not permitted to exercise, and to enjoy free circulation of air. Many poor animals are left to breathe the poison of filth which is left in barns and stables. Their lungs will not long remain healthy while inhaling such impurities. Disease is conveyed to the liver, and the entire system of the animal is diseased. They are killed, and prepared for the market, and people eat freely of this poisonous animal food. Much disease is caused in this manner. But the people cannot be made to believe that it is the meat they have eaten which has poisoned their blood, and caused their sufferings. Many die of disease caused wholly by meat eating, yet the world does not seem to be the wiser.... It may be doing its work surely upon the system, and yet the person for the time being realize nothing of it.—*How to Live*, 59.

475. Animals are frequently killed that have been driven quite a distance to the slaughter. Their blood has become heated. They are of full flesh, and have been deprived of healthy exercise, and when they

have to travel far, they become exhausted, and in that condition are killed for market. Their blood is highly inflamed, and those who eat of their meat, eat poison. Some are not immediately affected, while others are attacked with severe pain, and die from fever, cholera, or some unknown disease.... Some animals that are brought to the slaughter seem to realize what is to take place, and they become furious, and literally mad. They are killed while in this state, and their flesh is prepared for market. Their meat is poison, and has produced, in those who have eaten it, cramps, convulsions, apoplexy, and sudden death.—*How to Live*, 59, 60.

476. Swine have been prepared for market even while the plague wasupon them, and their poisonous flesh has spread contagious diseases, and great mortality has followed.—*How to Live*, 60.

477. Meat eating is doing its work, for the meat is diseased.—*Unpublished Testimonies*, August 30, 1896.

478. The flesh which they ate was diseased, and their entire systemwas becoming gross and corrupted.—*Unpublished Testimonies*, August 30, 1897.

479. Death was caused by the abundant eating of meat which at the lastwas tainted.—*Unpublished Testimonies*, November 5, 1896.

480. Pulmonary diseases, cancers, and tumors are startlingly commonamong animals. It is true that the inspectors reject many cattle that are diseased, but many are passed on to the market that ought to have been refused.... Thus unwholesome flesh has gone on the market for human consumption. In many localities even fish is unwholesome, and ought not to be used. This is especially so where the fish come in contact with the sewerage of large cities.... The fish that partake of the filthy sewerage of the drains may pass into waters far distant from the sewerage, and be caught in localities where the water is pure and fresh; but because of the unwholesome drainage in which they have been feeding, they are not safe to eat.—*Unpublished Testimonies*, January 19, 1895.

481. The fact that meat is largely diseased should lead us to make strenuous efforts to discontinue its use entirely.... It will be hard for some to do this, as hard as for the rum drinker to forsake his dram; but they will be better for the change.—*Unpublished Testimonies*, November 9, 1896.

CHAPTER XX. - STIMULANTS.

General Statements.

482. The use of unnatural stimulants is destructive to health, and hasa benumbing influence upon the brain, making it impossible to appreciate eternal things.—*Testimonies for the Church* 1:549.

483. Never be betrayed into indulging in the use of stimulants; forthis will result not only in reaction and loss of physical strength, but in a benumbed intellect.—*Testimonies for the Church* 4:214.

484. It is these hurtful stimulants that are surely undermining the constitution and preparing the system for acute diseases, by impairing nature's fine machinery, and battering down her fortifications erected against disease and premature decay.—*Testimonies for the Church* 1:549.

485. Because these stimulants produce for the time being such agreeable results, many conclude that they really need them, and continue their use. But there is always a reaction. The nervous system, having been unduly excited, borrowed power for present use from its future resources of strength. All this temporary invigoration of the system is followed by depression. In proportion as these stimulants temporarily invigorate the system, will be the letting down of the power of the excited organs after the stimulus has lost its force.—*Testimonies for the Church* 3:487.

486. Excitement will be followed by depression.—The Review andHerald, May 8, 1883.

TEA AND COFFEE

487. Tea has an influence to excite the nerves, and coffee benumbs thebrain; both are highly injurious.—*Testimonies for the Church* 4:365.

488. Tea, coffee, and flesh meats produce an immediate effect. Underthe influence of these poisons the nervous system is excited, and in some cases, for the time being, the intellect seems to be invigorated, and the imagination to be more vivid.—*Testimonies for the Church* 3:487.

489. To a certain extent, tea produces intoxication. It enters into the circulation, and gradually impairs the energy of body and mind. It stimulates, excites, and quickens the motion of the living machinery, forcing it to unnatural action, and thus gives the tea drinker the

impression that it is doing him great service, imparting to him strength. This is a mistake. Tea draws upon the strength of the nerves, and leaves them greatly weakened. When its influence is gone and the increased action caused by its use is abated, then what is the result?—Languor and debility corresponding to the artificial vivacity the tea imparted. When the system is already overtaxed and needs rest, the use of tea spurs up nature by stimulation to perform unwonted, unnatural action, and thereby lessens her power to perform, and her ability to endure; and her powers give out long before Heaven designed they should. Tea is poisonous to the system. Christians should let it alone.... The second effect of tea drinking is headache, wakefulness, palpitation of the heart, indigestion,
trembling of the nerves, and many other evils.—*Testimonies for the Church* 2:64, 65.

490. The influence of coffee is in a degree the same as tea, but theeffect upon the system is still worse. Its influence is exciting, and just in the degree that it elevates above par, it will exhaust and bring prostration below par. Tea and coffee drinkers carry the marks upon their faces. The skin becomes sallow, and assumes a lifeless appearance. The glow of health is not seen upon the countenance.

Tea and coffee do not nourish the system. The relief obtained from them is sudden, before the stomach has had time to digest them. This shows that what the users of these stimulants call strength is only received by exciting the nerves of the stomach, which convey the irritation to the brain, and this in turn is aroused to impart increased action to the heart, and short-lived energy to the entire system. All this is false strength, that we are the worse for having. They do not give a particle of natural strength.—*Testimonies for the Church* 2:65.

491. The stimulating diet and drink of this day are not conducive tothe best state of health. Tea, coffee, and tobacco are all stimulating, and contain poisons. They are not only unnecessary, but harmful, and should be discarded if we would add to knowledge temperance.—*The Review and Herald*, February 21, 1888.

492. There is need of a better understanding of the principles of healthreform. Temperance in eating, drinking, and dressing is essential. The advocates of temperance should place their standard on a broader platform. They would then be laborers together with God. With every iota of their influence they should encourage the spread of

reform principles. Let appetite rule instead of principle, and the whole machinery will be implicated. The violation of physical law is a violation of the law of God. Those who eat too much, and whose food is of an objectionable quality are easily led into dissipation.—*Unpublished Testimonies*, August 25, 1897.

493. He calls upon them to sacrifice their idols. They should lay asidesuch stimulants as tobacco, tea, and coffee.—*Testimonies for the Church* 1:224.

494. The highly seasoned flesh meats and tea and coffee, which somemothers encourage their children to use, prepare the way for them to crave stronger stimulants, as tobacco.—*Testimonies for the Church* 3:488.

TOBACCO

495. The use of tobacco encourages the appetite for liquor; and the useof tobacco and liquor invariably lessens nerve power.—*Testimonies for the Church* 3:488.

496. By the use of alcoholic drinks and narcotics and the flesh of diseased animals, man has distorted and crippled the Lord's divine arrangements. Nature does her best to expel the poisonous drug tobacco, but frequently she is overborne, gives up her struggle, and life is sacrificed in the conflict.—*Unpublished Testimonies*, January 11, 1897.

497. Tobacco, in whatever form it is used, tells upon the constitution.It is a slow poison. It affects the brain and benumbs the sensibilities so that the mind cannot discern spiritual things, especially those truths which would have a tendency to correct this filthy indulgence. Those who use tobacco in any form are not clear before God. In such a filthy practise it is impossible for them to glorify God in their bodies and spirits, which are his. And while they are using slow and sure poisons, which are ruining their health and debasing the faculties of the mind, God cannot approbate them. He may be merciful to them while they indulge in this pernicious habit in ignorance of the injury it is doing them; but when the matter is set before them in its true light, then they are guilty before God if they continue to indulge this gross appetite.—*Facts of Faith*, 126.

498. Tobacco is a poison of the most deceitful and malignant kind,having an exciting, then a paralyzing, influence upon the nerves of

the body. It is all the more dangerous because its effects upon the system are so slow, and at first scarcely perceivable.—*Facts of Faith*, 128.

499. Tobacco is a slow, insidious poison, and its effects are more difficult to cleanse from the system than those of liquor.—*Testimonies for the Church* 3:569.

500. Tobacco using is a habit which frequently affects the nervous system in a more powerful manner than does the use of alcohol. It binds the victim in stronger bands of slavery than does the intoxicating cup; the habit is more difficult to overcome. Body and mind are, in many cases, more thoroughly intoxicated with the use of tobacco than with spirituous liquors; for it is a more subtle poison.—*Testimonies for the Church* 3:562.

501. It is unpleasant, if not dangerous, to remain in a railroad car or ina crowded room that is not
thoroughly ventilated, where the atmosphere is impregnated with the properties of liquor and tobacco. The occupants give evidence by the breath and emanations from the body that the system is filled with the poison of liquor and tobacco.—*Testimonies for the Church* 3:562.

502. Many infants are poisoned beyond remedy by sleeping in bedswith their tobacco-using fathers. By inhaling the poisonous tobacco effluvium, which is thrown from the lungs and pores of the skin, the system of the infant is filled with poison. While it acts upon some infants as a slow poison, and affects the brain, heart, liver, and lungs, and they waste away and fade gradually; upon others it has a more direct influence, causing spasms, paralysis, and sudden death. The bereaved parents mourn the loss of their loved ones, and wonder at the mysterious providence of God, which has so cruelly afflicted them, when Providence designed not the death of these infants. They died martyrs to the filthy lust for tobacco. Every exhalation of the lungs of the tobacco slave poisons the air about him.—The Health Reformer, January 1, 1872.

503. Tobacco and liquor stupefy and defile the user. But the evil doesnot stop here. He transmits irritable tempers, polluted blood, enfeebled intellects, and weak morals to his children, and renders himself accountable for all the evil results that his wrong and dissipated course of life brings upon his family and the community.—*Testimonies for the Church* 4:30.

ALCOHOL

504. The tables of our American people are generally prepared in amanner to make drunkards....

By the use of tea and coffee an appetite is formed for tobacco, and this encourages the appetite for liquors.... Youth in general are governed by impulse and are slaves to appetite. In the glutton, the tobacco devotee, the wine-bibber, and the inebriate, we see the evil results of defective education.—*Testimonies for the Church* 3:563.

505. The only safe course is to touch not, taste not, handle not, tea,coffee, wines, tobacco, opium, and alcoholic drinks.—*Testimonies for the Church* 3:488.

506. If men would become temperate in all things, if they would touchnot, taste not, handle not, spirituous liquors and narcotics, reason would hold the reins of government in her hands, and control the animal appetites and passions.—*Testimonies for the Church* 3:561.

507. Persons may become just as really intoxicated on wine and cideras on stronger drinks, and the worst kind of inebriation is produced by these so-called milder drinks. The passions are more perverse; the transformation of character is greater, more determined and obstinate. A few quarts of cider or sweet wine may awaken a taste for strong drinks, and many who have become confirmed drunkards have thus laid the foundation of the drinking habit.... Moderate drinking is the school in which men are receiving an education for the drunkard's career. The taste for stimulants is cultivated; the nervous system is disordered; Satan keeps the mind in a fever of unrest; and the poor victim, imagining himself perfectly secure, goes on and on, until every barrier is broken down, every principle sacrificed.—*The Review and Herald*, March 25, 1884.

508. The Bible nowhere teaches the use of intoxicating wine, either asa beverage or as a symbol of the blood of Christ. We appeal to the natural reason whether the blood of Christ is better represented by the pure juice of the grape in its natural state, or after it has been converted into a fermented and intoxicating wine.... We urge that the latter should never be placed upon the Lord's table.... We protest that Christ never made intoxicating wine; such an act would have been contrary to all the teachings and examples of his life.... The wine which Christ

manufactured from water by a miracle of his power was the pure juice of the grape.—The Health Reformer, July 1, 1878.

EFFECTS OF THE USE OF ALCOHOLIC DRINKS

509. The use of tobacco and liquor invariably lessens nerve power.— Testimonies for the Church 3:489.

510. A tendency to disease of various kinds, as dropsy, liver complaint,trembling nerves, and the determination of the blood to the head, results from the habitual use of sour cider. By its use many bring upon themselves permanent disease. Some die of consumption or fall under the power of apoplexy from this cause alone. Some suffer from dyspepsia. Every vital function refuses to act, and the physician tells them they have liver complaint, when if they would break in the head of the cider barrel, and never give way to the temptation to replace it, their abused life forces would recover their vigor.—The Review and Herald, March 25, 1884.

511. A single glass of wine may open the door of temptation which willlead to habits of drunkenness.—Testimonies for the Church 4:578.

512. When the appetite for spirituous liquor is indulged, the man voluntarily places to his lips the draught which debases below the level of the brute him who was made in the image of God. Reason is paralyzed, the intellect is benumbed, the animal passions are excited, and then follow crimes of the most debasing character.—Testimonies for the Church 3:561.

513. The law authorizes the sale of liquor, and then has to build prisonsfor the victims; for nine tenths of those who are taken to prison are those who have learned to drink.—The Review and Herald, May 8, 1894.

514. How many frightful accidents occur through the influence of drink.... What is the portion of this terrible intoxicant that any man can take, and be safe with the lives of human beings? He can be safe only as he abstains from drink. No intoxicant should pass his lips; then if a disaster comes, men in responsible positions can do their best, and meet their record with satisfaction, whatever may be the issue.—The Review and Herald, May 29, 1894.

515. Liquor-drinking men may be seen everywhere. Their intellectis enfeebled, their moral powers are weakened, their sensibilities are

benumbed, and the claims of God and heaven are not realized, eternal things are not appreciated. The Bible declares that no drunkard shall inherit the kingdom of God.... Intemperance of any kind is the worst kind of selfishness.—*Testimonies for the Church* 4:30, 31.

CURE FOR THE LIQUOR HABIT

516. What cure would you advise for a person who thus indulges a habit that is rebuked even by

the beasts of the field? The word of God has denounced it: no drunkard shall enter the kingdom of God. What would you recommend to cure such an appetite? You would not say, "You may use strong drink moderately. Continue within bounds, but never indulge to excess." You would rather say, "There is no such thing as helping you unless you co-operate fully with my efforts, and sign the pledge of total abstinence. You have by indulgence made your habit second nature, and it cannot be controlled unless the moral power shall be aroused, and you look unto Jesus, trusting in the grace he shall give to overcome this unnatural craving." You would say, "You have lost your self-control. Your self-indulgence is not only a moral sin, but it has become a physical disease. You are not your own; you are God's property. He has purchased you with an infinite price, and every faculty is to be employed in his service. Keep your body in a healthy condition to do his will; keep your intellect clear and active to think candidly and critically, and to control all your powers."—*Unpublished Testimonies*, October 12, 1896.

ALCOHOL IN DISEASE

517. The taste created for the disgusting, filthy poison, tobacco, leadsto the desire for stronger stimulants, as liquor, which is taken on one plea or another, for some imaginary infirmity, or to prevent some possible disease.—*Testimonies for the Church* 4:30.

518. By advising friends and neighbors to take brandy for the sakeof their health, they are in danger of becoming agents for the destruction of their friends.... Physicians are responsible for making many drunkards.

Knowing what drink will

do for its lovers, they have taken upon themselves the responsibility of prescribing it for their patients. Did they reason from cause to effect, they would know that stimulants would have the same effect on each individual organ of the body that they have on the whole man. What excuse can doctors render for the influence they have exerted in making fathers and mothers drunkards?—*The Review and Herald*, May 29, 1894.

519. Go with me to yonder sick-room. There lies a husband and father, a man who is a blessing to society and to the cause of God. He has been suddenly stricken down by disease. The fire of fever seems consuming him. He longs for pure water to moisten the parched lips, to quench the raging thirst, and cool the fevered brow. But no; the doctor has forbidden water. The stimulus of strong drink is given, which adds fuel to the fire.... For a time nature wrestles for her rights, but at last, overcome, she gives up the contest, and death sets the sufferer free.— *Testimonies for the Church* 5:195.

520. Those who do not control their appetites in eating are guilty of intemperance.... With many, their first error is in making a god of their appetite, subsisting mostly on highly seasoned animal food, which produces a feverish state of the system, especially if pork is used freely. The blood becomes impure. The circulation is not equalized. Chills and fever follow. The appetite fails. They think something must be done, and perhaps send for ale, which stimulates for the time, but as soon as the influence of the ale is gone, they sink as much lower, and a continual use of the ale keeps them stimulated

and overexcited. They think that the ale was of so much benefit to them that they must continue its use. After a while it loses its influence; then they use a stronger beverage, until they give themselves up to every excess, and man formed in the image of his Maker degrades himself lower than the beasts. It required time to benumb the sensibilities of the mind. It was done gradually, but surely. *Facts of Faith*, 126.

CHAPTER XXI. - DRESS.

General Statements.

521. Our words, our actions, and our dress are daily, living preachers, gathering with Christ or scattering abroad. This is no trivial matter.—*Testimonies for the Church* 4:641.

522. Turn away from the fashion plates, and study the human organism.—*Christian Temperance and Bible Hygiene*, 91.

523. Christians should not take pains to make themselves a gazing-stock by dressing differently from the world. But if, when following out their convictions of duty in respect to dressing modestly and healthfully, they find themselves out of fashion, they should not change their dress in order to be like the world; but they should manifest a noble independence and moral courage to be right, if all the world differ from them. If the world introduces a modest, convenient, and healthful mode of dress, which is in accordance with the Bible, it will not change our relation to God or to the world to adopt such a style of dress. Christians should follow Christ and make their dress conform to God's word. They should shun extremes.—*Testimonies for the Church* 1:458.

524. In dress we should seek that which is simple, comfortable, convenient, and appropriate.—*The Review and Herald*, June 15, 1886.

525. A plain, direct testimony is now needed, as given in the wordof God, in regard to plainness of dress. This should be our burden. But it is too late now to become enthusiastic in making a test of this matter. There were some things which made the reform dress, which was once advocated, a decided blessing. With it the ridiculous hoops, which were then the fashion, could not be worn. The long dress skirts trailing on the ground and sweeping up the filth of the streets could not be patronized. But a more sensible style of dress has been adopted, which does not embrace these objectionable features. The fashionable part may be discarded, and should be by all who read the word of God. The dress of our people should be made most simple. The skirt and sack I have mentioned may be used, not that just that pattern and nothing else should be established, but a simple style as was represented in that dress. Some have supposed that the very pattern given was the pattern that all should adopt; this is not so, but something as simple as this would be the best we could adopt under the circumstances.... Simple dress should be the word; try your talent, my sisters, in this essential

reform.... Let our sisters dress plainly, as many do, in having the dress of good material, durable, modest, appropriate for the age; and let not the dress question fill the mind.—*Unpublished Testimonies*, July 4, 1897.

MENTAL AND MORAL INFLUENCE OF DRESS

526. The sum and substance of true religion is to own and continuallyacknowledge by words, by
dress, by deportment, our relationship to God.—*Testimonies for the Church* 4:582.

527. Perhaps no question has ever come up among us which has causedsuch development of character as has the dress reform.—*Testimonies for the Church* 4:636.

528. Simplicity of dress will make a sensible woman appear to the bestadvantage. We judge of a person's character by the style of dress worn. Gaudy apparel displays vanity and weakness. A modest, godly woman will dress modestly. A refined taste, a cultivated mind, will be revealed in the choice of simple and appropriate attire.—*Testimonies for the Church* 4:643.

529. We would not by any means encourage carelessness in dress. Letthe attire be appropriate and becoming. Though only a ten-cent calico, it should be kept neat and clean.—*Testimonies for the Church* 4:642.

530. Taste should be manifested as to colors. Uniformity in this respectis desirable so far as convenient. Complexion, however, may be taken into account. Modest colors should be sought for. When figured material is used, figures that are large and fiery, showing vanity and shallow pride in those who choose them, should be avoided. And a fantastic taste in putting on different colors is bad.—The Health Reformer, September 1, 1868.

531. Let the wearing of useless trimmings and adornments be discarded. Extravagance should never be indulged in to gratify pride. Our dress may be of good quality, made up with plainness and simplicity, for durability rather than for display.—*The Review and Herald*, November 21, 1878.

532. There is no need to make the dress question the main point of yourreligion. There is something richer to speak of. Talk of Christ; and

when the heart is converted, everything that is out of harmony with the word of God will drop off.—*The Signs of the Times*, July 1, 1889.

533. There is no use in telling you that you must not wear this or that,for if the love of these vain things is in your heart, your laying off your adornments will only be like cutting the foliage off a tree.—*The Review and Herald*, May 10, 1892.

534. "Thou shalt not follow a multitude to do evil." ... Be not hardenedby the deceitfulness of sin. Fashion is deteriorating the intellect and eating out the spirituality of our people.—*Testimonies for the Church* 4:647.

535. As soon as any have a desire to imitate the fashions of the world that they do not immediately subdue, just so soon God ceases to acknowledge them as his children.—*Testimonies for the Church* 1:137.

536. Those who have had the light upon the subjects of eating anddressing with simplicity, in obedience to physical and moral laws, and who turn from the light which points out their duty, will shun duty in other things. If they blunt their consciences to avoid the cross which they will have to take up to be in harmony with natural law, they will, in order to shun reproach, violate the ten commandments.—*Testimonies for the Church* 3:51.

INFLUENCE OF DRESS UPON THE BODY

537. Physical loveliness consists in symmetry—the harmonious proportion of parts.—*Christian Temperance and Bible Hygiene*, 94.

538. Dress reform ... includes every article of dress upon the person. Itlifts the weights from the hips by suspending the skirts from the shoulders. It removes the tight corsets, which compress the lungs, the stomach, and other internal organs, and induce curvature of the spine and an almost countless train of diseases. Dress reform proper provides for the protection and development of every part of the body.—*Testimonies for the Church* 4:635.

539. Woman's dress should be arranged so loosely upon the person,about the waist, that she can breathe without the least obstruction. Her arms should be left perfectly free, that she may raise them above her head with ease.... The compression of the waist by tight lacing prevents the waste matter from being thrown off through its natural channels. The most important of these is the lungs.... If the

lungs are cramped, they cannot develop; but their capacity will be diminished, making it impossible to take a sufficient inspiration of air.... The compression of the waist weakens the muscles of the respiratory organs. It hinders the process of digestion. The heart, liver, lungs, spleen, and stomach are crowded into a small compass, not allowing room for the healthful action of these organs.—*The Heath Reformer*, November 1, 1871; see also, *Counsels to Parents*, Teachers, and Students, 88.

540. The dress should fit easily, obstructing neither the circulation ofthe blood, nor a free, full, natural respiration.—*Christian Temperance and Bible Hygiene*, 89.

541. Our Creator made no mistake in fashioning the human body. Hegave appropriate space for the free action of every organ, and formed us in such a way that every muscle could come into play without trespassing upon the function of any other muscle.—*The Youth's Instructor*, September 14, 1893.

542. Lacing causes displacements, and this form of disease is increasing with each successive generation.—The Health Reformer, November 1, 1871.

543. Many have become lifelong invalids through their compliance with the demands of fashion. Displacements and deformities, cancers and other terrible diseases, are among the evils resulting from fashionable dress.—*Testimonies for the Church* 4:635.

544. Half the diseases of women are caused by unhealthful dress.— TheHealth Reformer, February 1, 1877.

HEAVY SKIRTS

545. The hips are not formed to bear heavy weights. The heavy skirts worn by women, their weight dragging down upon the hips, have been the cause of various diseases which are not easily cured, because the sufferers seem to be ignorant of the cause which has produced them, and they continue to violate the laws of their being by girding the waist and wearing heavy skirts, until they are made lifelong invalids.—*How to Live*, 64.

546. This heavy weight pressing upon the bowels, drags them downward, and causes weakness of the stomach, and a feeling of lassitude, which leads the sufferer to incline forward. This tends further

to cramp the lungs, and prevents their proper action. The blood becomes impure, the pores of the skin fail in their office, sallowness and disease result, and beauty and health are gone.... Every woman who values health should avoid hanging any weight upon the hips.—*Christian Temperance and Bible Hygiene*, 89.

CLOTHING OF THE EXTREMITIES

547. The most of us wear clothing enough, but many fail to give everypart of the body its due proportion.... If any part of the body should be favored with extra coverings, it should be the limbs and feet, which are at a distance from the great wheel of life, which sends the blood through the system. The limbs should ever be clothed with a warm covering to protect them from a chill current of air.... If the feet are clothed with good-sized, thick-soled, warm boots or shoes, for comfort rather than for fashion, the blood will be induced to circulate freely in the limbs and feet, as well as other portions of the body.... If we give the lungs and feet ample room to do the work God designed they should, we shall be rewarded with better health and a clearer conscience.—The Health Reformer, April 1, 1871.

548. There is but one woman in a thousand who clothes her limbs as sheshould.... Women should clothe their limbs as thoroughly as do men.—*How to Live*, 64.

549. The portions of the body close to the life springs, need less covering than the limbs which are remote from the vital organs. If the limbs and feet could have the extra coverings usually put upon the shoulders, lungs, and heart, and healthy circulation be induced to the extremities, the vital organs would act their part healthfully, with only their share of clothing.—*How to Live*, 73.

550. The extremities are chilled, and the heart has thrown upon it double labor, to force the blood into these chilled extremities; and when the blood has performed its circuit through the body, and returned to the heart, it is not the same vigorous, warm current which left it. It has been chilled in its passage through the limbs. The heart, weakened by too great labor and poor circulation of poor blood, is then compelled to still greater exertion, to throw the blood to the extremities which are never as healthfully warm as other parts of the body. The heart fails in its efforts, and the limbs become habitually cold; and the blood, which is chilled away from the extremities, is thrown back upon

the lungs and brain, and inflammation and congestion of the lungs or the brain is the result.—*How to Live*, 72.

551. It is impossible for women to have, habitually, chilled limbs and cold feet, without some of the internal organs' being congested.... The many extra coverings over the chest and back and lower part of the body, induce the blood to these parts, and the animal heat, thus retained, weakens and debilitates the delicate organs, and congestion and inflammation result.—The Health Reformer, May 1, 1872.

552. When the extremities, which are remote from the vital organs,are not properly clad, the blood is driven to the head, causing headache or nosebleed; or there is a sense of fulness about the chest producing cough or palpitation of the heart, on account of too much blood in that locality; or the stomach has too much blood, causing indigestion.—*Testimonies for the Church* 2:531.

LENGTH OF DRESS

553. The length of the fashionable dress is objectionable for several reasons:—

1.   It is extravagant and unnecessary to have a dress of such length thatit will sweep the sidewalk and street.

2.   A dress thus long gathers dew from the grass and mud from thestreets, and is therefore uncleanly.

3.   In its bedraggled condition it comes in contact with the sensitiveankles, which are not sufficiently protected, quickly chilling them, and thus endangering health and life. This is one of the greatest causes of catarrh and scrofulous swellings.

4.   The unnecessary length is an additional weight upon the hips andbowels.

5.   It hinders the walking, and is also often in other people's way.—*Testimonies for the Church* 1:459.

If women would wear their dresses so as to clear the filth of the street an inch or two, their dresses would be modest, and they could be kept clean much more easily, and would wear longer.—*Testimonies for the Church* 1:458.

554. You have worn too great an amount of clothing, and have debilitated the skin by so doing. You have not given your body a chance to breathe. The pores of the skin, or little mouths through which the body breathes, have become closed, and the system has been filled with impurities.—*Testimonies for the Church* 3:74.

555. I advise invalid sisters who have accustomed themselves to toogreat an amount of clothing, to lay it off gradually.—*Testimonies for the Church* 2:533.

556. Disease of every type is brought upon the body through the unhealthful, fashionable style of dress; and the fact should be made prominent that a reform must take place before treatment will effect a cure.—*Testimonies for the Church* 4:582.

CHAPTER XXII. - EXERCISE.

General Statements.

557. The human body may be compared to nicely adjusted machinery,which needs care to keep it in running order. One part should not be subjected to constant wear and pressure, while another part is rusting from inaction. While the mind is taxed, the muscles also should have their proportion of exercise. Every young person should learn how many hours may be spent in study, and how much time should be given to physical exercise.—*The Signs of the Times*, August 26, 1886.

558. There is quite a difference between weariness and exhaustion.—*A Solemn Appeal*, 64.

559. The compression of the waist will not allow free action of themuscles.—The Health Reformer, November 1, 1871.

560. Another precious blessing is proper exercise.—*Testimonies for the Church* 2:528.

561 They should go out and exercise every day, ... make it their object to do some good, working to the end of benefiting others.—*Testimonies for the Church* 2:531.

VARIETIES OF EXERCISE

Gymnastics.

562. The exercise of one muscle, while others are left with nothingto do, will not strengthen the inactive ones, any more than the continual exercise of one of the organs of the mind will develop and
strengthen the organs not brought into use. Each faculty of the mind and each muscle has its distinctive office, and all require to be exercised in order to become properly developed and retain healthful vigor. Each organ and muscle has its work to do in the living organism. Every wheel in the machinery must be a living, active, working wheel. Nature's fine and wonderful works need to be kept in active motion in order to accomplish the object for which they were designed. Each faculty has a bearing upon the others, and all need to be exercised in order to be properly developed. If one muscle of the body is exercised more than another, the one used will become much the larger, and will destroy the harmony and beauty of the development of the system. A variety of exercise will call into use all the muscles of the body.—*Testimonies for the Church* 3:77, 78.

563. It is not good policy to give up the use of certain muscles because pain is felt when they are exercised. The pain is frequently caused by the effort of nature to give life and vigor to those parts that have become partially lifeless through inaction. The motion of these long disused muscles will cause pain, because nature is awakening them to life.—*Testimonies for the Church* 3:78.

564. Exercise, to be of decided advantage to you, should be systematized, and brought to bear upon the debilitated organs that they may become strengthened by use.—*Testimonies for the Church* 3:76.

Useful Labor

565. When useful labor is combined with study, there is no need of gymnastic exercises; and much more benefit is derived from work performed in the
open air than from indoor exercise. The farmer and the mechanic each have physical exercise; yet the farmer is much the healthier of the two, for nothing short of the invigorating air and sunshine will fully meet the wants of the system. The former finds in his labor all the movements

that were ever practised in the gymnasium. And his movement room is the open fields; the canopy of heaven is its roof, the solid earth is its floor.—*The Signs of the Times*, August 26, 1886.

566. Brethren, when you take time to cultivate your gardens, thus gaining the exercise needed to keep the system in good working order, you are just as much doing the work of God as in holding meetings.—*Gospel Workers*, 174.

567. If work is performed without the heart's being in it, it is simplydrudgery, and the benefit which should result from the exercise is not gained.—The Health Reformer, May 1, 1873.

Passive Exercise

568. The movement cure is a great advantage to a class of patients whoare too feeble to exercise. But for all who are sick to rely upon it, making it their dependence, while they neglect to exercise their muscles themselves, is a great mistake.—*Testimonies for the Church* 3:76.

569. Many who depend on the movement cure could accomplish more for themselves by muscular exercise than the movements can do for them.—*Testimonies for the Church* 3:78.

Walking

570. There is no exercise that can take the place of walking. By it thecirculation of the blood is greatly improved.... Walking, in all cases where it is possible, is the best remedy for diseased bodies, because in this exercise all of the organs of the body are brought into use.—*Testimonies for the Church* 3:78.

571. When the weather will permit, all who can possibly do so oughtto walk in the open air every day, summer and winter.... A walk, even in winter, would be more beneficial to the health than all the medicine the doctors may prescribe. For those who can walk, walking is preferable to riding. The muscles and veins are enabled better to perform their work. There will be increased vitality, which is so necessary to health. The lungs will have needful action; for it is impossible to go out in the bracing air of a winter's morning without inflating the lungs.—*Testimonies for the Church* 2:529.

572. There is no exercise that will prove as beneficial to every partof the body as walking. Active walking in the open air will do more for

women, to preserve them in health if they are well, than any other means. Walking is also one of the most efficient remedies for the recovery of health of the invalid. The hands and arms are exercised as well as the limbs.—The Health Reformer, April 1, 1872.

When to Exercise

573. Exercise will aid the work of digestion. To walk out after a meal,hold the head erect, put back the shoulders, and exercise moderately, will be a great benefit. The mind will be diverted from self to the beauties of nature. The less the attention is called to the stomach after a meal, the better.—Testimonies for the Church 2:530.

574. Morning exercise, in walking in the free, invigorating air of heaven, or cultivating flowers, small fruits, and vegetables, is necessary to a healthful
circulation of the blood. It is the surest safeguard against colds, coughs, congestions of the brain and lungs, inflammation of the liver, the kidneys, and the lungs, and a hundred other diseases.—The Health Reformer, May 1, 1872.

575. A large class of women are content to hover over the stove, breathing impure air for one half or three fourths of the time, until the brain is heated and half benumbed. They should go out and exercise every day, even though some things indoors have to be neglected. They need the cool air to quiet distracted brains.—Testimonies for the Church 2:531.

576. Neither study nor violent exercise should be engaged in immediately after a full meal; this would be a violation of the laws of the system. Immediately after eating there is a strong draught upon the nervous energy. The brain force is called into active exercise to assist the stomach; therefore, when mind or body is taxed heavily after eating, the process of digestion is hindered. The vitality of the system, which is needed to carry on the work in one direction, is called away and set to work in another.—Testimonies for the Church 2:413.

Benefits Derived from Exercise

577. God designed that the living machinery should be in daily activity; for in this activity or motion is its preserving power.—The Health Reformer, May 1, 1873.

578. By active exercise in the open air every day the liver, kidneys, andlungs also will be strengthened to perform their work.—*Testimonies for the Church* 2:533.

579. If invalids who can would engage in light, useful labor in the openair a portion of each day, they would find physical exercise one of God's appointed agents for the benefit of man.—*The Health Reformer*, June 1, 1871.

580. If they worked intelligently, giving both mind and body a due shareof exercise, ministers would not so readily succumb to disease.—*Gospel Workers*, 173.

581. Healthy, active exercise is what you need. This will invigorate themind.—*Testimonies for the Church* 2:413.

582. There will be increased vitality, which is so necessary to health.—*Testimonies for the Church* 2:529.

583. Not only will the organs of the body be strengthened by exercise,but the mind also will acquire strength and knowledge through the action of these organs.—*Testimonies for the Church* 3:77.

584. The more we exercise, the better will be the circulation of theblood.—*Testimonies for the Church* 2:525.

585. If physical exercise were combined with mental exertion, the blood would be quickened in its circulation, the action of the heart would be more perfect, impure matter would be thrown off, and new life and vigor would be experienced in every part of the body.—*Testimonies for the Church* 3:490.

586. The proper use of their physical strength, as well as of the mentalpowers, will equalize the circulation of the blood, and keep every organ of the living machinery in running order.—*Special Testimonies On Education*, 352.

587. Judicious exercise will induce the blood to the surface, and thusrelieve the internal organs. Brisk, yet not violent, exercise in the open air, with cheerfulness of spirits, will promote the circulation, giving a healthful glow to the skin, and sending the blood, vitalized by the pure air, to the extremities.—*Testimonies for the Church* 2:530.

588. By judicious exercise they may expand the chest and strengthenthe muscles.... By giving heed to proper instruction, by following health principles in regard to the expansion of the lungs and culture of the voice, our young men and women may become speakers

that can be heard, and the exercise necessary to this accomplishment will prolong life.—*Christian Education*, 132.

589. A farmer who is temperate in all his habits usually enjoys goodhealth. His work is pleasant; and his vigorous exercise causes full, deep, and strong inspirations and exhalations, which expand the lungs and purify the blood, sending the warm current of life bounding through arteries and veins.... The student sits day after day in a close room, bending over his desk or table, his chest contracted, his lungs crowded. His brain is taxed to the utmost, while his body is inactive. He cannot take full, deep inspirations; his blood moves sluggishly; his feet are cold, his head hot.... Let them take regular exercise that will cause them to breathe deep and full, and they will soon feel that they have a new hold on life.—*The Signs of the Times*, August 26, 1886.

590. The diseased stomach will find relief by exercise.—*Testimonies for the Church* 2:530.

591. Exercise is important to digestion, and to a healthy condition ofbody and mind.—*Testimonies for the Church* 2:413.

592. Digestion will be promoted by physical exercise.—*Testimonies for the Church* 2:569.

593. Useful employment would bring into exercise the enfeebled muscles, enliven the stagnant blood in the system, and arouse the torpid liver to perform its work. The circulation of the blood would be equalized, and the entire system invigorated to overcome bad conditions.—The Health Reformer, January 1, 1871.

Results of Lack of Exercise

594. I frequently turn from the bedside of these self-made invalids,saying to myself, "Dying by inches, dying of indolence, a disease which no one but themselves can cure."—The Health Reformer, January 1, 1871.

595. Neglecting to exercise the entire body, or a portion of it, will bringon morbid conditions.—*Testimonies for the Church* 3:76.

596. The bloom of health fades from their cheeks, and disease fastensupon them, because they are robbed of physical exercise, and their habits are perverted generally.—*Testimonies for the Church* 3:158.

597. Continued inactivity is one of the greatest causes of debility ofbody and feebleness of mind.—*Testimonies for the Church* 2:524.

598. Inaction of any of the organs of the body will be followed bydecrease in size and strength of the muscles, and will cause the blood to flow sluggishly through the blood-vessels.—*Testimonies for the Church* 3:76.

599. In what contrast to the habits of the active farmer are those of thestudent who neglects physical exercise.... His blood moves sluggishly; his feet are cold; his head hot. How can such a person have health?—*The Signs of the Times*, August 26, 1886.

600. The studied habit of shunning the air and avoiding exercise, closesthe pores,—the little mouths through which the body breathes,— making it impossible
to throw off impurities through that channel. The burden of labor is thrown upon the liver, lungs, kidneys, etc., and these internal organs are compelled to do the work of the skin.—*Testimonies for the Church* 2:524.

601. The blood is not enabled to expel the impurities as it would ifactive circulation were induced by exercise.—*Testimonies for the Church* 2:529.

602. In some cases, want of exercise causes the muscles of the bowelsto become enfeebled and shrunken, and these organs that have become enfeebled for want of use will be strengthened by exercise.— *Testimonies for the Church* 3:78.

603. Moderate exercise every day will impart strength to the muscles,which without exercise become flabby and enfeebled.— *Testimonies for the Church* 2:533.

604. If invalids would recover health, they should not discontinue physical exercise; for they will thus increase muscular weakness and general debility. Bind up the arm, and permit it to remain useless, even for a few weeks, then free it from its bondage, and you will discover that it is weaker than the one you had been using moderately during the same time. Inactivity produces the same effect upon the whole muscular system.—*Testimonies for the Church* 2:529.

CHAPTER XXIII. - MANUAL TRAINING.

605. If all our workers were so situated that they could spend a fewhours each day in outdoor labor, and feel free to do this, it would be a blessing to them; they would be able to discharge more successfully the duties of their calling.—*Gospel Workers*, 173.

606. Manual occupation for the youth is essential.... The proper exercise of mind and body will develop and strengthen all the powers. Both mind and body will be preserved, and will be capable of doing a variety of work. Ministers and teachers need to learn in regard to these things, and they need to practise as well.—*Special Instruction on Educational Work* 14.

607. The people of this country have so little appreciation of the importance of industrious habits that the children are not educated to do real, earnest work. This must be a part of the education given to the youth.... We need schools to educate children and youth that they may be *masters* of labor, and not *slaves* of labor. Ignorance and idleness will not elevate one member of the human family. Ignorance will not lighten the lot of the hard toiler. Let the worker see what advantage he may gain in the humblest occupation, by using the ability God has given him as an endowment. Thus he can

become an educator, teaching others the art of doing work intelligently.... The Lord wants the physical strength; and you can reveal your love for him by the right use of your physical powers, doing the very work which needs to be done.... There is science in the humblest kind of work, and if all would thus regard it, they would see nobility in labor.... Let the educated ability be employed in devising improved methods of work. This is just what the Lord wants. There is honor in any class of work that is essential to be done. Let the law of God be made the standard of action, and it ennobles and sanctifies all labor.... We are not to be dwarfed in any kind of service for God. Whatever he has lent us is to be used intelligently for him. The man who exercises his faculties will surely strengthen them; but he must seek to do his best. There is need of intelligence and educated ability to devise the best methods in farming, in building, and in every other department, that the worker may not labor in vain.—*Special Instruction on Educational Work*

5.

608. Your means could not be used to better advantage than in providinga workshop furnished with tools for your boys, and equal facilities for your girls. They can be taught to love labor.—The Health Reformer, January 1, 1873.

609. Agriculture will open resources for self-support, and various othertrades also could be learned. This real, earnest work calls for a strength of intellect as well as of muscle. Method and tact are required even to raise fruits and vegetables successfully. And habits of industry will be found an important aid to the youth in resisting temptation. Here is opened a field to give vent to their pent-up energies, that, if not expended in useful employment, will be a continual source of trial to themselves and to their teachers. Many kinds of labor adapted to different persons may be devised. But the working of the land will be a special blessing to the worker.... This knowledge will not be a hindrance to the education essential for business or for usefulness in any line. To develop the capacity of the soil requires thought and intelligence.— *Special Instruction on Educational Work* 15.

610. Agriculture should be advanced by scientific knowledge.—*The Signs of the Times*, August 13, 1896.

611. Students sent to school to prepare to become evangelists, ministers, and missionaries to foreign countries, have received the idea that amusements are essential to keep them in physical health, when the Lord has presented it before them that the better way is to embrace in their education manual labor in place of amusement.... The education to be obtained in felling trees, tilling the soil, as well as in literature, is the education our youth should seek to obtain. Farther on printing-presses should be connected with our schools. Tent making also should be taken hold of. Buildings should be erected, and masonry should be learned.

There are also many things which the lady students may engage in. There is cooking, dressmaking, and gardening to be done. Strawberries should be planted, and plants and flowers cultivated.

Bookbinding also and a variety of trades should

be taken up. Thus the student will be putting into exercise bone, brain, and muscle, and will also be gaining knowledge. The greatest curse of our schools is idleness. It leads to amusements merely to please and gratify self. The students have had a superabundance of this way of passing their time. They are not prepared to go forth from the school with an all-round education.

The proper cooking of food is a most essential requirement. Something must be prepared to take the place of meat, and so well prepared that meat will not be desired. Culture on all points of life will make the youth useful after they shall leave the school to go to foreign countries. They will not then have to depend upon the people to whom they go to cook and sew for them, or to build their habitations; and they will have much more influence if they show that they know how to do work by the best methods and to produce the best results. This will be appreciated where means are difficult to obtain. Missionaries can thus teach others how to labor. A much smaller fund will be required to sustain such missionaries, and wherever they may go, all that they have gained in this line will give them standing.

It is also essential to understand the philosophy of medical missionary work. Wherever the students may go, they need education in the science of how to treat the sick. This will give them a welcome in any place, because there is suffering of every kind in every part of the world. Education, true education, means much.—*Unpublished Testimonies*, December 20, 1896.

CHAPTER XXIV. - HYGIENE.

Hygiene of the Home and Premises.

612. Dwellings, if possible, should be built upon high and dry ground.If a house be built where water settles around it, remaining for a time and then drying away, a poisonous miasma arises, and fever and ague, sore throat, lung diseases, and fevers will be the result.—*How to Live*, 64.

613. If every family realized the beneficial results of thorough cleanliness, they would make special efforts to remove every impurity from their persons and from their houses, and would extend their efforts to their premises. Many suffer decayed vegetable matter to remain about their premises. They are not awake to the influence of these things. There is constantly arising from the decayed substances an effluvium that is poisoning the air. By inhaling the impure air, the

blood is poisoned, the lungs become affected, and the whole system is diseased.—*How to Live*, 60.

614. Stubborn fevers and violent diseases have prevailed in neighborhoods and towns that had formerly been considered healthy, and some have died, while others have been left with broken constitutions to be crippled with disease for life. In many instances their own yards contained the agent of destruction, which sent forth deadly poison into the atmosphere to be inhaled by the family and the neighborhood. The slackness and recklessness sometimes witnessed is beastly, and the ignorance of the results of such things upon health is astonishing. Such places should be purified, especially in summer, by lime or ashes, or by a daily burial with earth.—*How to Live*, 61.

615. Shade-trees and shrubbery too close and dense around a houseare unhealthful; for they prevent a free circulation of air, and prevent the rays of the sun from shining through sufficiently. In consequence of this a dampness gathers in the house. Especially in wet seasons the sleeping-rooms become damp, and those who sleep in the beds are troubled with rheumatism, neuralgia, and lung complaints, which generally end in consumption. Numerous shade-trees cast off many leaves, which, if not immediately removed, decay, and poison the atmosphere. A yard, beautiful with scattering trees, and some shrubbery at a proper distance from the house, has a happy, cheerful influence upon the family, and if well taken care of, will prove no injury to health.—*How to Live*, 64.

616. Rooms that are not exposed to light and air become damp. Beds and bedding gather dampness, and the atmosphere in these rooms is poisonous, because it has not been purified by light and air. Various diseases have been brought on by sleeping in these fashionable, health-destroying apartments.... Sleeping-rooms especially should be well ventilated, and the atmosphere made healthful by light and air. Blinds should be left open several hours each day, the curtains put aside, and the room thoroughly aired; nothing should remain, even for a short time, which would destroy the purity of the atmosphere.—*How to Live*, 62.

617. Sleeping apartments should be large and so arranged as to have acirculation of air through them day and night.—*How to Live*, 63.

618. Rooms that are not freely ventilated daily, and bedding that has notbeen thoroughly dried and aired, are not fit for use. We feel confident that disease and great suffering are brought on by sleeping in rooms with closed and curtained windows, not admitting pure air and the rays of the sun.... The room may not have had an airing for months, nor the advantages of a fire for weeks, if at all. It is dangerous to health and life to sleep in these rooms until the outside air shall have circulated through them for several hours and the bedding shall have been dried by the fire. Unless this precaution is taken, the rooms and bedding will be damp. Every room in the house should be thoroughly ventilated every day, and in damp weather should be warmed by fires.... Every room in your dwelling should be daily thrown open to the healthful rays of the sun, and the purifying air should be invited in. This will be a preventive of disease.... If all would appreciate the sunshine, and expose every article of clothing to its drying, purifying rays, mildew and mold would be prevented. The confined air of unventilated rooms meets us with sickening odors of mildew and

mold, and the impurities exhaled by its inmates.... The emanations from damp, moldy rooms and clothing are poisonous to the system.— The Health Reformer, February 1, 1874.

HYGIENE OF THE PERSON

619. Strict habits of cleanliness should be observed. Many, while well, will not take the trouble to keep in a healthy condition. They neglect personal cleanliness, and are not careful to keep their clothing pure. Impurities are constantly and imperceptibly passing from the body, through the pores, and if the surface of the skin is not kept in a healthy condition, the system is burdened with impure matter. If the clothing worn is not often washed, and frequently aired, it becomes filthy with impurities which are thrown off from the body by sensible and insensible perspiration. And if the garments worn are not frequently cleansed from these impurities, the pores of the skin absorb again the waste matter thrown off. The impurities of the body, if not allowed to escape, are taken back into the blood, and forced upon the internal organs.—*How to Live*, 60.

620. In regard to cleanliness, God requires no less of his people now than he did of ancient Israel. A neglect of cleanliness will induce disease.—*How to Live*, 61.

621. The ten commandments spoken by Jehovah from Sinai cannot livein the hearts of persons of disorderly, filthy habits. If ancient Israel could not so much as listen to the proclamation of that holy law, unless they had obeyed the injunction of Jehovah,

and had cleansed their clothing, how can that sacred law be written upon the hearts of persons who are not cleanly in person, in clothing, or in their houses? It is impossible. Their profession may be as high as heaven, yet it is not worth a straw.... All who meet upon the Sabbath to worship God should, if possible, have a neat, well-fitting, comely suit to wear in the house of worship. It is a dishonor to the Sabbath, and to God and his house, for those who profess that the Sabbath is the holy of the Lord, and honorable, to wear the same clothing upon the Sabbath that they have worn through the week while laboring upon their farms, when they can obtain other.—*How to Live*, 59.

HYGIENE FOR CHILDREN

General Statements.

622. Several instances have come under my notice where children are being murdered by inches by the mistaken kindness of parents.— The Health Reformer, September 1, 1866.

623. The calm, self-possessed course the mother pursues in the treatment of her child has very much to do in molding the mind of the infant. If it is nervous and easily agitated, the mother's careful, unhurried manner will have a soothing and correcting influence, and the health of the infant can be very much improved.—*How to Live*, 39.

Diet

624. It ever has appeared to me to be cold, heartless business for mothers who can nurse their children to turn them from the maternal breast to the bottle. But in case that is necessary, the greatest care must be exercised to have the milk from a healthy cow, and to have the bottle, as well as the

milk, perfectly sweet. This is frequently neglected, and as the result, the infant is made to suffer needlessly. Disturbances of the stomach and bowels are liable to occur, and the much-to-be-pitied infant becomes diseased, if it were healthy when born.—The Health Reformer,

September 1, 1871.

Hired Nurses

625. Mothers sometimes depend upon a hireling.... A stranger performsthe duties of the mother, and gives from her breast the food to sustain life. Nor is this all. She also imparts her temper and her temperament to the nursing child. The child's life is linked to hers. If the hireling is a coarse type of woman, passionate and unreasonable; if she is not careful in her morals, the nursling will be, in all probability, of the same or similar type. The same quality of blood coursing in the veins of the hireling nurse is in that of the child.—The Health Reformer, September 1, 1871.

Frequent Feeding

626. Children are also fed too frequently, which produces feverishnessand suffering in various ways. The stomach should not be kept constantly at work, but should have its periods of rest. Without it children will be peevish and irritable and frequently sick.—The Health Reformer, September 1, 1866.

627. The first education that children should receive from the motherin infancy should be in regard to their physical health. They should be allowed only plain food, of that quality that would preserve to them the best condition of health, and that should be partaken of only at regular periods, not oftener than three times a day, and two meals would be better than three.

If children are disciplined aright, they will soon learn they can

receive nothing by crying and fretting. A judicious mother will act in training her children, not merely in regard to her own present comfort, but for their future good. And to this end she will teach her children the important lesson of controlling the appetite, and of self-denial, that they should eat, drink, and dress in reference to health.—How to Live, 47.

628. It is much easier to create an unnatural appetite than to correct andreform it after it has become second nature.... Meat given to children is not the best thing to insure success.... To educate your children to subsist upon a meat diet would be harmful to them.... Highly seasoned meats, followed by rich pastry, is wearing out the vital organs of the digestion of children. Had they been accustomed to plain,

wholesome food, their appetites would not have craved unnatural luxuries and mixed preparations.—*Unpublished Testimonies*, November 5, 1896. Fresh Air.

629. One great error of the mother in the treatment of her infant is, shedeprives it very much of fresh air, that which it ought to have to make it strong. It is a practise of many mothers to cover their infant's head while sleeping, and this, too, in a warm room, which is seldom ventilated as it should be. This alone is sufficient to greatly enfeeble the action of the heart and lungs, thereby affecting the whole system. While care may be needful to protect the infant from a draught of air or from any sudden and too great change, especial care should be taken to have the child breathe a pure, invigorating atmosphere. No disagreeable odor should remain in the nursery or about the child; such things are more dangerous to the feeble infant than to grown persons.—*How to Live*, 66.

630. But there is an evil greater than those already named. The infantis exposed to a vitiated air caused by many breaths, some of which are very offensive and injurious to the strong lungs of older people. The infant lungs suffer and become diseased by inhaling the atmosphere of a room poisoned by the tobacco user's tainted breath. Many infants are poisoned beyond remedy by sleeping in beds with their tobacco-using fathers. By inhaling the poisonous tobacco effluvium, which is thrown from the lungs and the pores of the skin, the system of the infant is filled with the poison. While it acts upon some as a slow poison, and affects the brain, heart, liver, and lungs, and they waste away and fade gradually, upon others it has a more direct influence, causing spasms, fits, paralysis, palsy, and sudden death.—*How to Live*, 68.

Dress of the Infant

631. The garments are made extravagantly long, and in order to keepthem up on the infant, its body is girded with tight bands, or waists, which hinder the free action of the heart and lungs. Infants are compelled to bear a needless weight because of the length of their garments, and thus clothed, they do not have free use of their muscles and limbs. Mothers have thought it necessary to compress the bodies of their infant children to keep them in shape, as if fearful that without tight bandages they would fall in pieces or become deformed. Do the animal creation become deformed because nature

is left to do her own work? Do the little lambs become deformed because they are not girded about with bands to give them shape? They are delicately and beautifully formed. Human infants are the most perfect, and yet the most helpless, of all the Creator's handiwork, and therefore their mothers should be instructed in regard to physical laws, so as to be capable of rearing them with physical, mental, and moral health. Mothers, nature has given our infants forms which need no girts or bands to perfect them. God has supplied them with bones and muscles sufficient for their support, and to guard nature's fine machinery within, before committing it to your care. The dress of the infant should be so arranged that its body will not be in the least compressed after taking a full meal.... Another great cause of mortality among infants and youth, is the custom of leaving their arms and shoulders naked. This fashion cannot be too severely censured. It has cost the lives of thousands. The air, bathing the arms and limbs and circulating about the armpits, chills these sensitive portions of the body so near the vitals, hinders the healthy circulation of the blood, and induces disease, especially of the lungs and brain.—*How to Live*, 67-69.

632. Mothers who dress their children in accordance with fashion, endanger their health and life. Fashion leaves the limbs of children unclad, save with one covering, or, at most, two. If they are exposed to the chill autumn, spring, or winter weather, their limbs are bathed in a current of cold air. Over

the heart, where is the greatest amount of vitality, there are from four to eight coverings. These unclad limbs and feet become habitually cold. While traveling, it is customary to see little girls dressed fashionably, but not healthfully. The upper portions of the body are abundantly clothed with warm cloaks, and over these are furs, while the limbs are scarcely covered.... Christian mother, why not clothe your daughter as comfortably and as properly as you do your son? ... His limbs are protected by from three to five thicknesses; hers by only one. Is she feebler? Then she needs the greater care. Is she indoors more, and therefore less protected against cold and storm? Then she needs double care.—The Health Reformer, January 1, 1873.

633. Societies are formed in our cities for the prevention of crueltyto dumb animals. It would be well to go still further, and, inasmuch as accountable intelligences, capable of obtaining life eternal, are of more value than the dumb beasts, there is greater need of societies to prevent

the cruelty of mothers in dressing their darling little girls in a manner to sacrifice them at the shrine of cruel fashion.—The Health Reformer, January 1, 1873.

Drugs

634. There is a disposition with many parents to dose children perpetually with medicine. They always have a supply on hand, and when any slight indisposition is manifested, caused by overeating or exhaustion, the medicine is poured down their throats, and if that does not satisfy them, they send for the doctor.... The child is drugged to death, and the parents console themselves that they
have done all they could for their children, and wonder why they must die when they did so much to save them.... Upon the gravestones of such children should be written, "Died of Drug Medication."—The Health Reformer, September 1, 1866.

Schools

635. Many mothers feel that they have not time to instruct their children, and in order to get them out of the way, and get rid of their noise and trouble, they send them to school. The schoolroom is a hard place for children who have inherited enfeebled constitutions. Schoolrooms generally have not been constructed in reference to health, but in regard to cheapness. The rooms have not been arranged so they could be ventilated as they should be without exposing the children to severe cold. The seats have seldom been made so that the children can sit with ease, and keep their little, growing frames in a proper posture to insure healthy action of the lungs and heart. Young children can grow into almost any shape, and can, by habits of proper exercise and positions of the body, obtain healthy forms. It is destructive to the health and life of young children to sit in the schoolroom, upon hard, ill-formed benches, from three to five hours a day, inhaling the air made impure by many breaths. The weak lungs become affected, the brain, from which the nervous energy of the whole system is derived, becomes enfeebled by being called into active exercise before the strength of the mental organs is sufficiently matured to endure fatigue.

In the schoolroom the foundation has been too surely laid for diseases of various kinds. But, more especially, the most delicate of all organs, the brain, has often been permanently injured by too great exercise. This has often caused inflammation, then dropsy of the head, and convulsions with their dreaded results.... Of those children who have apparently had sufficient force of constitution to survive this treatment, there are very many who carry the effects of it through life. The nervous energy of the brain becomes so weakened that after they have come to maturity it is impossible for them to endure much mental exercise. The force of some of the delicate organs of the brain seems to be expended....

During the first six or seven years of a child's life, special attention should be given to its physical training, rather than to the intellect. After this period, if the physical constitution is good, the education of both should receive attention.... Parents, especially mothers, should be the only teachers of such infant minds. They should not educate from books. The children generally will be inquisitive to learn the things of nature. They will ask questions in regard to the things they see and hear, and parents should improve the opportunity to instruct and patiently answer these little inquiries.—*How to Live*, 42, 44.

HYGIENE OF MOTHERHOOD

636. It is an error generally committed to make no difference in thelife of a woman previous to the birth of her children.—*Testimonies for the Church* 2:381.

637. In past generations, if mothers had informed themselves in regard to the laws of their being, they would have understood that their constitutional strength, as well as the tone of their morals, and their mental faculties, would in a great measure be represented in their offspring. Their ignorance upon this subject, where so much is involved, is criminal. Many women never should have become mothers. Their blood was filled with scrofula, transmitted to them from their parents, and increased by their gross manner of living. The intellect has been brought down and enslaved to serve the animal appetites, and children born of such parents have been poor sufferers, and of but little use to society....

Wives and mothers who otherwise would have had a beneficial influence upon society in raising the standard of morals, have been lost to society through multiplicity of home cares, because of the fashionable, health-destroying manner of cooking, and also in consequence of too frequent child-bearing. They have been compelled to needless suffering, the constitution has failed, and the intellect has become weakened by so great a draught upon the vital resources.... If the mother, before the birth of her offspring, had always possessed self-control, realizing that she was giving the stamp of character to future generations, the present state of society would not be so depreciated in character as at the present time.

Every woman about to become a mother, whatever may be her surroundings, should encourage constantly a happy, cheerful, contented disposition, knowing that for all her efforts in this direction she will be repaid tenfold in the physical as well as the moral character of her offspring.—*How to Live*, 37, 38.

638. Great care should be exercised to have the surroundings of the mother pleasant and happy.... Not half the care is taken of some women while they are bearing children that is taken of animals in the stable.—*Testimonies for the Church* 2:383.

Toiling Mothers

639. The mother, in many cases previous to the birth of her children, is permitted to toil early and late, heating her blood.... Her strength should have been tenderly cherished.... Her burdens and cares are seldom lessened, and that period, which should be to her of all others a time of rest, is one of fatigue, sadness, and gloom. By too great exertion on her part, she deprives her offspring of that nutrition which nature has provided for it, and by heating her own blood, she imparts to the child a bad quality of blood. The offspring is robbed of its vitality, robbed of physical and mental strength.—*How to Live*, 33.

Effect of the Mother's Overwork on the Infant

640. Many mothers, while nursing their infants, have been permitted to overlabor, and to heat their blood in cooking, and the nurseling has been seriously affected, not only with fevered nourishment from the mother's breast, but its blood has been poisoned by the unhealthful diet of the mother.... The infant will also be affected by the condition of the mother's mind. If she is unhappy, easily agitated, irritable, giving vent

to outbursts of passion, the nourishment the infant receives from its mother will be affected, often producing colic, spasms, and, in some instances causing convulsions.—*How to Live*, 39.

Diet

641. At this important period the labor of the mother should be lightened. Great changes are going on in her system. It requires a greater amount of blood, and therefore an increase of food of the most nourishing quality to convert into blood. Unless she has an abundant supply of nutritious food, she cannot retain her physical strength, and her offspring is robbed of vitality.... There will be an inability in the offspring to appropriate food which it can convert into good blood to nourish the system.... The extra draught upon the vitality of the mother must be considered and provided for.—*Testimonies for the Church* 2:381, 382.

Variable Appetite

642. But, on the other hand, the idea that women, because of theirspecial condition, may let the appetite run riot, is a mistake based on custom, but not on sound sense. The appetite of women in this condition may be variable, fitful, and difficult to gratify; and custom allows her to have anything she may fancy, without consulting reason as to whether such food can supply nutrition for her body and for the growth of her child. The food should be nutritious, but should not be of an exciting quality. Custom says that if she wants flesh meats, pickles, spiced food, or mince pies, let her have them; appetite alone is to be consulted. This is a great mistake, and does much harm. The harm cannot be estimated. If ever there is need of simplicity of diet and special care as to the quality of food eaten, it is at this important period. Women who possess
principle, and who are well instructed, will not depart from simplicity of diet at this time of all others. They will consider that another life is dependent upon them, and will be careful in all their habits, especially in diet.—*Testimonies for the Church* 2:382.

643. From the food the mother was compelled to receive, she could notfurnish a good quality of blood, and therefore gave birth to children filled with humors.—*Testimonies for the Church* 2:379.

Clothing

644. Her clothing also demands attention. Care should be taken toprotect the body from a sense of chilliness. She should not call vitality unnecessarily to the surface to supply the want of sufficient clothing.... The prosperity of mother and child depends much upon good, warm clothing, and a supply of nourishing food.—*Testimonies for the Church* 2:382.

645. Very many children are born with their blood tainted with scrofula,through the wrong habits of the mother in her eating and dressing. The very many miscarriages that now occur may generally be traced to fashionable dress.—*The Health Reformer, November 1, 1871.*

Hygiene of the Sick-Room.

646. When we do all we can on our part to have health, then may weexpect that blessed results will follow, and we can ask God in faith to bless our efforts for the preservation of health.—*How to Live, 64.*

647. Thousands have died for want of pure water and pure air, whomight have lived.... These blessings they need in order to become well. If they would become enlightened, and let medicine alone, and accustom themselves to outdoor exercise, and to air in their houses, summer and winter, and use soft water for drinking and bathing purposes, they would be comparatively well and happy instead of dragging out a miserable existence.—*How to Live, 56.*

648. If those who are well need the blessing of light and air, and needto observe habits of cleanliness in order to remain well, the sick are in still greater need of them in proportion to their debilitated condition.—*How to Live, 60.*

Ventilation

649. It is also of the greatest importance that the sick-room, from thefirst, be properly ventilated. This will be beneficial to the afflicted, and highly necessary to keep those well who are compelled to remain a length of time in the sick-room.—*How to Live, 54.*

650. There is a lamentable catalogue of evils which have their originin the sick-room, from which the pure air of heaven is excluded. All who breathe this poisonous atmosphere violate the laws of their being, and must suffer the penalty.—*How to Live, 58.*

651. Every breath of vital air in the sick-room is of the greatest value,although many of the sick are very ignorant on this point. They feel very much depressed, and do not know what the matter is. A draught of pure air through their room would have a happy, invigorating influence upon them.... The sick-room, if possible, should have a draught of air through it day and night. The draught should not come directly upon the invalid.—*How to Live*, 59.

652. In pleasant weather the sick in no case should be deprived of afull supply of fresh air.... Fresh air will prove more beneficial to the sick than medicine, and is far more essential to them than their food. They will do better and recover sooner deprived of food than of fresh air.... Their rooms may not always be so constructed as to allow the windows or doors to open in their rooms without the draughts coming directly upon them, and exposing them to take cold. In such cases windows and doors should be opened in an adjoining room, and thus let the fresh air enter the room occupied by the sick.—*How to Live*, 55.

653. If no other way can be devised, the sick, if possible, should beremoved to another room and another bed, while the sick-room, the bed and bedding, are being purified by ventilation.—*How to Live*, 60.

Temperature

654. It is of great value to the sick to have an even temperature in the room. This cannot always be correctly determined, if left to the judgment of the attendants, for they may not be the best judges of a right temperature. Some persons require more heat than others, and would be only comfortable in a room which to another would be uncomfortably warm. If each of these is at liberty to arrange the fires to suit her ideas of proper heat, the atmosphere in the sick-room will be anything but regular.... The friends of the sick, or attendants, who through anxiety and watching are deprived of sleep, and who
are suddenly awakened in the night from sleep to attend in the sick-room, are liable to chilliness. Such are not correct thermometers of the healthful temperature of a sick-room. These things may appear of small account, but they have very much to do with the recovery of the sick. In many instances life has been imperiled by extreme changes of the temperature of the sick-room.—*How to Live*, 54, 55.

655. While burning fevers are raging, there is but little danger of takingcold. But especial care is needful when the crisis comes, and fever

is passing away. Then constant watching may be necessary to keep vitality in the system—*How to Live*, 60.

656. The heated, oppressed atmosphere, deprived of vitality, benumbsthe sensitive brain.—*Testimonies for the Church* 1:702.

Cleanliness

657. If fevers enter a family, often more than one have the same fever.This need not be if the habits of the family are correct. If their diet is as it should be, and they observe habits of cleanliness and realize the necessity of ventilation, the fever need not extend to another member of the family. The reason that fevers prevail in families and expose the attendants, is because the sick-room is not kept free from poisonous infection, by cleanliness and proper ventilation.—*How to Live*, 57.

658. Many suffer decayed vegetable matter to remain about their premises. They are not awake to the influence of these things. There is constantly arising from these decaying substances an effluvium that is poisoning the air; by inhaling the impure air, the blood is poisoned, the lungs become affected, and the whole system is diseased. Disease of almost every description will be caused by inhaling the atmosphere affected by these decaying substances.—*How to Live*, 61.

Quiet

659. All unnecessary noise and excitement should be avoided in the sick-room, and the whole house should be kept as quiet as possible. Ignorance, forgetfulness, and recklessness have caused the death of many who might have lived had they received proper care from judicious, thoughtful attendants. The doors should be opened and shut with great care, and the attendants should be unhurried, calm, and self-possessed.—*How to Live*, 59.

660. Much harm has resulted to the sick from the universal custom ofhaving watchers at night. In critical cases this may be necessary; but it is often the case that more harm than good is done the sick by this practise.... Even one watcher will make more or less stir, which disturbs the sick. But where there are two, they often converse together, sometimes aloud, but more frequently in whispered tones, which is far more trying and exciting to the nerves of the sick than talking aloud.... Attendants upon the sick should, if possible, leave them to quiet and rest through the night, while they occupy a room adjoining.... The sick

as a general thing are taxed with too many visitors and callers, who chat with them, and weary them by introducing different topics of conversation, when they need quiet and undisturbed rest.... It is a mistaken kindness that leads so many, out of courtesy, to visit the sick. Often have they spent a sleepless, suffering night after receiving visitors. They have been more or less excited, and the reaction has been too great for their already debilitated energies, and as the result of these fashionable calls, they have been brought into very dangerous conditions, and lives have been sacrificed for the want of thoughtful prudence.... In very many instances these fashionable calls have turned the scale when the invalid was recovering, and the balance has borne them down to death. Those who cannot make themselves useful should be cautious in regard to visiting the sick.—*How to Live*, 58.

CHAPTER XXV. - THE ORGANS OF DIGESTION.

Physiology of the Digestive System.

661. The stomach has a controlling power upon the health of the entirebody.—The Health Reformer, October 1, 1871.

662. Anything which is taken into the stomach and converted into bloodbecomes a part of the being.—*Testimonies for the Church* 4:141.

663. The benefit you derive from your food does not depend so muchon the quantity eaten as on its thorough digestion, nor the gratification of the taste so much on the amount of food swallowed as on the length of time it remains in the mouth.... Eat slowly, and allow the saliva to mingle with the food.... Those who are excited, anxious, or in a hurry, cannot supply the necessary gastric juice.—*The Review and Herald*, July 29, 1884.

664. Thorough mastication is a benefit both to the teeth and the stomach.—The Review and Herald, May 8, 1883.

665. You are a nervous dyspeptic. The brain is closely connected with the stomach, and its power has so often been called to aid the weakened digestive organs that it is in its turn weakened, depressed, congested.—*Testimonies for the Church* 2:318.

666. It is important that we relish the food we eat. If we cannot do this,but eat mechanically, we fail to be nourished and built up as we

would be if we could enjoy the food we take into the stomach.—*Testimonies for the Church* 1:682.

667. Immediately after eating there is a strong draught upon the nervousenergy. The brain force is called into active exercise to assist the stomach; therefore, when the mind or body is taxed heavily after eating, the process of digestion is hindered. The vitality of the system, which is needed to carry on the work in one direction, is called away and set to work in another.—*Testimonies for the Church* 2:413.

668. The stomach, when we lie down to rest, should have its work alldone, that it may enjoy rest, as well as other portions of the body. The work of digestion should not be carried on through any period of the sleeping hours. After the stomach, which has been overtaxed, has performed its task, it becomes exhausted, which causes faintness.... The stomach becomes weary by being kept constantly at work.... Having no time for rest, the digestive organs become enfeebled, hence the sense of "goneness," and desire for frequent eating.... The stomach must have its regular periods for labor and rest.—*How to Live*, 56.

CAUSES OF INDIGESTION

669. The stomach has a controlling power upon the health of the entirebody.... The brain nerves are in strong sympathy with the stomach.—The Health Reformer, October 1, 1871.

670. Many are willingly ignorant of their own structure. They lead theirchildren in the same path of selfish indulgence which they have followed, causing them to suffer the penalty of the transgression of nature's laws. They go to distant countries to seek a better climate, but their stomachs will create for them a malarious atmosphere wherever they may locate. They bring upon themselves sufferings that no one can alleviate.—*Unpublished Testimonies*, August 25, 1897.

Hasty Eating

671. In order to have healthy digestion, food should be eaten slowly.Those who wish to avoid dyspepsia, and those who realize their obligation to keep all their powers in the condition which will enable them to render the best service to God, will do well to remember this. If your time to eat is limited, do not bolt your food, but eat less, and eat slowly.... Those who are excited, anxious, or in a great hurry would do

well not to eat until they have found rest or relief; for the vital powers, already severely taxed, cannot supply the necessary gastric juice.... Eat slowly, and allow the saliva to mingle with the food.—*The Review and Herald*, July 29, 1884.

Drinking at Meals

672. Food should not be washed down; no drink is needed with meals....The more liquid there is taken into the stomach with meals, the more difficult it is for the food to digest; for the liquid must first be absorbed.... Many make a mistake in drinking cold water with their meals. Taken with meals, water diminishes the flow of the salivary glands; and the colder the water, the greater the injury to the stomach. Ice-water or iced lemonade, drunk with meals, will arrest digestion until the system has
imparted sufficient warmth to the stomach to enable it to take up its work again.—*Ibid*.

673. Hot drinks are debilitating; and besides, those who indulge in theiruse become slaves to the habit.... But if anything is needed to quench thirst, pure water drunk some little time before or after the meal is all that nature requires. Never take tea, coffee, beer, wine, or any spirituous liquor. Water is the best liquid possible to cleanse the tissues.—*Ibid*.

Liquid Foods

674. Soups, puddings, and other articles of the kind are often eatentoo hot, and as a consequence the stomach is debilitated. Let them become partly cooled before they are eaten.—*Ibid*.

675. To eat largely of porridge would not insure health to the digestiveorgans; for it is too much like liquid.—*The Youth's Instructor*, May 31, 1894.

676. For those who can use them, good vegetables, prepared in a healthful manner, are better than soft mushes or porridge.—*Unpublished Testimonies*, January 11, 1897.

Too Frequent Eating

677. A second meal should never be eaten until the stomach has hadtime to rest from the labor of digesting the preceding meal.—*How to Live*, 55.

678. After the stomach has done its work for one meal, do not crowdmore work upon it before it has had a chance to rest, and to provide a sufficient supply of gastric juice for the next meal. Five hours at least should be given between each meal, and always bear in mind that if you would give it a trial, you would find that two meals would be better than three.—*Unpublished Testimonies*, August 30, 1896.

679. If a third meal be eaten at all, it should be light, and several hoursbefore going to bed. But with many the poor tired stomach may complain of weariness in vain. More food is forced upon it, which sets the digestive organs in motion, again to perform the same round of labor through the sleeping hours. The sleep is generally disturbed with unpleasant dreams, and in the morning they awake unrefreshed. There is a sense of languor and loss of appetite. A lack of energy is felt through the entire system. In a short time the digestive organs are worn out, for they have had no time to rest. Such persons become miserable dyspeptics, and wonder what has made them so. The cause has brought the sure result. If this practise is indulged in a great length of time, the health will become seriously impaired. The blood becomes impure, the complexion sallow, and eruptions will frequently appear. You will often hear complaints of frequent pains and soreness in the region of the stomach; and while performing labor, the stomach becomes so tired that they are obliged to desist from work, and rest. They seem to be at a loss to account for this state of things; for, setting this aside, they are apparently healthy.... After the stomach, which has been overtaxed, has performed its task, it is exhausted, which causes faintness. Here many are deceived, and think that it is the want of food that produces such feelings, and without giving the stomach time to rest, they take more food, which for the time removes the faintness....

The stomach becomes weary by being kept constantly at work disposing of food not the most healthful. Having no time for rest, the digestive organs become enfeebled, hence the sense of "goneness" and desire for frequent eating.—*How to Live*, 55.

680. Gluttonous feasts, and food taken into the stomach at untimelyseasons, leave an influence upon every fiber of the system.—The Health Reformer, June 1, 1878.

Improper Food Combinations

681. The less that condiments and desserts are placed upon our tables, the better it will be for all who partake of the food. All mixed and complicated foods are injurious to the health of human beings. Dumb animals would never eat such a mixture as is often placed in the human stomach.... Rich and complicated mixtures of food are health destroying.—*Unpublished Testimonies*, November 5, 1896.

682. Because it is the fashion, in harmony with morbid appetite, richcake, pies, and puddings, and every hurtful thing are crowded into the stomach. The table must be loaded down with variety or the depraved appetite cannot be satisfied. In the morning, these slaves to appetite often have impure breath and a furred tongue. They do not enjoy health, and wonder why they suffer with pains, headaches, and various ills. The cause has brought the sure result.—*How to Live*, 57.

683. If we would preserve the best health, we should avoid eating vegetables and fruit at the same meal. If the stomach is feeble, there will be distress, the brain will be confused, and unable to put
forth mental effort. Have fruit at one meal and vegetables at the next.—*The Youth's Instructor*, May 31, 1894.

684. I frequently sit down to the tables of the brethren and sisters andsee that they use a great amount of milk and sugar. These clog the system, irritate the digestive organs, and affect the brain. Anything that hinders the active motion of the living machinery, affects the brain very directly. And from the light given me, sugar, when largely used, is more injurious than meat.—*Testimonies for the Church* 2:370.

Overeating

685. Nearly all the members of the human family eat more than thesystem requires. This excess decays, and becomes a putrid mass.... If more food, even of a simple quality, is placed in the stomach than the living machinery requires, this surplus becomes a burden. The system makes desperate efforts to dispose of it, and this extra work causes a tired feeling. Some who are continually eating call this "all gone" feeling hunger, but it is caused by the overworked condition of the abused digestive organs.—*Unpublished Testimonies*, August 30, 1896.

686. They (ministers, students, etc.) closely apply their minds to books,and eat the allowance of a laboring man. Under such habits,

some grow corpulent, because the system is clogged. Others become lean, feeble, and weak, because their vital powers are exhausted in throwing off the excess of food; the liver becomes burdened, and unable to throw off the impurities in the blood, and sickness is the result.—*Testimonies for the Church* 3:490.

687. Often this intemperance is felt at once in the form of headache andindigestion and colic. A load
has been placed upon the stomach that it cannot care for, and a feeling of oppression comes. The head is confused, the stomach is in rebellion. But these results do not always follow overeating. In some cases the stomach is paralyzed. No sensation of pain is felt, but the digestive organs lose their vital force. The foundation of the human machinery is gradually undermined, and life is rendered very unpleasant.—*Unpublished Testimonies*, August 30, 1896.

688. The power of the brain is lessened by drawing so heavily upon itto help the stomach get along with its heavy burden.—*Testimonies for the Church* 2:363.

689. The brain nerve energy is benumbed and almost paralyzed byovereating—*Testimonies for the Church* 2:414.

Improper Clothing

690. The compression of the waist hinders the process of digestion. Theheart, liver, lungs, spleen, and stomach are crowded into a small compass, not allowing room for the healthful action of these organs.—*The Health Reformer*, November 1, 1871.

691. When the extremities are not properly clad, the blood is chilledback from its natural course, and thrown upon the internal organs, breaking up the circulation and producing disease. The stomach has too much blood, causing indigestion.—*Testimonies for the Church* 2:531.

Intemperance

692. Intemperance in eating, even of food of the right quality, willhave a prostrating influence upon the system.... Strict temperance in eating and drinking is highly essential for the healthy preservation and vigorous exercise of all the functions of the body.... Intemperance

commences at our tables, in the use of unhealthful food. After a time, through
continued indulgence, the digestive organs become weakened, and the food taken does not satisfy the appetite. Unhealthy conditions are established, and there is a craving for more stimulating food.—*Testimonies for the Church* 3:487.

HELPFUL SUGGESTIONS AS TO TREATMENT

Regular Habits.

693. The stomach must have its regular periods for labor and rest....With regular habits and proper food, the stomach will gradually recover.... Efforts should be made to preserve carefully the remaining strength of the vital forces, by lifting off every overtasking burden. The stomach may never fully recover health, but a proper course of diet will save further debility, and many will recover more or less, unless they have gone too far in gluttonous self-murder.—*How to Live*, 57.

694. A second meal should never be eaten until the stomach has hadtime to rest from the labor of digesting the preceding meal.—*How to Live*,

55.

695. The stomach becomes weary by being kept constantly at work;the remedy such require is to eat less frequently and less liberally, and be satisfied with plain, simple food, eating twice, or, at most, three times a day.—*How to Live*, 56.

Rest

696. The stomach must have careful attention. It must not be kept incontinual operation. Give this misused and much-abused organ some peace and quiet rest.—*Unpublished Testimonies*, August 30, 1896.

Exercise

697. Exercise will aid the work of digestion. To walk out after a meal,hold the head erect, put back
the shoulders, and exercise moderately, will be a great benefit.... The diseased stomach will find relief by exercise.—*Testimonies for the Church*

Air

698. He has not had the vitalizing air of heaven to help in the work ofdigestion.—*Testimonies for the Church* 2:374.

699. Pure, fresh air ... excites the appetite, renders the digestion of foodmore perfect, and induces sound, sweet sleep.—*Testimonies for the Church* 1:702.

Bathing

700. Bathing helps the bowels, stomach, and liver, giving energy andnew life to each. It also promotes digestion, and instead of the system's being weakened, it is strengthened.—*Testimonies for the Church* 3:70, 71.

Mental Influence

701. The less the attention is called to the stomach after a meal, thebetter. If you are in constant fear that your food will hurt you, it most assuredly will. Forget self, and think of something cheerful.—*Testimonies for the Church* 2:530.

702. At meal-time cast off all care and taxing thought. Do not be hurried, but eat slowly and with cheerfulness, your heart filled with gratitude to God for all his blessings.—*Gospel Workers*, 174.

703. You eat too much, and then you are sorry, and so you keep thinkingupon what you eat and drink. Just eat that which is for the best, and go right away, feeling clear in the sight of Heaven and not having remorse of conscience.—*Testimonies for the Church* 3:374.

CHAPTER XXVI. - THE LUNGS AND RESPIRATION.

Physiology of Respiration.

704. The health of the entire system depends upon the healthy action of the respiratory organs.—*How to Live*, 57.

705. In order to have good blood, we must breathe well.—The HealthReformer, November 1, 1871.

706. The lungs, in order to be healthy, must have pure air.—*How to Live*, 63.

707. Your lungs, deprived of air, will be like a hungry person deprived of food. Indeed, we can live longer without food than without air, which is the food that God has provided for the lungs.—*Testimonies for the Church* 2:533.

708. The strength of the system is, in a great degree, dependent upon the amount of pure, fresh air breathed. If the lungs are restricted, the quantity of oxygen received into them is also limited, the blood becomes vitiated, and disease follows.—The Health Reformer, February 1, 1877.

709. It is impossible to go out in the bracing air of a winter's morning without inflating the lungs.—*Testimonies for the Church* 2:529.

710. The compression of the waist by tight lacing prevents the waste matter from being thrown off through its natural channels. The most important of these is the lungs. In order for the lungs to do the work designed, they must be left free, without the slightest compression. If the lungs are cramped, they cannot develop; but their capacity will be diminished, making it impossible to take a sufficient inspiration of air. The abdominal muscles were designed to aid the lungs in their action. Where there is no compression of the lungs, the motion in full breathing will be observed to be mostly of the abdomen.... When tight lacing is practiced, the lower part of the chest has not sufficient room for action. The breathing, therefore, is confined to the upper portion of the lungs, where there is not sufficient room to carry on the work. But the lower part of the lungs should have the greatest freedom possible. The compression of the waist will not allow free action of the muscles of the respiratory organs.—The Health Reformer, November 1, 1871.

CAUSES OF DISEASES OF THE RESPIRATORY ORGANS

711. Many suffer decayed vegetable matter to remain about their premises.... There is constantly arising from these decaying substances an effluvium that is poisoning the air. By inhaling the impure air, the blood is poisoned, the lungs become affected, and the whole system is diseased.—*How to Live*, 61.

712. If a house be built where water settles around it, remaining for atime and then drying away, a poisonous miasma arises, and fever and ague, sore throat, lung diseases, and fevers will be the result.—*How to Live*, 64. 713. Especially in wet seasons the sleeping-rooms become damp, and those who sleep in the beds are troubled with rheumatism, neuralgia, and lung complaints, which generally end in consumption.—*How to Live*, 64.

Poor Ventilation

714. Many families suffer from sore throat, lung diseases, and livercomplaints, brought upon them by their own course of action.... They keep their windows and doors closed, fearing they will take cold if there is a crevice to let in the air. They breathe the same air over and over, until it becomes impregnated with the poisonous impurities and waste matter thrown off from their bodies, through the lungs and the pores of the skin.—*How to Live*, 63.

715. For invalids who have feeble lungs, nothing can be worse than anoverheated atmosphere.—*Testimonies for the Church* 2:527.

716. The heated, oppressed atmosphere, deprived of vitality, benumbsthe sensitive brain. The lungs contract, the liver is inactive.—*Testimonies for the Church* 1:702.

Improper Breathing

717. Stomach, liver, lungs, and brain are suffering for want of deep, fullinspirations of air, which would electrify the blood and impart to it a bright, lively color, and which alone can keep it pure, and give tone

and vigor to every part of the living machinery.—*Testimonies for the Church* 2:67.

Improper Use of the Voice

718. Speaking from the throat, letting the words come out from theupper extremity of the vocal organs, all the time fretting and irritating them, is not the best way to preserve health or to increase the efficiency of these organs.—*Testimonies for the Church* 2:616.

719. Careful attention and training should be given to the vocal organs.They are strengthened by right use, but become enfeebled if improperly used. Their excessive use will, if often repeated, not only injure the organs of speech, but will bring an undue strain upon the whole nervous system. The delicate harp of a thousand strings becomes worn, gets out of repair, and produces discord instead of melody.... It is not necessary to talk in a loud voice or in a high key; this does great injury to the speaker.... The human voice is a precious gift of God; it is a power for good, and the Lord wants his servants to preserve its pathos and melody. The voice should be cultivated so as to promote its musical quality, that it may fall pleasantly upon the ear and impress the heart. But the vocal organs are strangely abused, greatly to the injury of the speaker and the discomfort of the hearers.—*Special Testimonies for Ministers and Workers* 7:9.

720. They injure the throat and vocal organs ... when it is not calledfor.... This is in consequence of the unnatural position of the body, and the manner of holding the head.—*Testimonies for the Church* 2:617.

721. Your dislike for physical taxation, while talking and exercisingyour throat, makes you liable to disease of the throat and lungs.... You should not let the labor come upon the upper part of the vocal organs, for this will constantly wear and irritate them, and will lay the foundation for disease. The action should come upon the abdominal muscles; the lungs and throat should be the channel, but should not do all the work.—*Testimonies for the Church* 3:311.

722. Many speak in a rapid way, and in a high, unnatural key; but ifthey continue such a practise, they will injure the throat and lungs, and as a result of continual abuse the weak and inflamed organs will become diseased in a serious way, and they will fall into consumption.—*Christian Education*, 125.

723. There is need that among our ministers careful attention shouldbe given to the culture of the voice, or many will lie down in untimely graves.—*Christian Education*, 133.

Proper Use of the Voice

724. The proper use of the vocal organs will bring benefit to the physical health, and increase your usefulness and influence.—*Christian Education*, 132.

Improper Dress

725. The extremities are chilled.... The heart fails in its efforts, and thelimbs become habitually cold; and the blood, which is chilled away from the extremities, is thrown back upon the lungs and brain, and inflammation and congestion of the lungs or the brain is the result.... If the limbs and feet could have the extra coverings usually put upon the shoulders, lungs, and heart, and healthy circulation be induced to the extremities, the vital organs would act their part healthfully, with only their share of clothing.

I appeal to you mothers, do you not feel alarmed and heart-sick by seeing your children pale and dwarfed, suffering with catarrh, influenza, croup, scrofulous swellings appearing upon the face and neck, inflammation and congestion of the lungs and brain? Have you studied from cause to effect? Leaving their arms and legs insufficiently protected has been the cause of a vast amount of disease and premature death.—*How to Live*, 72.

726. It is essential to health that the chest should have room to expand fully, so that the lungs may be enabled to take full inspirations of air. Many who have died of consumption might have lived their allotted term of life had they dressed in accordance with the laws of their being. The strength of the system is, in a great degree, dependent upon the amount of fresh air breathed. If the lungs are restricted, the quantity of oxygen received into them is also limited, the blood becomes vitiated, and disease follows.—The Health Reformer, February 1, 1877.

727 The arms' being naked exposes the infant to constant cold, and congestion of lungs or brain. These exposures prepare the way for the infant to become sickly and dwarfed.—*How to Live*, 71.

Immoderate Eating

728. Catarrhal difficulties, kidney disease, headache, and heart troublesare the result of immoderate eating.—*Unpublished Testimonies*, August 30, 1896.

Liquor

729. By the habitual use of sour cider many bring upon themselvespermanent disease. Some die of consumption or fall under the power of apoplexy from this cause alone.—*The Review and Herald*, March 25, 1884.

Drugs

730. Every poisonous preparation in the vegetable and mineral kingdoms, taken into the system, will leave its wretched influence, affecting the liver and lungs.—*Facts of Faith*, 140.

CARE OF THE RESPIRATORY ORGANS

Exercise.

731. Morning exercise, walking in the free, invigorating air of heaven,or cultivating flowers, small
fruits, and vegetables, is necessary to a healthful circulation of the blood. It is the surest safeguard against colds, coughs, congestion of the brain, inflammation of the liver, the kidneys, and the lungs, and a hundred other diseases.—The Health Reformer, September 1, 1868.

732. A walk, even in winter, would be more beneficial to the healththan all the medicine the doctors may prescribe.... There will be increased vitality, which is so necessary to health. The lungs will have needful action; for it is impossible to go out in the bracing air of a winter's morning without inflating the lungs.—*Testimonies for the Church* 2:529.

Fresh Air

733. The strength of the system is, in a great degree, dependent uponthe amount of pure air breathed.—The Health Reformer, February 1, 1877.

734. In the cool of the evening it may be necessary to guard from chilliness by extra clothing, but they should give their lungs air.—*Testimonies for the Church* 2:527.

735. Many labor under the mistaken idea that if they have taken cold,they must carefully exclude the outside air, and increase the temperature of their room until it is excessively hot. The system may be deranged, the pores closed by waste matter, and the internal organs suffering more or less inflammation, because the blood has been chilled back from the surface and thrown upon them. At this time of all others the lungs should not be deprived of pure, fresh air. If pure air is ever necessary, it is when any part of the system, as the lungs or stomach, is diseased.—*Testimonies for the Church* 2:530.

736. Air is the free blessing of Heaven, calculated to electrify the wholesystem.—*Testimonies for the Church* 1:701.

CHAPTER XXVII. - THE HEART AND BLOOD.

Physiology of the Circulatory System.

737. Perfect health depends upon perfect circulation.—*Testimonies for the Church* 2:531.

738. The more active the circulation the more free from obstructionsand impurities will be the blood. The blood nourishes the body. The health of the body depends upon the healthful circulation of the blood.—The Health Reformer, May 1, 1873.

739. At every pulsation of the heart, the blood should be propelled tothe extremities quickly and easily in order to have health.... The current of human life is struggling to go its accustomed rounds, and should not be hindered in its circuit through the body by the imperfect manner in which women clothe their limbs.—The Health Reformer, May 1, 1872.

740. The limbs were not formed by our Creator to endure exposure,as was the face. The Lord provided the face with an immense circulation, because it must be exposed. He provided, also, large veins and nerves for the limbs and feet, to contain a large amount of the current of

human life, that the limbs might be uniformly as warm as the body.—*Testimonies for the Church* 2:531.

741. The limbs and feet have large arteries, to receive a large amountof blood, that warmth, nutrition,
elasticity, and strength may be imparted to them. But when the blood is chilled from these extremities, their blood-vessels contract, which makes the circulation of the necessary amount of blood in them still more difficult.—The Health Reformer, April 1, 1872.

742. The extremities are chilled, and the heart has thrown upon it double labor, to force the blood into these chilled extremities; and when the blood has performed its circuit through the body, and returned to the heart, it is not the same vigorous, warm current which left it. It has been chilled in its passage through the limbs. The heart, weakened by too great labor and poor circulation of poor blood, is then compelled to still greater exertion, to throw the blood to the extremities which are never as healthfully warm as other parts of the body. The heart fails in its efforts, and the limbs become habitually cold; and the blood, which is chilled away from the extremities, is thrown back upon the lungs and brain, and inflammation and congestion of the lungs or the brain is the result.—*How to Live*, 72.

Nervous Control of the Circulatory System

743. The nerves control the circulation of the blood; ... for instance, youare impressed that if you bathe, you will become chilly. The brain sends this intelligence to the nerves of the body, and the blood-vessels, held in obedience to your will, cannot perform their office and cause a reaction after the bath.—*Testimonies for the Church* 3:70.

744. You have a determined will, which causes the mind to react uponthe body, unbalancing the circulation, and producing congestion in certain organs; and you are sacrificing health to your feelings.—*Testimonies for the Church* 5:310.

745. The exercise of the brain in study without corresponding physicalexercise has a tendency to attract the blood to the brain, and the circulation of the blood through the system becomes unbalanced. The brain has too much blood and the extremities too little.—*Testimonies for the Church* 3:138.

Causes of Diseases of the Blood and Circulation

746. Those who are not in health have impurities of the blood.—*Testimonies for the Church* 3:70.

747. A bad circulation leaves the blood to become impure, inducescongestion of the brain and lungs, and causes diseases of the heart, the liver, and the lungs.—The Health Reformer, April 1, 1872.

748. By interrupting the circulation of the blood, the entire system isderanged.—The Health Reformer, November 1, 1870.

749. The chief if not the only reason why many become invalids is thatthe blood does not circulate freely, and the changes in the vital fluid which are necessary to life and health do not take place. They have not given their bodies exercise nor their lungs food, which is pure, fresh air; therefore it is impossible for the blood to be vitalized, and it pursues its course sluggishly through the system.—*Testimonies for the Church* 2:525.

750. Foul blood will surely becloud the moral and intellectual powers,and arouse and strengthen the baser passions of your nature.—*Testimonies for the Church* 2:404.

Innutrition

751. Flesh meats, butter, cheese, rich pastry, spiced foods, and condiments are freely partaken
of by both old and young.... The blood making organs cannot convert such things into good blood.—*Christian Temperance and Bible Hygiene*, 47.

752. In order to make a good quality of blood, we must have the right kind of food, prepared in a right manner.—*Testimonies for the Church* 1:682.

753. A poor quality of food, cooked in an improper manner, and insufficient in quantity, cannot make good blood. Flesh meats and rich food and an impoverished diet will produce the same results.—*Testimonies for the Church* 2:368.

Errors in Diet

754. Anything which is taken into the stomach and converted into blood, becomes a part of the being. Children should not be allowed to eat gross articles of food, such as pork, sausage, spices, rich cakes, and pastry; for by so doing their blood becomes fevered, the nervous system unduly excited, and the morals are in danger of being affected.—*Testimonies for the Church* 4:141.

755. Indulging in eating too frequently, and of too large quantities,overtaxes the digestive organs, and produces a feverish state of the system. The blood becomes impure, and then diseases of various kinds follow.—*Facts of Faith*, 133.

756. Catarrhal difficulties, kidney disease, headache, and heart troublesare the result of immoderate eating.—*Unpublished Testimonies*, August 30, 1896.

757. Your health is greatly injured by overeating and eating at impropertimes. This causes a determination of the blood to the brain.... You are in danger of apoplexy; and if you continue to disobey the laws of health, your life will be cut short suddenly.—*Testimonies for the Church* 4:501, 502.

758. The liver becomes burdened, and unable to throw off the impuritiesin the blood, and sickness is the result.—*Testimonies for the Church* 3:490.

759. While fever is raging, food may irritate and excite the blood; butas soon as the strength of the fever is broken, nourishment should be given in a careful, judicious manner.—*Testimonies for the Church* 2:384.

Flesh Meats

760. Flesh meats will depreciate the blood. Cook meat with spices, andeat it with rich cakes and pies, and you have a bad quality of blood. The system is too heavily taxed in disposing of this kind of food.—*Testimonies for the Church* 2:368.

761. The eating of flesh meats has made a poor quality of blood andflesh. Your systems are in a state of inflammation, prepared to take on disease. You are liable to acute attacks of disease, and to sudden death, because you do not possess the strength of constitution to rally and resist disease.—*Testimonies for the Church* 2:61.

762. When we feed on flesh, the juices of what we eat pass into thecirculation....Thus a feverish condition is created, because the animals are diseased, and ... we plant the seeds of disease in our own tissue and blood.—*Unpublished Testimonies*, November 5, 1896.

Pork

763. Subsisting mostly on highly seasoned animal food produces a feverish state of the system, especially if pork is used freely. The blood becomes impure, the circulation is not equalized.—*Facts of Faith*, 126.

764. Pork, although one of the most common articles of diet, is one of the most injurious. God did not prohibit the Hebrews from eating swine's flesh merely to show his authority, but because it was not a proper article of food for man. It would fill the system with scrofula, and especially in that warm climate produce leprosy and disease of various kinds.... Swine's flesh, above all other flesh meats, produces a bad state of the blood.... It is impossible for the flesh of any living creature to be healthy when filth is its natural element, and when it feeds upon every detestable thing. The flesh of swine is composed of what they eat. If human beings eat their flesh, their blood and their flesh will be corrupted by impurities conveyed to them through the swine.—*How to Live*, 58.

765. Cancers, tumors, and inflammatory diseases are largely caused by meat eating.... Flesh diet cannot make good blood.—*Unpublished Testimonies*, November 5, 1896.

Impure Air

766. If the lungs are restricted, the quantity of oxygen received into them is also limited, the blood becomes vitiated, and disease follows.—The Health Reformer, February 1, 1877.

767. For fear of taking cold they persist from year to year in... living in an atmosphere almost destitute of vitality. It is impossible for this class to have a healthy circulation.—*Testimonies for the Church* 2:526.

768. Such can test the matter, and be convinced of the unhealthy air in their close rooms, by entering them after they have remained a while in the open air. Then they can have some idea of the impurities they have conveyed to the blood through the inhalations of the lungs.—*How to Live*, 63.

769. By inhaling the impure air, the blood is poisoned, the lungs become affected, and the whole system is diseased.—*How to Live*, 61.

Lack of Exercise

770. Inaction of any of the organs of the body will be followed by decrease in size and strength of the muscles, and will cause the blood

to flow sluggishly through the blood-vessels.—*Testimonies for the Church* 3:76.

771. The blood is not enabled to expel the impurities as it would ifactive circulation were induced by exercise.—*Testimonies for the Church* 2:529.

772. The exercise of the brain in study, without corresponding physicalexercise, has a tendency to attract the blood to the brain, and the circulation of the blood through the system becomes unbalanced.—*Testimonies for the Church* 3:138.

Improper Clothing

773. Parents who dress their children with their extremities naked, ornearly so, are sacrificing the life and health of their children to fashion. If these parts are not so warm as the body, the circulation is not equalized.... The blood is driven to the head, causing headache or nosebleed; or there is a sense of fulness about the chest; producing cough or palpitation of the heart, on account of too much blood in that locality; or the stomach has too much blood, causing indigestion... The blood is chilled back from its natural course, and thrown upon the internal organs, breaking up the circulation and producing disease.—*Testimonies for the Church* 2:531.

774. Look at the tight-fitting waists of the dresses of these children. Itis impossible for their lungs to have full action. The heart and liver cannot do their work, thus compressed.....Look at their limbs,
unclad except by the slight covering of cotton stockings .... The air chills the limbs, the life current is driven back from its natural course, and the limbs are robbed of their proportion of blood. The blood, which should be induced to the extremities by their being properly clad, is thrown back upon the internal organs. There is too much blood in the head. The lungs are congested or the liver is burdened; by interrupting the circulation of the blood, the entire system is deranged.—The Health Reformer, November 1, 1870.

775. The artificial hair and pads covering the base of the brain heat andexcite the spinal nerves centering in the brain. The head should ever be kept cool. The heat caused by these artificial coverings induces the blood to the brain. The action of the blood upon the lower or animal organs of the brain, causes unnatural activity, tends to recklessness in

morals, and the mind and heart are in danger of being corrupted.—The Health Reformer, October 1, 1871.

Lack of Cleanliness

776. The impurities of the body, if not allowed to escape, are taken backinto the blood, and forced upon the internal organs.—How to Live, 60.

Heredity

777. From the food the mother was compelled to receive, she could notfurnish a good quality of blood, and therefore gave birth to children filled with humors.—Testimonies for the Church 2:379.

Drugs

778. The disease which the drug was given to cure may disappear,but only to reappear in a new form, such as skin diseases, ulcers, painful, diseased joints, and sometimes in a more dangerous and deadly form. The liver, heart, and brain are frequently affected by drugs, and often all these organs
are burdened with disease.... These organs, which should be in healthy condition, are enfeebled, and the blood becomes impure.—How to Live, 61.

HOW IMPROVED

Exercise.

779. The more we exercise, the better will be the circulation of theblood....Those who accustom themselves to proper exercise in the open air. will generally have a good and vigorous circulation.— Testimonies for the Church 2:525.

780. Brisk, yet not violent, exercise in the open air, with cheerfulness ofspirits, will promote the circulation, giving a healthy glow to the skin, and sending the blood, vitalized by the pure air, to the extremities.— Testimonies for the Church 2:530.

781. There is no exercise that can take the place of walking. By it thecirculation of the blood is greatly improved.—*Testimonies for the Church* 3:78.

782. Physical labor, a diversion from mental, will draw the blood from the brain.... The circulation of the blood will be better equalized.—*Testimonies for the Church* 2:569.

Fresh Air

783. In order to have good blood, we must breathe well.—*The HealthReformer*, November 1, 1871.

784. The influence of pure, fresh air is to cause the blood to circulatehealthfully through the system.—*Testimonies for the Church* 1:702.

785. The chief if not the only reason why many become invalids, is thatthe blood does not circulate freely, and the changes in the vital fluid which are necessary to life and health do not take place.
They have not given their bodies exercise nor their lungs food, which is pure, fresh air; therefore it is impossible for the blood to be vitalized, and it pursues its course sluggishly through the system.—*Testimonies for the Church* 2:525.

Water Drinking

786. Pure water to drink and fresh air to breathe invigorate the vitalorgans, purify the blood, and help nature in her task of overcoming the bad conditions of the system.—*How to Live*, 55.

787. Water is the best liquid possible to cleanse the tissues.—*The Review and Herald*, July 29, 1884.

Clothing

788. To secure a good circulation of the current of human life, all partsof the body must be suitably clad.—*The Health Reformer*, April 1, 1872.

Bathing

789. Bathing frees the skin from the accumulation of impurities whichare constantly collecting, and keeps the skin moist and supple,

thereby increasing and equalizing the circulation.—*Testimonies for the Church* 3:70.

790. A bath, properly taken, fortifies against cold, because the circulation is improved, ... for the blood is brought to the surface, and a more easy and regular flow of the blood through all the blood-vessels is obtained.—*Testimonies for the Church* 3:71.

Chapter XXVIII. - The Skin and its Functions.

Physiology of the Skin.

Elimination.

791. Impurities are constantly and imperceptibly passing from the body,through the pores, and if the surface of the skin is not kept in a healthy condition, the system is burdened with impure matter.—*How to Live*, 60.

792. The burden of labor is thrown upon the liver, lungs, kidneys, etc., and these internal organs are compelled to do the work of the skin.—*Testimonies for the Church* 2:524.

793. The skin needs to be carefully and thoroughly cleansed, that thepores may do their work in freeing the body from impurities.—*Testimonies for the Church* 3:70.

794. You have not given your body a chance to breathe. The pores ofthe skin, or the little mouths through which the body breathes, have become closed, and the system has been filled with impurities.—*Testimonies for the Church* 3:74.

795. Its million little mouths are closed, because they are clogged by theimpurities of the system, and for want of air.—*Testimonies for the Church* 1:701.

796. They breathe the same air over and over, until it becomes impregnated with the poisonous impurities and waste matter thrown off from their
bodies through the lungs and the pores of the skin.—*How to Live*, 63.

Absorption

797. If the garments worn are not frequently cleansed from these impurities, the pores of the skin absorb again the waste matter thrown

off. The impurities of the body, if not allowed to escape, are taken back into the blood, and forced upon the internal organs.—*How to Live*, 60.

798. Many are ignorantly injuring their health and endangering theirlives by using cosmetics... When they become heated, ... the poison is absorbed by the pores of the skin, and is thrown into the blood. Many lives have been sacrificed by this means alone.—The Health Reformer, October 1, 1871.

IMPAIRED ACTION OF THE SKIN

Impure Air.

799. The surface of the skin is nearly dead because it has no air tobreathe. Its million little mouths are closed, because they are clogged by the impurities of the system, or for want of air.—*Testimonies for the Church* 1:701.

800. The effects produced by living in close, ill-ventilated rooms arethese: .... The body becomes relaxed; the skin becomes sallow; digestion is retarded; and the system is peculiarly sensitive to the influence of cold. A slight exposure produces serious diseases. Great care should be exercised not to sit in a draught or in a cold room when weary or when in a perspiration.—*Testimonies for the Church* 1:702.

801. For fear of taking cold they persist from year to year in ... living inan atmosphere almost destitute of vitality .... The skin becomes debilitated, and more sensitive to any change in the atmosphere.—*Testimonies for the Church* 2:526.

Improper Clothing

802. Additional clothing is put on, and the heat of the room increased.The next day they require a little more heat and a little more clothing, in order to feel perfectly warm; and thus they humor every changing feeling until they have but little vitality to endure any cold.... If you add clothing, let it be but little, and exercise, if possible, to regain the heat you need.—*Testimonies for the Church* 2:526.

803. You have worn too great an amount of clothing, and have debilitated the skin by so doing.—*Testimonies for the Church* 3:74.

804. The unnatural heat caused by artificial hair and pads about thehead, induces the blood to the brain, producing congestion, and

causing the natural hair to fall off.—The Health Reformer, October 1, 1871.

Improper Diet

805. With many the poor, tired stomach may complain of wearinessin vain. More food is forced upon it, which sets the digestive organs in motion, again to perform the same round of labor.... These become miserable dyspeptics.... If this practise be indulged in for a great length of time, the health becomes seriously impaired. The blood becomes impure, the complexion sallow, and eruptions frequently appear.—How to Live, 55.

Drugs

806. This is the effect of calomel.... It frequently manifests itself intumors, ulcers, and cancers, years after it has been introduced into the system.—How to Live, 59.

807. The disease, which the drug was given to cure may disappear, butonly to reappear in a new
form, such as skin diseases, ulcers, painful, diseased joints, and sometimes in a more dangerous and deadly form.—How to Live, 61.

808. Ladies may resort to cosmetics to restore the tint of the complexion, but they cannot thus bring back the glow of healthful feelings to the heart. That which darkens and makes dingy the skin also clouds the spirits and destroys cheerfulness and peace of mind.—The Health Reformer, February 1, 1877.

COMPENSATORY ACTION OF THE INTERNAL ORGANS

809. Those who are not in health have impurities in the blood, and theskin is not in a healthy condition.—Testimonies for the Church 3:70.

810. The studied habit of shunning the air and avoiding exercise closesthe pores,—the little mouths through which the body breathes,—making it impossible to throw off impurities through that channel. The burden of labor is thrown upon the liver, lungs, kidneys, etc., and these internal organs are compelled to do the work of the skin.—Testimonies for the Church

2:524.

811. These pores have become clogged and cannot perform the taskallotted to them, and so the internal organs have a double task thrown upon them, and the whole system is deranged.—The Health Reformer, September 1, 1866.

TREATMENT

Proper Clothing.

812. If you add clothing, let it be but little, and exercise, if possible, toregain the heat you need. If you positively cannot engage in active exercise, warm yourselves by the fire; but as soon as you are warm, lay off your extra clothing, and remove from the fire.— *Testimonies for the Church* 2:526.

Exercise

813. If those who can, would engage in some active employment totake the mind from themselves, they would generally forget that they were chilly, and would not receive harm.—*Testimonies for the Church* 2:526.

Bathing

814. Bathing frees the skin from the accumulation of impurities, which are constantly collecting, and keeps the skin moist and supple.— *Testimonies for the Church* 3:70.

815. Twice a week she should take a general bath, as cool as will beagreeable, a little cooler every time, until the skin is toned up.— *Testimonies for the Church* 1:702.

816. Upon rising in the morning, most persons would be benefited bytaking a sponge bath, or, if more agreeable, a hand bath, with merely a wash-bowl of water; this will remove impurities from the skin.—*How to Live*, 63.

817. Frequent bathing is very beneficial, especially at night just beforeretiring, or upon rising in the morning. It will take but a few moments to give the children a bath, and to rub them until their bodies

are in a glow. This brings the blood to the surface, relieving the brain.—*Christian Temperance and Bible Hygiene*, 141.

818. Bathe frequently in pure soft water, followed by gentle rubbing.—*How to Live*, 54.

CHAPTER XXIX. - THE BRAIN AND THE NERVOUS SYSTEM.

The Physiology of the Nervous System.

819. Each faculty of the mind and each muscle has its distinctive office,and all require to be exercised in order to become properly developed and retain healthful vigor.—*Testimonies for the Church* 3:77.

820. Every organ of the body was made to be servant of the mind.—*Testimonies for the Church* 3:136.

821. The brain is the capital of the body, the seat of all the nervousforces and of mental action. The nerves proceeding from the brain control the body. By the brain nerves, mental impressions are conveyed to all the nerves of the body as by telegraph wires; and they control the vital action of every part of the system. All the organs of motion are governed by the communications they receive from the brain.—*Testimonies for the Church* 3:69.

822. The senses ... are the avenues to the soul.—*Testimonies for the Church* 3:507.

823. The brain nerves which communicate with the entire system arethe only medium through which Heaven can communicate with man, and affect his inmost life. Whatever disturbs the circulation of the electric currents in the nervous system, lessens the strength of the vital powers, and the result is a

deadening of the sensibilities of the mind.—*Testimonies for the Church* 2:347.

824. Any part of the body that is not treated with consideration willtelegraph its injury to the brain.—*Christian Education*, 125.

825. The nervous system, having been unduly excited, borrowed powerfor present use from its future resources of strength.—*Testimonies for the Church* 3:487.

826. Anything that hinders the active motion of the living machinery,affects the brain very directly.—*Testimonies for the Church* 2:370.

827. A calm, clear brain and steady nerve are dependent upon a well-balanced circulation of the blood.—The Health Reformer, November 1, 1871.

Examples of Nervous Control

828. When the minds of ministers, school-teachers, and students are continually excited by study, and the body is allowed to be inactive, the nerves of emotion are taxed, while the nerves of motion are inactive.—*Testimonies for the Church* 3:490.

829. Immediately after eating there is a strong draught upon the nervousenergy.... Therefore, when the mind or body is taxed heavily after eating, the process of digestion is hindered. The vitality of the system, which is needed to carry on the work in one direction, is called away and set to work in another.—*Testimonies for the Church* 2:413.

830. The very food they place before their children is such as to irritatethe tender coats of the stomach. This excitement is communicated, through the nerves, to the brain, and the result is that the animal passions are aroused, and control the moral powers. Reason is thus made a servant to the lower qualities of the mind.—*Testimonies for the Church* 4:140.

Opium

831. This drug poison, opium, gives temporary relief from pain, butdoes not remove the cause of pain. It only stupefies the brain, rendering it incapable of receiving impressions from the nerves. While the brain is thus insensible, the hearing, the taste, and the sight are affected. When the influence of opium wears off, and the mind arouses from its state of paralysis, the nerves, which have been cut off from communication with the brain, shriek out louder than ever ... because of the additional outrage the system has sustained in receiving this poison.—*How to Live*, 56.

SYMPATHETIC NERVOUS DISTURBANCES

832. God himself has formed us with distinctive organs and faculties.These he designs should act together in harmony. If we injure one, all are affected.—The Health Reformer, January 1, 1873.

833. Every wrong habit which injures the health of the body, reacts ineffect upon the mind.—The Health Reformer, February 1, 1877.

834. The brain is the citadel of the whole man, and wrong habits ofeating, dressing, or sleeping affect the brain, and prevent the attaining of that which the student desires,—a good mental discipline. Any part of the body that is not treated with consideration will telegraph its injury to the brain.—Christian Education, 125.

835. It is impossible for the brain to do its best work when the digestivepowers are abused. Many eat hurriedly of various kinds of food, which set up
a war in the stomach, and thus confuse the brain.... At meal-time cast off care and taxing thought. Do not be hurried, but eat slowly and with cheerfulness, your heart filled with gratitude to God for all his blessings; and do not engage in brain labor immediately after a meal. Exercise moderately, and give a little time for the stomach to begin its work.—Gospel Workers, 174.

836. When the mind or body is taxed heavily after eating, the processof digestion is hindered. The vitality of the system, which is needed to carry on the work in one direction, is called away and set to work in another.—Testimonies for the Church 2:413.

837. What the users of these stimulants call strength is only receivedby exciting the nerves of the stomach, which convey the irritation to the brain, and this in turn is aroused to impart increased action to the heart.—Testimonies for the Church 2:65.

838. Those who are changing from three meals a day to two, will atfirst be troubled more or less with faintness, especially about the time they have been in the habit of eating the third meal. But if they persevere for a short time, this faintness will disappear.—How to Live, 56.

CAUSES OF NERVOUS DISEASES

839. Anything that hinders the active motion of the living machineryaffects the brain very directly.—*Testimonies for the Church* 2:370.

Unhealthful Surroundings

840. It is destructive to the health and life of young children to sit in theschoolroom upon hard, ill-formed benches, from three to five hours a day, inhaling the impure air cause by many breaths. The weak lungs become affected, the brain, from which the nervous energy of the whole system is derived, becomes enfeebled by being called into active exercise before the strength of the mental organs is sufficiently matured to endure fatigue.—*How to Live*, 43.

841. In the schoolroom the foundation has been too surely laid fordiseases of various kinds. But more especially the most delicate of all organs, the brain, had often been permanently injured by too great exercise. This has often caused inflammation, then dropsy of the head, and convulsions with their dreaded results.... In those children who have survived, the nervous energy of the brain becomes so weakened that after they come to maturity it is impossible for them to endure much mental exercise. The forces of some of the delicate organs of the brain seem to be expended.—*How to Live*, 43.

Abuse of the Mind

842. The mind which is allowed to be absorbed in story reading is being ruined. The practice results in air-castle building and a sickly sentimentalism. The imagination becomes diseased, and there is a vague unrest, a strange appetite for unwholesome mental food. Thousands are today in insane asylums whose minds became unbalanced by novel reading.—*The Signs of the Times*, January 4, 1905.

843. The memory is greatly injured by ill-chosen reading, which hasa tendency to unbalance the reasoning powers, and to create nervousness, weariness of the brain, and prostration of the entire system.—*Testimonies for the Church* 4:497.

844. The exercise of the brain in study, without corresponding physicalexercise, has a tendency to attract the blood to the brain, and the circulation of the blood through the system becomes unbalanced. The brain has too much blood, and the extremities too little.—*Christian Education*, 9.

845. Minds are often abused, and goaded on to madness by pursuingone line of thought; the excessive employment of the brain power and the neglect of the physical creates diseased conditions of the system.—*Special Instruction on Educational Work* 14.

846. Doubt, perplexity, and excessive grief often sap the vital forces, and induce nervous disease of a most debilitating and distressing character.—*The Review and Herald*, October 16, 1883.

Irregular Habits

847. The mind does not wear out or break down so often on accountof diligent employment and hard study, as on account of eating improper food at improper times, and of careless inattention to the laws of health.... Diligent study is not the principal cause of the breaking down of the mental powers. The main cause is improper diet, irregular meals, and a lack of physical exercise. Irregular hours for eating and sleeping sap the brain forces.—*The Youth's Instructor*, May 31, 1894.

Insufficient Air

848. Stomach, liver, lungs, and brain are suffering for the want of deep,full inspirations of air.—*Testimonies for the Church* 2:67.

Improper Dress

849. Artificial hair and pads covering the base of the brain, heat andexcite the nerves centering in the brain.... The heat caused by these artificial coverings induces the blood to the brain, producing congestion. In consequence of the brain's being congested its nerves lose their healthy action.—The Health Reformer, October 1, 1871.

850. Their limbs, as well as their arms, are left almost naked.... Theheart, weakened by too great labor, fails in its efforts, and the limbs become habitually cold; and the blood, which is chilled away from the extremities, is thrown back upon the lungs and brain, and inflammation and congestion of the lungs or the brain is the result.— *How to Live*, 71, 72.

Errors in Diet

851. The brain is closely connected with the stomach, and its powerhas so often been called to aid the weakened digestive organs that it is in its turn weakened, depressed, congested.—*Testimonies for the Church* 2:318.

852. The brain-nerve energy is benumbed and almost paralyzed by overeating.—*Testimonies for the Church* 2:414.

853. Your health is greatly injured by overeating and eating at impropertimes. This causes a determination of the blood to the brain. The mind becomes confused, and you have not the proper control of yourself. You appear like a man whose mind is unbalanced. You make strong moves, are easily irritated, and view things in an exaggerated and perverted light.—*Testimonies for the Church* 4:501.

854. If the stomach is burdened with too much food, even of a simplecharacter, the brain force is called to the aid of the digestive organs. There is a benumbed sensation upon the brain. It is almost impossible to keep the eyes open.... The brain is almost paralyzed in consequence of the amount of food eaten.—*Testimonies for the Church* 2:603.

855. Nature bears abuse as long as she can without resisting, then she arouses and makes a mighty effort to rid herself of the incumbrances and evil treatment she has suffered. Then come headache, chills, fever, nervousness, paralysis, and other evils too numerous to mention.—*Testimonies for the Church* 2:69.

856. Children should not be allowed to eat gross articles of food, suchas pork, sausage, spices, rich cakes, and pastry; for by so doing their blood becomes fevered, the nervous system unduly excited, and the morals are in danger of being affected.—*Testimonies for the Church* 4:141.

857. Some animals that are brought to the slaughter seem to realizewhat is to take place, and they become furious, and literally mad. They are killed while in this state, and their flesh prepared for market. Their meat is poison, and has produced in those who have eaten it, cramps, convulsions, apoplexy, and sudden death.—*How to Live*, 60.

Stimulants

858. The appetite for liquor is encouraged by the preparation of foodwith condiments and spices. These cause a feverish state of the

system.... The effect of such food is to cause nervousness.—*The Review and Herald*, November 6, 1883.

859. To a certain extent tea produces intoxication.... Tea draws uponthe strength of the nerves, and leaves them greatly weakened.... When the system is already overtaxed and needs rest, the use of tea spurs up nature by stimulation to unwonted, unnatural action, and thereby lessens her power to perform and her ability to endure; and her powers give out long before Heaven designed they should.
Tea is poisonous to the system.... The second effect of tea drinking is headache, wakefulness, palpitation of the heart, indigestion, trembling of the nerves, and many other evils.—*Testimonies for the Church* 2:64.

860. The influence of coffee is in a degree the same as tea, but theeffect upon the system is still worse. Its influence is exciting, and just in the degree that it elevates above par, it will exhaust and bring prostration below par.... The relief obtained from them [tea and coffee] is sudden, before the stomach has had time to digest them. This shows that what the users of these stimulants call strength is only received by exciting the nerves of the stomach, which convey the irritation to the brain, and this in turn is aroused to impart increased action to the heart, and short-lived energy to the entire system. All this is false strength, that we are the worse for having.—*Testimonies for the Church* 2:65.

861. Tobacco is a poison of the most deceitful and malignant kind,having an exciting, then a paralyzing, influence upon the nerves,—*Facts of Faith*, 128.

862. Tobacco-using is a habit which frequently affects the nervous system in a more powerful manner than does the use of alcohol.—*Testimonies for the Church* 3:562.

863. While it [tobacco] acts upon some [infants who are compelledto inhale its fumes] as a slow poison, and affects the brain, heart, liver, and lungs, and they waste away and fade gradually, upon others it has a more direct influence, causing spasms, paralysis, and sudden death.—*How to Live*, 68.

864. A tendency to disease of various kinds, as dropsy, liver complaint,trembling nerves, and a determination of blood to the head, results from the habitual use of sour cider.... Some die of consumption or fall under the power of apoplexy from this cause alone.—*The Review and Herald*, March 25, 1884.

Drugs

865. The drugs given to stupefy, whatever they may be, derange thenervous system.—*How to Live*, 57.

866. The liver, heart, and brain are frequently affected by drugs, and often all these organs are burdened with disease, and the unfortunate subjects, if they live, are invalids for life, wearily dragging out a miserable existence.—*How to Live*, 61.

867. Witness the mildest protracted influence of nux vomica upon the human system. As its introduction, the nervous energy was excited to extraordinary action to meet this drug poison. This extra excitement was followed by prostration, and the final result has been paralysis of the nerves.—*How to Live*, 58.

868. Poisonous medicines, or something called a soothing cordial, ... ispoured down the throat of the abused infant.... If it recovers, it must bear about more or less in its system the effects of that poisonous drug, and it is liable to spasms, heart disease, dropsy of the brain, or consumption. Some infants are not strong enough to bear even a trifle of drug poisons; and as nature rallies to meet the intruder, the vital forces of the tender infant are too severely taxed, and death ends the scene.—*How to Live*, 70.

Vice

869. Impure thoughts lead to impure actions.... Some ... are in dangerof paralysis of the brain. Already the moral and intellectual powers are weakened and benumbed.—*Testimonies for the Church* 2:408, 409.

870. Many sink into an early grave, while others have a sufficient forceof constitution to pass this ordeal.... Nature will make them pay the penalty for the transgression of her laws ... by numerous pains in the system, ... neuralgia, ... affection of the spine.—*A Solemn Appeal*, 63, 64.

TREATMENT FOR NERVOUS DISORDERS

Improve the General Health.

871. The mind and body are intimately connected. If the former isto be firm and well balanced, the latter should be in the best possible condition. Conscience and right principles of life should be sustained

by firm, quiet nerves, a healthy circulation, and the activity and strength of general health.—The Health Reformer, November 1, 1877.

Fresh Air

872. Air, air, the precious boon of heaven, which all may have, willbless you with its invigorating influence if you will not refuse it entrance. Welcome it, cultivate a love for it, and it will prove a precious soother of the nerves.... It refreshes the body, ... while at the same time its influence is decidedly felt upon the mind, imparting a degree of composure and serenity.... It induces sound, sweet sleep.—Testimonies for the Church 1:702.

Diet

873. You were in danger of being stricken down by paralysis, one half of you becoming dead. A denial of appetite is salvation to you.—Testimonies for the Church 1:546.

874. All these brethren need to adhere more strictly and perseveringlyto a healthful, spare diet, for all are in danger of congested brains, and paralysis may fell one or more or all of them, if they continue living carelessly or recklessly.—Testimonies for the Church 1:588.

875. You should use the most simple food, prepared in the most simplemanner, that the fine nerves of the brain be not weakened, benumbed, or paralyzed.—Testimonies for the Church 2:46.

Exercise

876. Healthy, active exercise is what you need. This will invigorate themind. Neither study nor violent exercise should be engage in immediately after a full meal.—Testimonies for the Church 2:413.

877. Physical labor, a diversion from mental, will draw the blood fromthe brain.—Testimonies for the Church 2:569.

878. Morning exercise, in walking in the free, invigorating air of heaven, ... is the surest safeguard against colds, coughs, congestions of the brain and lungs, ... and a hundred other diseases.—The Health Reformer, May 1, 1872.

879. The proper exercise of mind and body will develop and strengthenall the powers. Both mind and body will be preserved, and

will be capable of doing a variety of work.... The proper use of the physical strength as well as the mental powers will equalize the circulation of the blood, and keep every organ of the living machinery in running order.... Every faculty of the mind may be exercised with comparative safety if the physical powers are equally taxed, and the subject of thought varied. We need
a change of employment, and nature is a living, healthful teacher.—*Special Instruction on Educational Work* 14.

The Bath

880. The bath is a soother of the nerves.—*Testimonies for the Church* 3:70.

Mental Influence

881. Some ... have a powerful will, which, exercised in the right direction, would be a potent means of controlling the imagination and thus resisting disease.—*Testimonies for the Church* 2:524.

882. You are capable of controlling your imagination and overcomingthese nervous attacks. You have will power, and you should bring it to your aid.—*Testimonies for the Church* 5:310.

883. Bring to your aid the power of the will, which will resist cold andwill give energy to the nervous system.—*Testimonies for the Church* 2:533.

884. The consciousness of right-doing is the best medicine for diseasedbodies and minds.—*Testimonies for the Church* 1:502.

The Bible

885. The Bible is a soother of the nerves, and imparts solidity of mindand firm principles.—*The Review and Herald*, November 28, 1878.

CHAPTER XXX. - AUTO-INTOXICATION, OR SELF-POISONING.

886. The more active the circulation, the more free will be the bloodfrom obstructions and impurities.—The Health Reformer, May 1, 1873.

TOXINS GENERATED

887. Impurities are constantly and imperceptibly passing from the bodythrough the pores, and if the skin is not kept in a healthy condition, the system is burdened with impure matter. If the garments worn are not frequently cleansed from these impurities, the pores of the skin absorb again the waste matter thrown off. The impurities of the body, if not allowed to escape, are taken back into the blood, and forced upon the internal organs. Nature, to relieve herself of poisonous impurities, makes an effort to free the system, which effort produces fevers and what is termed disease.—How to Live, 60.

888. Many families suffer with sore throat, and lung diseases, and livercomplaints, brought upon them by their own course of action.... They keep their windows and doors closed, fearing they will take cold if there is a crevice open to let in the air. They breathe the same air over and over until it becomes impregnated with the poisonous impurities and waste matter thrown off from their bodies through the lungs and the pores
of the skin. These impurities are conveyed to the blood through the inhalations of the lungs.—How to Live, 63.

889. Many are made sick by the indulgence of appetite.... So many varieties are introduced into the stomach that fermentation is the result. This condition brings on acute disease, and death frequently follows.—Unpublished Testimonies, August 25, 1897.

890. If physical exercise were combined with mental exertion, the blood would be quickened in its circulation, the action of the heart would be more perfect, impure matter would be thrown off, and new life and vigor would be experienced in every part of the body.... They

closely apply their minds to books, and eat the allowance of a laboring man. Under such habits some grow corpulent, because the system is clogged. Others become lean, feeble, and weak, because their vital powers are exhausted in throwing off the excess of food; the liver becomes burdened and unable to throw off the impurities in the blood, and sickness is the result.—*Testimonies for the Church* 3:490.

DEFECTIVE ELIMINATION

891. The studied habit of shunning the air and avoiding exercise closes the pores, ... making it impossible to throw off impurities through that channel. The burden of labor is thrown upon the liver, lungs, kidneys, etc., and these internal organs are compelled to do the work of the skin. Thus persons bring diseases upon themselves by their wrong habits.—*Testimonies for the Church* 2:524.

CHAPTER XXXI. - COLDS.

Causes of Colds.

892. Many labor under the mistaken idea that if they have taken cold,they must carefully exclude the outside air, and increase the temperature of their room until it is excessively hot. The system may be deranged, the pores closed by waste matter, and the internal organs suffering more or less inflammation, because the blood has been chilled back from the surface and thrown upon them.—*Testimonies for the Church* 2:530.

893. The effects produced by living in close, ill-ventilated rooms arethese: ... The body becomes relaxed; the skin becomes sallow; digestion is retarded, and the system is peculiarly sensitive to the influence of cold. A slight exposure produces serious diseases. Great care should be exercised not to sit in a draught or in a cold room when weary, or when in a perspiration.—*Testimonies for the Church* 1:702.

894. If the child has taken cold, it is generally due to the wrong management of the mother. If its head is covered as well as its body while sleeping, in a short time it will be in a perspiration, caused by

labored breathing, because of the lack of pure, vital air. When it is taken from beneath the covering, it is almost sure to take cold. The arms' being naked exposes the infant to constant cold, and congestion of the lungs or brain.

These exposures prepare the

way for the infant to become sickly and dwarfed.—*How to Live*, 71.

895. When we overtax our strength, and become exhausted, we areliable to take cold, and at such times there is danger of disease's assuming a dangerous form.—*Testimonies for the Church* 3:13.

CLOTHING

896. When the extremities, which are remote from the vital organs,are not properly clad, the blood is driven to the head, causing headache or nosebleed; or there is a sense of fulness about the chest, producing cough or palpitation of the heart, on account of too much blood in that locality.—*Testimonies for the Church* 2:531.

897. An abundance of clothing about the chest, where is the great wheel of life, induces the blood to the lungs and brain, and produces congestion.—The Health Reformer, April 1, 1872.

898. A dress thus long gathers dew from the grass, ... and in its bedraggled condition it comes in contact with the sensitive ankles, which are not sufficiently protected, quickly chilling them, and is one of the greatest causes of catarrh and of scrofulous swelling, and endangers of health and life.—*How to Live*, 62.

899. Drug takers are never well. They are always taking cold, which causes extreme suffering, because of the poison all through their system.—*Facts of Faith*, 137.

HELPFUL HINTS CONCERNING COLDS

900. At this time, of all others, the lungs should not be deprived of pure,fresh air. If pure air is ever necessary, it is when any part of the system, as the lungs or stomach, is diseased. Judicious

exercise would induce the blood to the surface, and thus relieve the internal organs. Brisk, yet not violent, exercise in the open air, with cheerfulness of spirits, will promote the circulation, giving a healthy glow to the skin, and sending the blood, vitalized by the pure air, to the extremities.—*Testimonies for the Church* 2:530.

901. Bring to your aid the power of the will, which will resist cold, andwill give energy to the nervous system.—*Testimonies for the Church* 2:533.

902. Instead of increasing the liability to cold, a bath, properly taken,fortifies against cold, because the circulation is improved, ... for the blood is brought to the surface, and a more easy and regular flow of blood through all the blood-vessels is obtained.—*Testimonies for the Church* 3:71.

903. Morning exercise, in walking in the free invigorating air of heaven,... is the surest safe-guard against colds, coughs, congestions of the brain and lungs, ... and a hundred other diseases.—The Health Reformer, May 1, 1872.

904. Twice a week she should take a general bath, as cool as will beagreeable, a little cooler every time, until the skin is toned up.—*Testimonies for the Church* 1:702

CHAPTER XXXII. - FEVERS AND ACUTE DISEASES.

Causes of Acute Diseases.

905. Nature is burdened and endeavors to resist your efforts to crippleher. Chills and fevers are the result of those attempts to rid herself of the burden you lay upon her.—*Testimonies for the Church* 2:68.

906. Nature, to relieve herself of poisonous impurities, makes an effort to free the system, which effort produces fevers and what is termed disease.—*How to Live*, 60.

907. Nature bears abuse as long as she can without resisting, then she arouses, and makes a mighty effort to rid herself of the incumbrances and evil treatment she has suffered. Then come headache, chills, fevers, nervousness, paralysis, and other evils too numerous to mention.—*Testimonies for the Church* 2:69.

Diet

908. When we feed on flesh, the juices of what we eat pass into the circulation. A feverish condition is created, because the animals are

diseased; and by partaking of their flesh we plant the seeds of disease in our own tissue and blood. Then, when exposed to the changes in a malarious atmosphere, to epidemics and contagious diseases, the system feels their effects; it is not in a condition to resist disease.— *Unpublished Testimonies*, November 5, 1896.

909. Highly seasoned animal food produces a feverish state of the system; especially if pork is used freely, the blood becomes impure, the circulation is not equalized, and chills and fever follow.—*Facts of Faith*, 126.

910. Many times your children have suffered from fever and ague brought on by improper eating, when their parents were accountable for their sickness.—*Testimonies for the Church* 4:502.

911. Children should not be allowed to eat gross articles of food, suchas pork, sausage, spices, rich cakes, and pastry; for by so doing their blood becomes fevered.—*Testimonies for the Church* 4:141.

912. Thousands have indulged their perverted appetites, have eaten agood meal, as they call it, and as the result have brought on a fever or some other acute disease, and certain death.—*Testimonies for the Church* 2:69.

Ventilation.

913. The effects produced by living in close, ill-ventilated rooms are these: The system becomes weak and unhealthy, the circulation is depressed, the blood moves sluggishly through the system because it is not purified and ventilated by the pure, invigorating air of heaven. The mind becomes depressed and gloomy, while the whole system is enervated, and fevers and other acute diseases are liable to be generated.—*Testimonies for the Church* 1:702, 703.

Infection.

914. If fevers enter a family, often more than one have the same fever.This need not be if the habits of the family are correct. If their diet is as it should be, and they observe habits of cleanliness, and realize the necessity of ventilation, the fever need not extend
to another member of the family. The reason that fevers prevail in families, exposing the attendants, is because the sick-room is not kept free from poisonous infection by cleanliness and proper ventilation.—

915. Families have been afflicted with fevers, some have died, and theremaining portion of the family circle have almost murmured against their Maker because of their distressing bereavements, when the sole cause of all their sickness and death has been the result of their own carelessness. The impurities about their own premises have brought upon them contagious diseases.... Disease of almost every description will be caused by inhaling the atmosphere affected by these decaying substances. There is constantly arising from them an effluvium that is poisoning the air.—*Facts of Faith*, 141.

916. If a house be built where water settles around it, remaining for atime and then drying away, a poisonous miasma arises, and fever and ague, sore throat, lung diseases, and fever will be the result.—*How to Live*, 64.

Helpful Suggestions.

917. In nine cases out of ten the indisposition of children can be tracedto some indulgence of the perverted appetite. Perhaps it is an exposure to cold, want of fresh air, irregularity in eating, or improper clothing; and all the parents need to do is to remove the cause, and secure for their children a period of quiet and rest or abstinence for a short time from food. An agreeable bath, of the proper temperature, will remove impurities from the skin,
and the unpleasant symptoms may soon disappear.—The Health Reformer, October 1, 1866.

918. Reduce the feverish state of the system by a careful and intelligentapplication of water. These efforts will help nature in her struggle to free the system of impurities.... The use of water can accomplish but little if the patient does not feel the necessity of also strictly attending to his diet.—*How to Live*, 60.

919. If, in their fevered state, water had been given them to drink freely,and applications had also been made externally, long days and nights of suffering would have been saved, and many precious lives spared. But thousands have died with raging fevers consuming them, until the fuel which fed the fever was burned up, the vitals consumed, and have died in the greatest agony, without being permitted to have water to allay their burning thirst. Water, which is allowed a senseless

building to put out the raging elements, is not allowed human beings to put out the fire which is consuming the vitals.—*How to Live*, 62.

920. The blessed, heaven-sent water, skilfully applied, would quenchthe devouring flame, but it is set aside for poisonous drugs.—*Testimonies for the Church* 5:195.

921. In cases of severe fever, abstinence from food for a short timewill lessen the fever, and make the use of water more effectual. But the acting physician needs to understand the real condition of the patient, and not allow him to be restricted in diet for a great length of time until his system becomes enfeebled. While the fever is
raging, food may irritate and excite the blood; but as soon as the strength of the fever is broken, nourishment should be given in a careful, judicious manner. If food is withheld too long, the stomach's craving for it will create fever, which will be relieved by a proper allowance of food of the right quality. It gives nature something to work upon. If there is a great desire expressed for food, even during the fever, to gratify that desire with a moderate amount of simple food would be less injurious than for the patient to be denied. When he can get his mind upon nothing else, nature will not be overburdened with a small portion of simple food.—*Testimonies for the Church* 2:384, 385.

922. The sick-room, if possible, should have a draught of air throughit day and night. The draught should not come directly upon the invalid. While burning fevers are raging, there is but little danger of taking cold. But especial care is needful when the crisis comes, and the fever is passing away. Then constant watching may be necessary to keep vitality in the system.—*How to Live*, 59, 60.

CHAPTER XXXIII. - MORAL MALADIES.

General Statements.

923. Immorality abounds everywhere. Licentiousness is the special sinof the age. Never did vice lift its deformed head with such boldness as now.—*Testimonies for the Church* 2:346.

924. A lethargy of unconscious sensualism, through indulgence of aperverted appetite, a constant submitting of soul and body and spirit to moral defilement, is upon the people.... And these lustful appetites, with their destroying power, have been transmitted from parents to children, and so intensified that the names of those who bear them are recorded in the books of heaven as transgressors of God's law.— *Unpublished Testimonies*, January 2, 1897.

925. Moral pollution has done more than every other evil to cause the race to degenerate. It is practised to an alarming extent, and brings on disease of almost every description. Even very small children, infants, being born with natural irritability of the sexual organs, find momentary relief in handling them, which only increases the irritation, and leads to a repetition of the act, until as habit is established which increases with their growth. These children, generally puny and dwarfed, are prescribed for by physicians, and drugged; but the evil is not removed. The cause still exists.—*Testimonies for the Church* 2:391.

926. Many might have been saved if they had been carefully instructedin regard to the influence of this practise upon their health. They were ignorant of the fact that they were bringing much suffering upon themselves.—*A Solemn Appeal*, 55.

Diet

INDUCING CAUSES OF IMMORALITY

927. If ever there was a time that the diet should be of the most simplekind, it is now. Meat should not be placed before our children. Its influence is to excite and strengthen the lower passions, and has a

tendency to deaden the moral powers.... The less feverish the diet, the more easily can the passions be controlled.—*Testimonies for the Church* 2:352.

928. You place upon your tables butter, eggs, and meat, and your children partake of them. They are fed with the very things that will excite their animal passions, and then you come to meeting and ask God to bless and save your children.—*Testimonies for the Church* 2:362.

929. The very food they place before their children is such as to irritatethe tender coats of the stomach. This excitement is communicated, through the nerves, to the brain, and the result is that the animal passions are aroused, and control the moral powers.—*Testimonies for the Church* 4:140.

930. By indulging in a wrong course of eating and drinking, thousandsupon thousands are ruining their health, and not only is their health ruined, but their

morals are corrupted, because diseased blood flows through their veins.—*Unpublished Testimonies*, August 30, 1896.

Idleness

931. To relieve the young from healthful labor is the worst possiblecourse a parent can pursue. Their life is then aimless, the mind and hands unoccupied, the imagination active, and left free to indulge in thoughts that are not pure and healthful. In this condition they are inclined to indulge still more freely in that vice which is the foundation of all their complaints.... Some mothers with their own hands open the door and virtually invite the devil in, by permitting their children to remain in idleness.—*A Solemn Appeal*, 58.

Wicked Associates

932. Children who are experienced in this vice seem to be bewitched bythe devil until they can impart their vile knowledge to others.—*A Solemn Appeal*, 54.

933. Neighbors may permit their children to come to your house, tospend the evening and the night with your children. Here is a trial, and a choice for you, to run the risk of offending your neighbors by sending their children to their own homes, or gratify them, and let them lodge with your children, and thus expose them to be instructed in that

knowledge which would be a lifelong curse to them.—*A Solemn Appeal*, 56.

934. If you are situated so that their intercourse with young associatescannot always be overruled as you would wish to have it, then let them visit your children in your presence, and in no case allow these associates to lodge in the same bed, or even in the same room. It will be far easier to prevent an evil than to cure it afterward.—*A Solemn Appeal*, 58.

Fortify Minds against Evil

REMEDIAL AGENCIES

935. Mothers, it is a crime for you to allow yourselves to remain in ignorance in regard to the habits of your children. If they are pure, keep them so. Fortify their young minds, and prepare them to detest this health-and-soul-destroying vice. Shield them from becoming contaminated by associating with every young companion.—*A Solemn Appeal*, 58.

Regulate the Diet

936. The less feverish the diet, the more easily can the passions becontrolled.—*Testimonies for the Church* 2:352.

Useful Labor

937. Give your children physical labor, which will call into exercisethe nerves and the muscles. The weariness attending such labor will lessen their inclination to indulge in vicious habits. Idleness is a curse. It produces licentious habits.—*Testimonies for the Church* 2:349.

938. Active employment will give but little time to invite Satan's temptations. They may be often weary, but this will not injure them. Nature will restore their vigor and strength in their sleeping hours, if her laws are not violated. And the thoroughly tired person has less inclination for secret indulgence.—*A Solemn Appeal*, 62.

RESULTS OF IMPURE HABITS

939. Moral pollution has done more than any other evil to cause the race to degenerate.... It brings on disease of almost every description.—*Testimonies for the Church* 2:391.

940. Industry does not weary and exhaust one fifth part as much as thepernicious habit of self-abuse.—*Testimonies for the Church* 2:349.

941. Secret indulgence is, in many cases, the only real cause of thenumerous complaints of the young. This vice is laying waste the vital forces and debilitating the system; and until the habit which produced the result is broken off, there can be no permanent cure.—*A Solemn Appeal*, 58.

Physical Effects

942. The sensitive nerves of the brain have lost their healthy tone by morbid excitation to gratify an unnatural desire for sensual indulgence.—*Testimonies for the Church* 2:347.

943. Let us view the results of this vice upon the physical strength.Have you not marked the lack of healthy beauty, of strength and power of endurance, in your dear children? Have you not felt saddened as you watched the progress of disease upon them, which has baffled your skill and that of physicians? You listen to numerous complaints of headache, catarrh, dizziness, nervousness, pain in the shoulders and side, loss of appetite, pain in the back and limbs, wakeful, feverish nights, tired feelings in the morning, and great exhaustion after exercising. As you have seen the beauty of health disappearing, and have marked the sallow countenance or the unnaturally flushed face, have you been aroused sufficiently to look beneath the surface, to inquire into the cause of this physical decay? Have you observed the astonishing mortality among the youth?—*A Solemn Appeal*, 49.

944. In those who indulge in this corrupting vice before attaining theirgrowth, the evil effects are more plainly marked, and recovery from its effects is more nearly hopeless. The frame is weak and stunted, the muscles are flabby; the eyes become small, and appear at times swollen; the memory is treacherous, and becomes sieve-like; and the inability to concentrate the thoughts upon study increases.—*Testimonies for the Church* 2:402.

945. The young indulge to quite an extent in this vice before the age ofpuberty, without experiencing at the time, to any very great degree, the evil results upon the constitution. But at this critical period, while

merging into manhood and womanhood, nature makes them feel the previous violation of her laws.—*A Solemn Appeal*, 57.

946. Many sink into an early grave, while others have sufficient forceof constitution to pass this ordeal. If the practise is continued from the age of fifteen and upwards, nature will protest against the abuse she has suffered and continues to suffer, and will make them pay the penalty of the transgression of her laws, especially from the ages of thirty to forty-five, by numerous pains in the system, and various diseases, such as affection of the liver and lungs, neuralgia, rheumatism, affection of the spine, diseased kidneys, and cancerous humors.... There is often a sudden breaking down of the constitution; and death is the result.—*A Solemn Appeal*, 63, 64.

Mental Effects

947. Have you not noticed that there was a deficiency in the mentalhealth of your children? that their course seemed to be marked with extremes? that they were absent-minded? that they started nervously when spoken to, and were easily irritated? Have you not noticed that, when occupied upon a piece of work, they would look dreamingly, as though
the mind was elsewhere? And when they came to their senses, they were unwilling to own the work as coming from their hands, it was so full of mistakes, and showed such marks of inattention. Have you not been astonished at their wonderful forgetfulness? The most simple and oft-repeated directions would often be forgotten. They might be quick to learn, but it would be of no special benefit to them; the mind would not retain it. What they might learn through hard study, when they would use their knowledge, is missing, lost through their sieve-like memories. Have you not noticed their reluctance to engage in active labor, and their unwillingness to perseveringly accomplish that which they have undertaken, which taxes the mental as well as the physical strength?—*A Solemn Appeal*, 50.

948. Have you not witnessed the gloomy sadness upon the countenance,and frequent exhibitions of a morose temper in those who once were cheerful, kind, and affectionate? They are easily excited to jealousy, disposed to look upon the dark side, and when you are laboring for their good, imagine that you are their enemy, that you needlessly reprove and restrain them.—*A Solemn Appeal*, 50.

949. And have you inquired, Where will all this end? as you have looked upon your children from a moral point of view? Have you not noticed the increase of disobedience in your children, and their manifestations of ingratitude and impatience under restraint? Have you not been alarmed at their disregard of parental authority, which has bowed down the heart of their parents with grief, and
prematurely sprinkled their heads with gray hair? Have you not witnessed the lack of that noble frankness in your children which they once possessed, and which you admired in them? Some children even express in their countenances a hardened look of depravity. Have you not felt distressed and anxious as you have seen the strong desire in your children to be with the other sex, and their overpowering disposition to form attachments when quite young? ... Mothers, the great cause of these physical, mental, and moral evils is secret vice, which inflames the passions, fevers the imagination, and leads to fornication and adultery. This vice is laying waste the constitution of very many, and preparing them for diseases of almost every description.—*A Solemn Appeal*, 53.

950. Upon their very countenances is imprinted the sin of Sodom. Acontinuance of these sins will bring the sure and terrible results. They will suddenly be destroyed, and that without remedy. They will receive the sentence, "He that is unjust, let him be unjust still; and he which is filthy, let him be filthy still."—*Unpublished Testimonies*, January 11, 1897.

CHAPTER XXXIV. - RATIONAL REMEDIES FOR DISEASE.

EFFORTS OF NATURE TO RESIST DISEASE

951. Nature alone possesses restorative powers. She alone can buildup her exhausted energies, and repair the injuries she has received by inattention to her fixed laws.—*How to Live*, 57.

952. Nature alone is the effectual restorer.—*How to Live*, 60.

953. Nature, to relieve herself of poisonous impurities, makes an effort to free the system, which effort produces fevers, and what is termed disease.—*How to Live*, 60.

954. Nature bears abuse as long as she can without resisting, then she arouses, and makes a mighty effort to rid herself of the incumbrances and evil treatment she has suffered. Then come headache, chills, fevers, nervousness, paralysis, and other evils too numerous to mention.—*Testimonies for the Church* 2:69.

955. Nature is loath to give up her hold on life. She is unwilling tocease her struggle.—*How to Live*, 63.

956. Give nature a chance, and she will rally and again perform her partnobly and well.—*Testimonies for the Church* 1:549.

957. Nature was doing her best to rid the system of an accumulation ofimpurities, and could she have been left to herself, aided by the common blessings of Heaven, such as pure air and pure water, a speedy and safe cure would have been effected.—*How to Live*, 60.

958. All the credit should be ascribed to nature's restorative power.—*How to Live*, 50.

ASSISTANCE WE MAY RENDER NATURE

959. Only seek to assist nature in her efforts, by removing every obstruction, and then leave her to recover the exhausted energies of the system.—*How to Live*, 54.

960. There are many ways of practising the healing art; but there is onlyone way that Heaven approves. God's remedies are the simple agencies of nature, that will not tax or debilitate the system through their powerful properties. Pure air and water, cleanliness, a proper diet,

purity of life, and a firm trust in God are remedies for the want of which thousands are dying; yet these remedies are going out of date because their skilful use requires work that the people do not appreciate. Fresh air, exercise, pure water, and clean, sweet premises are within the reach of all with but little expense.—*Testimonies for the Church* 5:443.

961. Keep the patient free from excitement, and every influence calculated to depress. Her attendants should be cheerful and hopeful. She should have a simple diet, and should be allowed plenty of pure, soft water to drink. Bathe frequently in pure, soft water, followed by gentle rubbing. Let the light and air be freely admitted into the room. She must have quiet and undisturbed rest.—*How to Live*, 54, 55.

WATER DRINKING

962. Water is the best liquid possible to cleanse the tissues.... Drinksome little time before or after the meal.—*The Review and Herald*, July 29, 1884.

963. Fast for one or two meals, and drink only pure, soft water. The lossof a meal or two will enable the overburdened system to overcome slight indispositions; and even graver difficulties may sometimes be overcome by this simple process.—The Health Reformer, February 1, 1871.

964. Their sallow skins indicate that they are bilious.... Observe regular habits of rising early.... Eat sparingly, thus relieving the system of unnecessary burden, and encourage cheerfulness; take proper exercise in the open air, bathe frequently, and drink freely of pure, soft water.—The Health Reformer, January 1, 1871.

965. If they would become enlightened, ... and accustom themselvesto outdoor exercise, and to air in their houses, summer and winter, and use soft water for drinking and bathing purposes, they would be comparatively well and happy, instead of dragging out a miserable existence.—*How to Live*, 56.

BATHING

966. Many have never experienced the beneficial effects of water, andare afraid to use one of heaven's greatest blessings.—*How to Live*, 62.

967. The use of water can accomplish but little if the patient does notfeel the necessity of also strictly attending to his diet.—*How to Live*, 60.

FREQUENCY OF THE BATH

968. Persons in health should ... by all means bathe as often as twicea week. Those who are not in health have impurities of the blood.... The skin needs to be carefully and thoroughly cleansed, that the pores may do their work in freeing the body from impurities; therefore feeble persons who are diseased surely need the advantages and blessings of bathing as often as twice a week, and frequently even more than this is positively necessary.—*Testimonies for the Church* 3:70.

969. Frequent bathing is very beneficial, especially at night just beforeretiring, or upon rising in the morning.—*Christian Temperance and Bible Hygiene*, 141.

MANNER OF GIVING THE BATH

970. A bath, properly taken, fortifies against cold, because the circulation is improved; ... for the blood is brought to the surface, and a more easy and regular flow of the blood through all the blood-vessels is obtained.—*Testimonies for the Church* 3:71.

971. Reduce the feverish state of the system by a careful and intelligentapplication of water.—*How to Live*, 60.

972. If, in their fevered state, water had been given them to drink freely,and applications had also been made externally, long days and nights of suffering would have been saved, and many precious lives spared.—*How to Live*, 62.

973. The fire of fever seems consuming him. He longs for pure waterto moisten the parched lips, to quench the raging thirst, and to cool the fevered brow.... The blessed, heaven-sent water, skilfully applied, would quench the devouring flame.—*Testimonies for the Church* 5:195.

974. Twice a week she should take a general bath, as cool as will beagreeable, a little cooler every time, until the skin is toned up.—*Testimonies for the Church* 1:702.

975. It will take but a few moments to give the children a bath and torub them until their bodies are in a glow.—*Christian Temperance and Bible Hygiene*, 141.

EFFECTS OF THE BATH

976. Whether a person is sick or well, respiration is more free and easyif bathing is practised. By it the muscles become more flexible, the body and mind are alike invigorated, the intellect is made brighter, and every faculty becomes livelier. The bath is a soother of the nerves. It promotes general perspiration, quickens the circulation, overcomes obstructions in the system, and acts beneficially on the kidneys and the urinary organs. Bathing helps the bowels, stomach, and liver, giving energy and new life to each. It also promotes digestion, and instead of the system's being weakened, it is strengthened. Instead of increasing the liability to cold, a bath, properly taken, fortifies against cold, because the circulation is improved, and the uterine organs, which are more or less congested, are relieved; for the blood is brought to the surface, and a more easy and regular flow of the blood through all the blood-vessels is obtained.—*Testimonies for the Church* 3:70.

977. Nature, to relieve herself of poisonous impurities, makes an effortto free the system, which effort produces fevers and what is termed disease. But even then, if those who are afflicted would assist nature in her efforts by the use of pure, soft water, much suffering would be prevented.—*How to Live*, 60.

SUNLIGHT

978. This is one of nature's most healing agents.—*Testimonies for the Church* 2:527.

979. If you would have your homes sweet and inviting, make thembright with air and sunshine, remove your heavy curtains, open the windows, throw back the blinds, and enjoy the rich sunlight, even if it be at the expense of the colors of your carpets.—*Testimonies for the Church* 2:527.

980. If the windows were freed from blinds and heavy curtains, andthe air and sun permitted to enter freely the darkened rooms, there would be seen a change for the better in the mental and physical health

of the children. The pure air would have an invigorating influence upon them, and the sun that carries healing in its beams would soothe and cheer, and make them happy, joyous, and healthy.—The Health Reformer, April 1, 1871.

981. The confined air of unventilated rooms meets us with sickeningodors of mildew and mold, and the impurities exhaled from its inmates.... The emanations from damp, moldy rooms and clothing are poisonous to the system.... If all would appreciate the sunshine, and expose every article of clothing to its drying, purifying rays, mildew and mold would be prevented.... This is the only way rooms can be kept from impurities.... Every room in our dwellings should be daily thrown open to the healthful rays of the sun, and the purifying air should be invited in. This will be a preventive of disease.—The Health Reformer, February 1, 1874.

982. Exercise, and a free and abundant use of the air and sunlight, ...would give life and strength to the emaciated.—*Testimonies for the Church* 2:531.

983. The feeble one should press out into the sunshine as earnestlyand naturally as do the shaded plants and vines. The pale and sickly grain blade that has struggled up out of the cold of early spring, puts out the natural and healthy deep green after enjoying for a few days the health-and-life-giving rays of the sun. Go out into the light and warmth of the glorious sun, you pale and sickly ones, and share with vegetation its life-giving, health-dealing power.—The Health Reformer, May 1, 1871.

RELATION OF THE MIND TO THE BODY

984. But few realize the power the mind has over the body.—*Testimonies for the Church* 3:184.

985. The sympathy which exists between the mind and the body isvery great; when one is affected, the other responds.—*Testimonies for the Church* 4:60.

986. The burden of sin, with its unrest and unsatisfied desires, liesat the very foundation of a large share of the maladies which the sinner suffers.—*Testimonies for the Church* 4:579.

987. Sickness of the mind prevails everywhere. Nine tenths of thediseases from which men suffer have their foundation here. Perhaps

some living home trouble is, like a canker, eating to the very soul and weakening the life forces. Remorse for sin sometimes undermines the constitution and unbalances the mind.—*Testimonies for the Church* 5:443.

HELP FOR THE BODY THROUGH THE MIND

988. Great wisdom is needed ... in order to cure the body through the mind. But few realize the power that the mind has over the body. A great deal of the sickness which afflicts humanity has its origin in the mind, and can only be cured by restoring the mind to health. There are very many more than we imagine who are sick mentally. To deal with men and women whose minds as well as bodies are diseased, is nice work.—*Testimonies for the Church* 3:184.

INFLUENCE OF THE WILL

989. Thousands are sick and dying around us who might get well andlive if they would; but their imagination holds them. They fear that they will be made worse if they labor to exercise, when this is just the change they need to make them well. Without this, they never can improve. They should exercise the power of the will, rise above their aches and debility, and engage in useful employment, and forget that they have aching backs, sides, lungs, and heads.—*Testimonies for the Church* 3:76.

990. I have met many who were really sufferers through their imagination. They lacked will power to rise above and combat disease of body and mind; and therefore they were held in suffering bondage.— The Health Reformer, January 1, 1871.

991. You have a determined will, which causes the mind to react uponthe body, unbalancing the circulation, and producing congestion in certain organs; and you are sacrificing health to your feelings.... And yet you are capable of controlling your imagination, and overcoming these nervous attacks.—*Testimonies For The Church ?:5.310.*

992. The nerves .. control the vital action of every part of the system. Ifyour mind is impressed and fixed that a bath will injure you, the mental impression is communicated to all the nerves of the body. The nerves control the circulation of the blood; therefore the blood is,

through the impression of the mind, confined to the blood-vessels, and the good effects of the bath are lost. All this is because the blood is prevented by the mind and will from flowing readily, and from coming to the surface to stimulate, arouse, and promote the circulation. For instance, you are impressed that if you bathe you will become chilly. The brain sends this intelligence to the nerves of the body, and the blood-vessels, held in obedience to your will, cannot perform their office and cause a reaction after the bath.—*Testimonies for the Church* 3:70.

993. Let the mind become intelligent, and the will be placed on theLord's side, and there will be a wonderful improvement in the physical health. But this can never be accomplished in mere human strength.—*The Medical Missionary*, 216.

994. Keep the power of the will awake; for the will, aroused and rightlydirected, is a potent soother of the nerves.—*Testimonies for the Church* 1:557.

995. Bring to your aid the power of the will, which will resist cold, andwill give energy to the nervous system.—*Testimonies for the Church* 2:533.

CHEERFULNESS PRODUCTIVE OF HEALTH

996. A contented mind, a cheerful spirit, is health to the body andstrength to the soul. Nothing is so fruitful a cause of disease as depression, gloominess, and sadness.—*Testimonies for the Church* 1:702.

997. That which brings sickness of body and mind to nearly all is dissatisfied feelings and discontented repinings.—*Testimonies for the Church* 1:566.

998. Heart-sickness makes many dyspeptics; for mental trouble hasa paralyzing influence upon the digestive organs.—*Testimonies for the Church* 3:184.

999. The less the attention is called to the stomach after a meal, thebetter. If you are in constant fear that your food will hurt you, it most assuredly will.—*Testimonies for the Church* 2:530.

1000. We should encourage a cheerful, hopeful, peaceful frame of mind; for our health depends upon our so doing.—*Testimonies for the Church* 3:13.

1001.   Cheerfulness and a clear conscience are better than drugs, and will be an effective agent in your restoration to health.—The Health Reformer, June 1, 1871.

DOING GOOD A REMEDY FOR DISEASE

1002.   You who are suffering with poor health, there is a remedy for you. If thou clothe the naked, and bring the poor that are cast out to thy house, and deal thy bread to the hungry, "then shall thy light break forth as the morning, and thine health shall spring forth speedily." Doing good is an excellent remedy for disease.—*Testimonies for the Church* 2:29.

1003.   The consciousness of right-doing is the best medicine for diseased bodies and minds. He who is at peace with God has secured the most important requisite to health. The blessing of the Lord is life to the receiver.—*The Signs of the Times*, June 15, 1882.

1004.   The condition of the mind has much to do with the health of the physical system. If the mind is free and happy, under a consciousness of right-doing and a sense of satisfaction in causing happiness
to others, it will create a cheerfulness that will react upon the whole system, causing a freer circulation of the blood and a toning up of the entire body.—*Testimonies for the Church* 4:60.

1005.   Doing good is a work that benefits both giver and receiver. If you forget self in your interest for others, you gain a victory over your infirmities. The satisfaction you will realize in doing good will aid you greatly in the recovery of the healthy tone of the imagination. The pleasure of doing good animates the mind and vibrates through the whole body.—*Testimonies for the Church* 2:534.

1006.   The blessing of God is a healer; and those who are abundant in benefiting others, will realize that wondrous blessing in their hearts and lives.—*Testimonies for the Church* 4:60.

RESTORATIVE POWER OF THE SPIRIT OF GOD

1007.   The influence of the Spirit of God is the very best medicine for disease. Heaven is all health; the more deeply heavenly influences are realized, the more sure will be the recovery of the believing invalid.—*Christian Temperance and Bible Hygiene*, 13.

1008. Sickness of the mind prevails everywhere. Nine tenths of thediseases from which men suffer have their foundation here.... The religion of Christ, so far from being the cause of insanity, is one of its most effectual remedies; for it is a potent soother of the nerves.—*Testimonies for the Church* 5:443.

1009. In nine cases out of ten the knowledge of a sin-pardoning Saviourwould make them better both in mind and body.—*Testimonies for the Church* 5:448.

1010. Many carry a violated conscience, and can be reached only bythe principles of Bible religion.—*Testimonies for the Church* 3:168.

1011. A sore, sick heart, a discouraged mind, needs mild treatment;and it is through tender sympathy that this class of minds can be healed. The physician should first gain their confidence, and then point them to the all-healing Physician. If their minds can be directed to the Burden-Bearer, and they can have faith that he will have an interest in them, the cure of their diseased bodies and minds will be sure.—*Testimonies for the Church* 3:184.

1012. A person whose mind is quiet and satisfied in God is in the pathway to health.—*The Review and Herald*, 1880, No. II.

1013. The assurance of God's approval will promote physical health. Itfortifies the soul against doubt, perplexity, and excessive grief, that so often sap the vital forces and induce nervous diseases of a most debilitating and distressing character.—The Review and Herald, October 16, 1883.

1014. The exalting influence of the Spirit of God is the best restorativefor the sick.—*Testimonies for the Church* 1:556.

CHAPTER XXXV. - PRAYER FOR THE SICK.

1015.　　　It is labor lost to teach people to go to God as a healer of their infirmities, unless they are educated also to lay aside every wrong practise.—*Unpublished Testimonies*, August 25, 1897.

CAUTIONS

1016.　　　Many have expected that God would keep them from sicknessmerely because they have asked him to do so. But God did not regard their prayers, because their faith was not made perfect by works. God will not work a miracle to keep those from sickness who have no care for themselves, but are continually violating the laws of health, and make no effort to prevent disease. When we do all we can on our part to have health, then we may expect that the blessed results will follow, and we can ask God in faith to bless our efforts for the preservation of health. He will then answer our prayer, if his name can be glorified thereby. But let all understand that they have a work to do. God will not work in a miraculous manner to preserve the health of persons who are taking a sure course to make themselves sick, by their careless inattention to the laws of health.—*How to Live*, 64.

1017.　　　In such cases of affliction where Satan has control of the mind,before engaging in prayer there should be the closest self-examination to discover if
there are not sins which need to be repented of, confessed, and forsaken. Deep humility of soul before God is necessary, and firm, humble reliance upon the blood of Christ alone. Fasting and prayer will accomplish nothing while the heart is estranged from God by a wrong course of action.—*Testimonies for the Church* 2:146.

1018.　　　If we regard iniquity in our hearts, the Lord will not hear us.... When we come to him, we should pray that we may enter into and accomplish his purpose, and that our desires and interests may be lost in his.—*Testimonies for the Church* 2:148.

1019.　　　What word has God for those who ignore the light that is shining abroad, and then ask to be prayed for that they may be sanctified and healed?—The same word that he had for Cain: "If thou doest well, shalt thou not be accepted? And if thou doest not well, sin lieth at the door."—*Unpublished Testimonies*, August 25, 1897.

INSTRUCTION

1020.   Some, if they should regain their health, would indulge in someheedless transgression of nature's laws.—*Unpublished Testimonies*.

1021.   We should first find out if the sick one has been withholdingtithes or has made trouble in the church.—*Unpublished Testimonies*.

1022.   There are very many more than we imagine that are sick mentally.... A sore, sick heart, a discouraged mind, needs mild treatment, and it is through tender sympathy that this class of minds can be directed to the Burden-Bearer, and if they can have faith that he will have an interest in them, the cure of their diseased bodies and minds will be sure.—*Testimonies for the Church* 3:184.

1023.   After the physicians [of the Health Institute] have done what theycan in behalf of the sick, they ask God to work with their efforts, and restore the suffering invalids to health. This he has done in some cases in answer to the prayer of faith. And this he will continue to do, if they are faithful, and put their trust in him.—*Testimonies for the Church* 2:184.

1024.   God does not work miracles where he has provided means bywhich the work may be accomplished.—*The Review and Herald*, July 17, 1888.

1025.   Faith without intelligent works is dead, being alone. Faith inthe healing power of God will not save unless it is combined with good works.—*Unpublished Testimonies*, August 25, 1897.

1026.   God will not work a miracle to change natural causes which youcan control.—*The Signs of the Times*, May 8, 1884.

1027.   Many would not endure the time of trial, and will therefore belaid away.—*Unpublished Testimonies*.

1028.   Where the way is clear for the offering up of prayer for the sick,the case should be committed to the Lord in calm faith, not with a storm of excitement. He alone is acquainted with the past life of the individual, and knows what his future will be.... All that we are required to do is to ask God to raise up the sick if in accordance with his will, believing that he hears the reasons which we present, and the fervent prayers offered. If the Lord sees that it will best honor him, he will answer our prayers. But to urge recovery without submission to his will, is not right.... All that can be done in praying for the sick is earnestly to importune God in their behalf, and in perfect confidence rest the matter in his hands.... If the life of the sick can glorify him, we pray that they may live; nevertheless, not as we will, but as he wills. Our faith can be just as firm, and more reliable, by committing the desire to the all-wise God, and without feverish anxiety, in perfect confidence, trusting all to him.... Our petitions must not take the form of a command, but of intercession for him to do the thing we desire of him.—*Testimonies for the Church* 2:147-149.

1029.　　The strong desire for recovery leads to earnest prayer; and thisis right. God is our refuge in sickness as in health.—*Testimonies for the Church* 5:315.

1030.　　Prayer will give the sick an abiding confidence.—*Testimonies for the Church* 5:443.

1031.　　Jesus can limit the power of Satan. He is the physician in whomthe sin-sick soul may trust to heal the maladies of the body as well as of the soul.—*Testimonies for the Church* 5:448.

1032.　　I would come before the Lord with this petition: "Lord, we cannot read the heart of this sick one, but thou knowest whether it is for the good of his soul and for the glory of thy name to raise him to health. In thy great goodness, compassionate this case, and let healthy action take place in the system. The work must be entirely thine own. We have done all that human skill can do; now, Lord, we lay this case at thy feet, work as only God can work, and if it be for thy good and for thy glory, arrest the progress of disease and heal this sufferer." ... But after I have prayed earnestly for the sick, what then? Do I cease to do all I can for their recovery?—No, I work all the more earnestly, with much prayer that the Lord may bless the means which his own hand has provided; that he may give sanctified wisdom to co-operate with him in the recovery of the sick.—*Unpublished Testimonies*, March 11, 1892.

1033.　　In praying for the sick, it is essential to have faith; for it is inaccordance with the word of God.... Sometimes answers to our prayers come immediately, sometimes we have to wait patiently and continue earnestly to plead for the things we need. Our faith is illustrated by the case of the importunate solicitor for bread.... If our petitions are indited by the Lord, they will be answered.—*Ibid*.

1034. We all desire an immediate answer to our prayers, and we aretempted to become discouraged if it does not come. Now my experience has taught me that this is a great mistake. The delay is for our special benefit.... Faith strengthens through continual exercise. This waiting does not mean that because we ask the Lord to heal, there is nothing for us to do. We are to make the very best use of the means which the Lord in his gracious goodness has provided for us in our very necessities.... I have looked to God in faith, and have used every benefit that hygienic methods have provided, of which we could avail ourselves. This was my duty.... In treatment we have used water in a variety of ways, always asking the Lord to give wisdom in all our efforts, and to put his blessing upon every laudable
means employed for the recovery of health.... As a reasonable being, through the grace of God I shall take advantage of the blessings of the Lord which he has placed within my reach.—*Unpublished Testimonies*, March 11, 1892.

1035. I have seen so much of carrying matters to extremes, even inpraying for the sick, that I have felt that this part of our experience requires much earnest, sanctified thinking, else we shall make movements that we may call faith, but that are nothing less than presumption. Persons worn down with affliction need to be counseled wisely that they may move discreetly; and while they place themselves before God to be prayed for that they may be healed, they are not to neglect methods of restoration to health that are in accordance with nature's laws. If, in praying for healing, they refuse to use the simple remedies provided by God to alleviate pain and to aid nature in her work, lest it be a denial of faith, they are talking an unwise position. It is not a denial of faith, it is in strict harmony with the plans of God.... One word from God, one touch of the divine finger, would have cured Hezekiah instantly, but special directions were given to take a fig and lay it on the affected part, and Hezekiah was raised to life. In everything we need to move along the line of God's providence. The human agent should have faith, and should co-operate with divine power, using every facility, taking advantage of everything that to his intelligence is beneficial, and working in harmony with natural laws; in doing this he neither denies nor hinders faith.—*Ibid*.

1036.　　　　Should the Lord work a miracle to restore the wonderful machinery which human beings have impaired through their own carelessness and inattention and their indulgence of appetite and passions, by doing the very things that the Lord has told them they should not do, he would be ministering to sin, which is the transgression of his own law.—*Unpublished Testimonies*, May 19, 1897.

1037.　　　　The relations between God and each soul are as distinct and full as though there were not another soul for whom he gave his beloved Son.... Keep your wants, your joys, your sorrows, your cares, and your fears before God.... The Lord is very pitiful and of tender mercy. His heart of love is touched by our sorrows, and even by our utterance of them.... Nothing that in any way concerns our peace is too small for him to notice. There is no chapter in our experience too dark for him to read; there is no perplexity too difficult for him to unravel. No calamity can befall the least of his children, no anxiety harass the soul, no joy cheer, no sincere prayer escape the lips, of which our Heavenly Father is unobservant, or in which he takes no immediate interest. "He healeth the broken in heart, and bindeth up their wounds."—*Steps to Christ*, 117.

CHAPTER XXXVI. - DRUGS.

1038.　　　　Many, instead of seeking to remove the poisonous matter from the system, take a more deadly poison into the system to remove a poison already there.—*How to Live*, 64.

1039.　　　　Many parents substitute drugs for judicious nursing.— The Health Reformer, September 1, 1886.

MODE OF ACTION

1040.　　　　Drugs never cure disease; they only change its form and location.... When drugs are introduced into the system, for a time they seem to have a beneficial effect. A change may take place, but the disease is not cured. It will manifest itself in some other form.... The disease which the drug was given to cure may disappear, but only to reappear in a new form, such as skin diseases, ulcers, painful, diseased joints, and sometimes in a more dangerous and deadly form.... Nature keeps struggling, and the patient suffers with different ailments, until there is a sudden breaking down in her efforts, and death follows.—*How to Live*, 60.

1041.　　　Every additional drug given to the patient ... will complicate thecase, and make the patient's recovery more hopeless.... An evil, simple in the beginning, which nature aroused herself to overcome, and which she would have done if left to

herself, aided by the common blessings of Heaven, has been made tenfold worse by introducing drug poisons into the system, which cause of themselves a destructive disease, forcing into extraordinary action the remaining life forces to war against and overcome the drug intruder.—*How to Live*, 57.

1042.　　　Sick people who take drugs do appear to get well. With somethere is sufficient life force for nature to draw upon to so far expel the poison from the system that the sick, having a period of rest, recover. But no credit should be allowed the drugs taken, for they only hindered nature in her efforts. All the credit should be ascribed to nature's restorative powers.—*How to Live*, 50.

1043.　　　Powerful poisons are often administered, which fetter nature in all her friendly efforts to recover from the abuse the system has suffered.—*How to Live*, 49.

RESULTS OF DRUG MEDICATION

1044.　　　Drugging should be forever abandoned; for while it does notcure any malady, it enfeebles the system, making it more susceptible to disease.—*Testimonies For The Church ?:5.311*.

1045.　　　There are more who die from the use of drugs than all who wouldhave died of disease had nature been left to do her own work.—*How to Live*, 61.

1046.　　　Medicines have no power to cure, but will most generally hindernature in her efforts.—*How to Live*, 62.

1047.　　　Medicine deranges nature's fine machinery, and breaks down theconstitution. It kills, but never cures.—*How to Live*, 57.

1048.　　　The endless variety of medicines in the market, the numerousadvertisements of new drugs and mixtures, all of which claim to do wonderful cures, kill hundreds where they benefit one.... Yet people keep dosing, and continue to grow weaker until they die. Some will have medicine at all events. Then let them take these hurtful mixtures and the various deadly poisons upon their own responsibility. God's servants should not administer medicines which they know will leave behind injurious effects upon the system, even if they do relieve present suffering. Every poisonous preparation in the vegetable and mineral kingdoms, taken into the system, will leave its wretched influence, affecting the liver and lungs, and deranging the system generally.—*Facts of Faith*, 140.

1049.　　　The sick are in a hurry to get well, and the friends of the sick areimpatient. They will have medicine, and if they do not feel that powerful influence upon their systems which their erroneous views lead them to think they should feel, they impatiently change to another physician. The change often increases the evil. They go through a course of medicine equally as dangerous as the first, and more fatal, because the two treatments do not agree, and the system is poisoned beyond remedy.—*How to Live*, 62.

1050.　　　Although the patient may recover, yet the powerful effort naturewas required to make to over-come the poison, injured the constitution, and shortened the life of the patient. There are many who do not die under the influence of drugs, but there are
very many who are left useless wrecks, hopeless, gloomy, and miserable sufferers, a burden to themselves and to society.—*How to Live*, 50.

1051 Everywhere you go you will see deformity, disease, and imbecility, which in very many cases can be traced directly back to drug poisons.—*How to Live*, 51.

1052. Drugs given to stupefy, whatever they may be, derange the nervous system.—*How to Live*, 57.

THE USE OF DRUGS IN OUR INSTITUTIONS

1053.　　　Our institutions are established that the sick may be treated byhygienic methods, discarding almost entirely the use of drugs. There is a terrible account to be rendered to God by men who have so little regard for human life as to treat the body ruthlessly, in dealing out drugs.... We are not excusable if, through ignorance, we destroy God's building by taking into the stomach poisonous drugs under a variety of names we do not understand. It is our duty to refuse all such prescriptions. We want sanitariums where maladies may be cured by nature's own provisions, and where the people may be taught how to treat themselves when sick; where they will learn to eat temperately of wholesome food, and to be educated to discard all narcotics, tea, coffee, fermented wines, and stimulants of all kinds, and the flesh of dead animals.—*Unpublished Testimonies*, December 4, 1896.

1054. Drug medication, as it is generally practised, is a curse. Educateaway from drugs, use them less and less, and depend more upon hygienic agencies. Nature will respond to God's remedies,—pure air,
pure water, proper exercise, and a clear conscience.—*Unpublished Testimonies*, 1888.

1055. To use drugs while continuing evil habits is certainly inconsistent, and greatly dishonors God by dishonoring the body which he has made. Yet for all this, stimulants and drugs continue to be prescribed and freely used; while the hurtful indulgences that produce the disease are not discarded. The use of tea, coffee, tobacco, opium, wine, beer, and other stimulants gives nature a false support. Physicians should understand how to treat the sick through the use of nature's remedies. Pure air, pure water, and healthful exercise should be employed in the treatment of the sick.—*Unpublished Testimonies*, 1892.

1056. Many physicians are not as thorough and intelligent as they should be in the practise of their profession. They resort to drugs, when greater skill and knowledge would teach them a more excellent way. Lives have been lost which might have been saved if drugs had not been resorted to. As a rule, the less frequently they are employed, the better the patient will prosper.—*Unpublished Testimonies*, 1888.

1057. Make use of the remedies that God has provided. Pure air, sunshine, and the intelligent use of water are beneficial agents in the restoration of health. But the use of water is considered too laborious. It is easier to employ drugs than to use natural remedies.

In treating the sick, the physician will seek God for wisdom; then, instead of placing his dependence upon drugs and expecting that medicine will bring health to his patients, he will use nature's
restoratives, and employ natural means whereby the sick may be aided to recover. The Lord will hear and answer the prayers of the Christian

physician.—*Unpublished Testimonies*, 1888.

1058.   A great amount of good can be done by enlightening all to whomwe have access, as to the best means, not only of curing the sick, but of preventing disease and suffering. The physician who endeavors to enlighten his patients as to the nature and causes of their maladies, and to teach them how to avoid disease, may have up-hill work; but if he is a conscious reformer, he will talk plainly of the ruinous effects of self-indulgence in eating, drinking, and dressing, of the overtaxation of the vital forces that has brought his patients where they are. He will not increase the evil by administering drugs till exhausted nature gives up the struggle, but will teach the patients how to form correct habits, and to aid nature in her work of restoration by a wise use of her own simple remedies.—*Christian Temperance and Bible Hygiene*, 121.

1059.   The question of health reform is not agitated as it must be andwill be. A simple diet and the entire absence of drugs, leaving nature free to recuperate the wasted energies of the body, would make our sanitariums far more effectual in restoring the sick to health.— *Unpublished Testimonies*, August 30, 1896.

CHAPTER XXXVII. - THE MISSIONARY NURSE.

NEED OF NURSES

1060. In almost every church there are young men and women who might receive an education either as physicians or nurses. They will never have a more favorable opportunity than now. I would urge that this subject be considered prayerfully, that special effort be made to select those youth who give promise of usefulness and moral strength. Let these receive an education at our Sanitarium at Battle Creek, to go out as missionaries wherever the Lord may call them to labor.—*The Medical Missionary*, 216.

QUALIFICATIONS OF NURSES

1061. I could wish that there were one hundred nurses in training wherethere is one. It ought to be thus. Both men and women can be much more useful as medical missionaries than as missionaries without a medical education.—*The Medical Missionary*, 215.

1062. Attendants should be cheerful and hopeful.—*How to Live*, 54.

1063. The attendants should be unhurried, calm, and self-possessed.—*How to Live*, 59.

1064. The mother may be an intelligent nurse and physician of herown dear children. It is her right to have an understanding of her own and her children's organisms, that she may know how to treat her children in sickness.—The Health Reformer, June 1, 1873.

THE NURSE'S DUTY TO HERSELF

1065. It is the duty of attendants and nurses in the sick-room to havea special care for their own health, especially in critical cases of fever and consumption. One person should not be kept closely confined to the sick-room. It is safer to have two or three to depend upon, who are careful and understanding nurses, these alternating and sharing the care and confinement of the sick-room. Each should have exercise in the open air as often as possible. This is important to sick-bed attendants, especially if the friends of the sick are among that class who continue to regard air, if admitted into the sick-room, as an enemy, and will not allow the windows raised or the doors opened. The sick and the attendants are in this case compelled to breathe the atmosphere from day to day, because of the inexcusable ignorance of the friends of the sick.—*How to Live*, 56.

1066.　　　If attendants are awake to the subject of health, and realize thenecessity of ventilation for their own benefit, as well as that of the patient, and the relatives, as well as the sick, oppose the admission of air and light into the sick-room, the attendants should have no scruples of conscience in leaving the sick-room. They should feel themselves released from their obligations to the sick. It is not the duty of one or more to risk the liability of incurring disease and endangering their lives by breathing the poisonous atmosphere. If the sick will fall victims to their own erroneous ideas, and will shut out of the room the most essential of heaven's blessings, let
them do so, but not at the peril of those who ought to live.—*How to Live*, 57.

SUGGESTIONS TO NURSES

1067.　　　It is of great value to the sick to have an even temperature in the room. This cannot always be correctly determined, if left to the judgment of attendants, for they may not be the best judges of a right temperature.—*How to Live*, 54.

1068.　　　Few realize the effect of a mild, firm manner, even in the care ofan infant. The fretful, impatient mother or nurse creates feverishness in the child in her arms, whereas a gentle manner tends to quiet the nerves of the little one.—The Health Reformer, November 1, 1878.

1069.　　　Where there are two watchers, they often converse together, sometimes aloud, but more frequently in whispered tones, which is far more trying and exciting to the nerves of the sick than talking aloud.... Attendants upon the sick should, if possible, leave them to quiet and rest through the night, while they occupy a room adjoining. All unnecessary noise and excitement should be avoided in the sick-room, and the whole house should be kept as quiet as possible. Ignorance, forgetfulness, and recklessness have caused the death of many who might have lived had they received proper care from judicious, thoughtful attendants.—*How to Live*, 59.

CHAPTER XXXVIII. - MEDICAL STUDENTS.

NEED OF MEDICAL STUDENTS

1070. I am intensely interested in the education of medical studentsas missionaries. This will prove a means of introducing the truth where otherwise it would not find an entrance.—*Unpublished Testimonies*, October 2, 1895.

1071. I can see that in the Lord's providence the medical missionarywork is to be a great entering wedge, whereby the diseased soul may be reached.—*Ibid.*

1072. What a field of usefulness is open before the medical missionary! Jesus Christ was in every sense of the word a missionary of the highest type, combining with his missionary work that of the great Physician, healing all manner of diseases.... Every physician ought to be a Christian, and if he is, he bears with him a cure for the soul as well as the body. He is doing the work of an apostle as well as of a physician.... How essential that the missionary should understand the diseases which afflict the human body, that he may combine the physician, trained to care for diseased bodies, with the faithful, conscientious shepherd of the flock, giving sacredness and double efficiency to the service! The Lord, in his great goodness and matchless love, has been urging it upon his human instrumentalities that the education of missionaries
is not really complete unless they have a knowledge of how to treat the sick and suffering. If the importance of this branch of missionary education had been felt, many who have lost their lives might have lived. Had they had an intelligent knowledge of the human body and how to treat its maladies, they could have reached many darkened minds that have not been reached.—*Ibid.*

1073.   Devout persons, both men and women, are wanted now to goforth as medical missionaries. Let them cultivate their physical and mental powers and their piety to the utmost. Every effort should be made to send forth intelligent workers. The same grace that came from Jesus Christ to Paul and Apollos, which caused them to be distinguished for their spiritual excellencies, can be received now, and will bring into working order many devoted missionaries.—*Unpublished Testimonies*, February 19, 1893.

1074.   I consider that there is nothing that can give character to thework like a proper taking up of the work of hygienic treatment for the sick.—*Unpublished Testimonies*, February 10, 1897.

1075.   As religious aggression subverts the liberties of our nation, thosewho would stand for freedom of conscience will be placed in unfavorable positions. For their own sake they should, while they have opportunity, become intelligent in regard to disease, its causes, prevention, and cure. Those who do this will find a field of labor anywhere. There will be suffering ones, plenty of them, who will need help, not only among those of our own faith, but largely
among those who know not the truth.—*The Signs of the Times*, September 16, 1892.

1076.   I would advise young men and women to give heed to this matter.Perilous times are before us. The whole world will be involved in perplexity and distress. Diseases of every kind will be upon the human family, and such ignorance as now prevails concerning the laws of health will result in great suffering and the loss of many lives that might be saved.—*The Signs of the Times*, September 16, 1893.

1077.   There is no missionary field more important than that occupiedby the faithful, God-fearing physician. There is no field where a man may accomplish greater good, or win more jewels to shine in the crown of his rejoicing.—*Testimonies for the Church* 5:448.

1078.   More of the right kind of men are needed to devote themselvesto this profession.—*Testimonies for the Church* 5:446.

QUALIFICATIONS OF MEDICAL STUDENTS

1079.   A physician can do much better work if he has physical strength.If he is feeble, he cannot endure the wearing labor incident to his calling. A man who has a weak constitution, who is a dyspeptic, or who has not perfect self-control, cannot become qualified to deal with all classes of disease. Great care should be taken not to encourage persons who might be useful in some less responsible position, to study medicine at a great outlay of time and means, when there is no reasonable hope that they will succeed.—*Testimonies For The Church ?:5.447*.

1080. Painstaking effort should be made to induce suitable men to qualify themselves for this work. They should be men whose characters are based

upon the broad principles of the word of God, men who possess a natural energy, force, and perseverance that will enable them to reach a high standard of excellence. It is not every one who can make a successful physician. Many have entered upon the duties of this profession every way unprepared. They have not the requisite knowledge; neither have they the skill and tact, the carefulness and intelligence, necessary to insure success.—*Testimonies for the Church* 5:446.

1081. Those who take the lives of others in their hands must be men who have been marked as making life a success. They must be men of judgment and wisdom, men who can sympathize, and feel to the depths, men whose whole being is stirred when they witness suffering.—*Testimonies for the Church* 2:385.

1082. There are those who have entered the medical profession whoshould have chosen some other calling. They are unsympathetic. They seem to think the proper way is to withhold all words of sympathy, and gird up their compassion so that not a particle of it shall be drawn out. They are cold and uncommunicative, and leave no warm, cheering influence. They seem to think words of tenderness and compassion are an evidence of weakness.—*Counsels to Physicians and Medical Students*, 28.

1083. God will surely advance the humble, faithful, praying, whole-souled medical missionary, as he advanced Daniel and his fellows.—*The Signs of the Times*, October 2, 1893.

1084. The duties and qualifications of a physician are not small. Thestudents need daily to lift

responsibilities, that they may become burden-bearers.... There is only one power that can make these students what they ought to be, and keep them steadfast. It is the grace of God and the power of the truth exerting a saving influence upon the life and character. These students, who intend to deal with suffering humanity, will find no graduating place this side of heaven. Every bit possible of that knowledge that is termed science should be acquired, while the seeker daily acknowledges that the fear of God is the beginning of wisdom. Every item of experience and everything that can strengthen the mind, should be cultivated to the utmost of their power, while at the same time they should seek God for his wisdom, their consciences illuminated, quick, and pure; for unless they are guided by the wisdom from above, they become an easy prey to the deceptive power of Satan. They become inflated, large in their own eyes, pompous, and self-sufficient. The principle of worldly policy will most assuredly lead into difficulties. The truth, God's truth, must be cherished in the heart, and held in the strength of God, or the powers of Satan will wrench it from you. You need to be self-reliant and yet teachable, that you may have strength to be faithful to duty. To trust to your own resources, your own wisdom or strength, is folly. You will be brought to confusion if you do this. You can walk securely only when you follow the counsel of God.—*Counsels to Physicians and Medical Students*, 17.

1085.   Knowledge and science must be vitalized by the Spirit of God inorder to serve the noblest
purposes. The Christian alone can make the right use of knowledge. Science, in order to be fully appreciated, must be viewed from a religious standpoint.—*Christian Education*, 32.

ADVICE TO MEDICAL STUDENTS

1086.   I wish I could set before the medical student the true responsibility that rests upon him and his work. There is not one in one hundred who has a just sense of his position, his work, his accountability to God, and how much God will do for him if he will make him his trust. The very first lesson he should learn is that of dependence upon God. Make God your counselor at every step. The worldly and the nominal Christian may insinuate that in order to be successful you must be politic, you must at times depart from the strictest rectitude; but be not deluded. These temptations find a ready welcome in the heart of man; but I speak that which I know. Pamper not self. Throw not open a door for the enemy to take possession of the citadel of the soul. There is danger in the first and slightest departure from the strictest veracity. In your work, be true to yourself. Preserve your God-given dignity in the fear of God. There is in your case the necessity of getting hold and keeping hold of the arm of infinite power.—*Counsels to Physicians and Medical Students*, 23.

1087.　　　By studying the word of God diligently medical students arefar better prepared for all other studies; for enlightenment always comes with an earnest study of the word of God. Let it be understood by medical missionaries that the better they become acquainted with God and Jesus

Christ whom he has sent, the better they become acquainted with

Bible history, the better qualified they will be to do their work.... There should be most faithful teachers who strive to make the students understand their lessons, not by explaining everything themselves, but by letting the students explain thoroughly every passage which they read. Let the inquiring minds of the students be respected.—*Unpublished Testimonies*, December 1, 1895.

1088.　　　Learn all they can of the principles of truth, and discard error.—*Christian Education*, 38.

1089.　　　In this age there is danger for every one who shall enter uponthe study of medicine. Often his instructors are world-wise men, and his fellow students infidels, who have no thought of God, and he is in danger of being influenced by these irreligious associations. Nevertheless, some have gone through the medical course, and have remained true to principle. They would not continue their studies on the Sabbath; and they have proved that men may become qualified for the duties of a physician, and not disappoint the expectations of those who furnish them means to obtain an education.—*Testimonies for the Church* 5:447.

1090.　　　Students may receive their diplomas, and yet their education bebut just begun.... The one who best knows himself works in all humility. He feels like making no proud boasts; he bears a weight of responsibility as he sees the woes of suffering humanity, and he will not take human life into his hand to deal with even the bodies of men without connecting with the experienced Physician, regarding him as a father and himself as a child to be

instructed and corrected, if in error.... Students should work up an experience beginning at the lower round of the ladder, and by careful, earnest, thoughtful exertion, climb round after round, religion, Bible religion, being the mainspring of action. They cannot expect to be ranked by the side of those of experience who have devoted their time, their energies, and their souls to the work for years, unless they shall give evidence of capabilities of mind and intelligence in practise.... They must be content to come up gradually, and prove their ability by showing in lesser matters that they sense the responsibility laid upon them. Many do not love the taxing, burden-bearing part. They will deal with the sick, but never lift the load. They take every thing very easily. The sick may approach the last crisis that wrings the heart of the older physician with intense pain because a life is going out and he can devise no means of saving it, and another physician connected with him will not sense the danger or devote time to close thought and severe mental effort. He works as a machine. He is as calm as a summer's evening, when he should be pressed as a cart beneath the sheaves. Had he more intensity of feeling, he would not throw off the burden for an instant, but by close thinking, by earnest prayer, would study to devise ways and means yet untried, and would perhaps be able to save not only the life, but, through Christ, the soul of the patient.—*Counsels to Physicians and Medical Students*, 11-13.

1091.   Students should be willing to work under those of experience, toheed their suggestions, to
follow their advice, and to go as far as possible in thought, training, and intelligent enterprise, but never to infringe upon a rule, never to disregard one principle that has been interwoven in the upbuilding of the institution. The dropping down is easy enough; the disregard of regulations is natural to the heart inclined to selfish ease and gratification. It is so much easier to tear down than to build up. One man with careless ideas may do more in this work of letting down the standard than ten men with all their efforts can do to counteract and stay the demoralizing influence....

There are many who are in such haste to climb to distinction that they skip some of the rounds of the ladder, and have, in so doing, lost essential experience, which they should have in order to become intelligent workers. In their zeal the knowledge of many things looks unimportant to them. They skim over the surface, and do not go deep and thorough, climbing round after round of the ladder of progress by a slow and painful process, thus gaining an experience which will enable them to help others to ascend. We want men and women who are more thorough, and who feel it their duty to improve every talent lent them, that they may finally double their intrusted capital.—*Counsels to Physicians and Medical Students*, 15.

1092.   A responsibility to spread the knowledge of hygienic principlesrests upon all who have enjoyed the benefits of health reform.... There must be a revival in regard to this matter; for God purposes to accomplish much through this agency.—Special Testimony to Ministers and Workers

CHAPTER XXXIX. - THE MISSIONARY PHYSICIAN.

1093.   The duties of the physician are arduous. Few realize the mentaland physical strain to which he is subjected. Every energy and capability must be enlisted with the most intense anxiety in the battle with disease and death. Often he knows that one unskilful movement of the hand, even but a hair's breadth, in the wrong direction may send a soul unprepared into eternity.—*Testimonies for the Church* 5:446.

1094.   The physician who endeavors to enlighten his patients as to thenature and causes of their maladies, and to teach them how to avoid disease, may have up-hill work.—*Christian Temperance and Bible Hygiene*, 121.

1095.   Why should the Christian physician, who is believing, expecting,looking, waiting, and longing for the coming and kingdom of Christ, when sickness and death will no longer have power over the saints, expect more pay for his services than the Christian editor or the Christian minister? He may say that his work is more wearing. That is yet to be proved. Let him work as he can endure it, and not violate the laws of life which he teaches to his patients. There are no good reasons why he should overwork and receive large pay for it, more than the minister or the editor. Let all who act a part in the
institute and receive pay for their services, act on the same liberal principle.—*Testimonies for the Church* 1:640.

1096.   The physicians should keep well. They must not get sick byoverlabor, or by any imprudence on their part.... The privilege of getting away from the Health Institute should occasionally be accorded to all the physicians, especially to those who bear burdens of responsibilities. If there is such a scarcity of help that this cannot be done, more help should be secured. To have physicians overworked, and thus disqualified to perform the duties of their profession, is a thing to be dreaded.—*Testimonies for the Church* 3:182.

CHRISTIAN PHYSICIANS

1097.   Satan is the originator of disease; and the physician is warringagainst his work and power.—*Testimonies for the Church* 5:443.

1098.   Every energy and capability must be enlisted with the most intense anxiety in the battle with disease and death.—*Ibid.*, 202.

1099.   He will be firm as a rock as to principle, yet kind and courteousto all. He will feel the responsibility of his position, and his practise will show that he is actuated by pure, unselfish motives, and a desire to adorn the doctrine of Christ in all things.—*Ibid.*, 195.

1100.   The physician should know how to pray.—*Ibid.*, 199.

1101.   Both the health of the body and the salvation of the soul are ina degree dependent upon the course of the physicians. It is of the utmost consequence that they be right, that they have not only scientific knowledge, but the knowledge of God's will and ways.—*Testimonies for the Church* 4:566.

1102.   The young physician has access to the God of Daniel. Throughdivine grace and power, he may become as efficient in his calling as Daniel was in his exalted position. But it is a mistake to make a scientific preparation the all-important thing, while religious principles that lie at the very foundation of a successful practise are neglected. Many are lauded as skilful men in their profession, who scorn the thought that they need to rely upon Jesus for wisdom in their work. But if these men who trust in their knowledge of science were illuminated by the light of heaven, to how much greater excellence might they attain! How much stronger would be their powers, with how much greater confidence could they undertake difficult cases! The man who is closely connected with the great Physician of soul and body, has the resources of heaven and earth at his command, and he can work with a wisdom, an unerring precision, that the godless man cannot possess.—*Testimonies for the Church* 5:448.

1103.   The physician needs more than human wisdom and power thathe may know how to minister to the many perplexing cases of disease of the mind and heart with which he is called to deal. If he is ignorant of the power of divine grace, he cannot help the afflicted one, but may aggravate the difficulty; but if he has a firm hold upon God, he will be able to help the diseased, distracted mind.—*Ibid.*, 200.

1104.   If he takes counsel of God, he will have the great Healer to workwith his efforts, and he will move with the greatest caution, lest by his mismanagement he injure one of God's creatures.—*Ibid.*, 195.

SCIENTIFIC ATTAINMENTS OF PHYSICIANS

1105.   Many have entered upon the duties of this profession every way unprepared. They have not the requisite knowledge; neither have they the skill and tact, the carefulness and intelligence, necessary to insure success.—*Testimonies for the Church* 5:446.

1106.   Many physicians are not as thorough and intelligent as they ought to be in the practise of their profession. They resort to drugs, when greater skill and knowledge would teach them a more excellent way.—*Unpublished Testimonies*, 1888.

1107.   When physicians understand physiology in its truest sense, theiruse of drugs will be very much less, and finally they will cease to use them at all. The physician who depends upon drug medication in his practise shows that he does not understand the delicate machinery of the human organism.—*Unpublished Testimonies*, October 12, 1896.

1108.   A skilful physician must understand the nature of various diseases, and must have a thorough knowledge of the human structure. He must be prompt in attending to the patients. He knows that delays are dangerous. When his experienced hand is laid upon the pulse of the sufferer, and he carefully notes the peculiar indications of the malady, his previous knowledge enables him to determine concerning the nature of the disease and the treatment necessary to arrest its progress.—*Testimonies for the Church* 4:267.

1109.   If he is an intelligent physician, he will be able to trace diseaseto its cause.—*Testimonies for the Church* 5:439.

1110.   If he will be observing and honest, he cannot help acknowledgingthat sin and disease bear to each other the relationship of cause and effect. The physician should be quick to see this, and to act accordingly.—*Ibid.*, 200.

1111.   There are constant temptations for physicians to exalt scienceabove the God who is the ruler of the universe. There is danger that physicians will, little by little, leave the simplicity of Bible faith in the power of God.—*Unpublished Testimonies*, April 15, 1892.

1112.   All who engage in the acquisition of knowledge should aim to reach the highest round of progress. Let them advance as fast and as far as they can; let their field of study be as broad as their powers can compass, making God their wisdom; clinging to him who is infinite in knowledge, who can reveal the secrets hidden for ages, who can solve the most difficult problems for minds that believe in him who only hath immortality, dwelling in the light that no man can approach unto.... The same principles run through the spiritual and the natural worlds.—*Special Testimonies On Education*, 216.

THE PHYSICIAN'S RELATION TO THE LAWS OF HEALTH

1113.   It is wilful sin in them to be ignorant of the laws of health or indifferent to them; for they are looked up to as wise above other men.—*Testimonies for the Church* 5:441.

1114.   If they do not put to a practical use the knowledge they have ofthe laws that govern their own being, if they prefer present gratification to soundness of mind and body, they are not fit to be intrusted with the lives of others.—*Ibid.*, 198.

1115.   He [the physician] is expected to indulge in no habit that willweaken the life forces.—*Ibid.*, 197.

1116.   The physicians in our institutions must be imbued with the living principles of health reform. Men will never be truly temperate until the grace of Christ is an abiding principle in the heart.—*Unpublished Testimonies*, October 12, 1896.

1117.   Men are wanted at the Institute who will have the fear of Godbefore them, who can minister to sick minds, and keep prominent the health reform from a religious standpoint.—*Testimonies for the Church* 3:168.

1118.   If a man who assumes so grave a responsibility as that of a physician, sins against himself in not conforming to nature's laws, he will reap the consequences of his own doings, and abide her righteous decision, from which there can be no appeal.... His capabilities for doing good are lessened. He will lead others in the path his own feet are traveling. Hundreds will follow the example of one intemperate physician, feeling that they are safe in doing what the doctor does. And in the day of God he will meet the record of his own course, and be called to give an account for all the good he might have done, but did not do, because by his own voluntary act he weakened his physical and mental powers by selfish indulgence.—*Testimonies for the Church* 5:442.

THE PHYSICIAN'S RELATION TO HIS PATIENTS

1119.   He will not look upon his patient as a mere piece of human mechanism, but as a soul to be saved or lost.—*Testimonies for the Church* 5:445.

1120.   Unless the physicians can obtain the confidence of their patients,they can never help them.—*Testimonies for the Church* 3:79.

1121.   Never should a physician neglect his patients.—*Unpublished Testimonies.*

1122.   The work of the Christian physician does not end with healingthe maladies of the body; his efforts should extend to the diseases of the mind, to the saving of the soul. It may not be his duty, unless asked, to present any theoretical points of truth, but he may point his patients to Christ. The lessons of the divine Teacher are ever appropriate. He should call the attention of the repining to the ever fresh tokens of the love and care of God, to his wisdom and goodness as manifested in his created works. The mind can then be led through nature up to nature's God, and centered on the heaven which he has prepared for those who love him.—*Testimonies for the Church* 5:443.

1123.   Physicians who would be successful in the treatment of diseaseshould know how to minister to a diseased mind.—*Testimonies for the Church* 3:169.

1124.   It should be the work of the God-fearing physician to guide themind of patients to right principles. If patients are left to their own natural bias, they will indulge appetite, because it is a habit, at the expense of health and life.... True, their appetite craves unwholesome

articles of food, and the disuse of these things will be felt strongly. But the only right course to be pursued in these cases is to educate the conscience, to lay before the patients the effect of these things upon the physical and
mental powers to weaken the constitution and induce disease.—*Unpublished Testimonies*, February 1, 1888.

1125.　　　Let your influence be persuasive, binding people to your heartbecause you love Jesus, and because these precious souls are his purchased possession. This is a great work. If, by your Christ-like words and actions, you make impressions that will kindle in their hearts a hungering and thirsting after righteousness and truth, you are a co-laborer with Christ.... Enlighten their minds by means of talks and lectures, in regard to the effects of tea, coffee, and flesh meats, and thus lead them to a voluntary correction of their habits.—*Ibid*.

1126.　　　When he has gained the confidence of the afflicted by relievingtheir sufferings and bringing them back from the verge of the grave, he may teach them that disease is the result of sin; and that it is the fallen foe who seeks to allure them to health-and-soul-destroying practises. He may impress their minds with the necessity of denying self, and obeying the laws of life and health. In the minds of the young especially he may instil right principles.—*Testimonies for the Church* 5:444.

1127.　　　It seldom does any good to talk in a censuring manner to patientswho are diseased in body and mind. But few who have moved in the society of the world, and who view things from the worldling's standpoint, are prepared to have a statement of facts in regard to themselves presented before them. The truth even is not to be spoken at all times. There is a fit time and opportunity to speak, when words will not offend.—*Testimonies for the Church* 3:182.

1128.　　　The physician should be a strictly temperate man.... He knowsthat much of the suffering he seeks to relieve is the result of intemperance and other forms of selfish indulgence. He is called to attend young men, and men in the prime of life and in mature age, who have brought disease upon themselves by the use of tobacco. If he is an intelligent physician, he will be able to trace disease to its cause; but unless he is free from the use of tobacco himself, he will hesitate to put his finger upon the plague-spot, and faithfully unfold to his patients the *cause* of their sickness. He will fail to urge upon the young the necessity of overcoming the habit before it becomes fixed.... If he uses the weed himself, how can he present to the inexperienced youth its injurious effects, not only upon themselves, but upon those around them?—*Testimonies for the Church* 5:439.

1129.   How can he place the feet of others on the ladder of progress,while he himself is treading the downward way?—*Ibid.*, 197.

1130.   The practising physician will instruct those who do not understand how to preserve the strength and health they already have, and how to prevent disease by a wise use of heaven's remedies,—pure water, air, and diet.—*Testimonies for the Church* 1:490.

THE PHYSICIAN'S RELATION TO SOCIETY

1131.   If he does the work enjoined upon him by the Ruler of the universe, he will protest against iniquity in every form and in every degree; he will exert his authority and influence on the side of self-denial and strict, undeviating obedience to the just requirements of God.—*Testimonies for the Church* 5:441.

1132.   Such a physician will possess a heaven-born dignity, and will be apowerful agent for good in the world. Although he may not be appreciated by those who have no connection with God, yet he will be honored of Heaven. In God's sight he will be more precious than gold, even the gold of Ophir.—*Ibid.*

1133.   If you are a Christian and a competent physician, you are qualified to do tenfold more good as a missionary for God than if you were to go forth merely as a preacher of the word.—*The Medical Missionary*, 216.

1134.   While brought in contact with the world, you should be on yourguard that you do not seek too ardently for the applause of men, and live for their opinion.—*Testimonies for the Church* 4:568.

CHAPTER XL. - MEDICAL MISSIONARY WORK.

THE PRESENT NEED

1135.   The prosperity of the medical missionary work is in God's order.This work must be done; the truth must be carried to the highways and hedges.—*Special Testimony to Ministers and Workers*, No. 10, 30.

1136.   Why has it not been understood from the word of God that the work being done in medical missionary lines is a fulfilment of the scriptures? "Go out quickly into the streets and lanes of the city, and bring hither the poor, and the maimed, and the halt, and the blind.... Go out into the highways and hedges and compel them to come in, that my house may be filled."—*The Review and Herald*, May 25, 1897.

1137.   The educational work in medical missionary lines is a great advance step toward awakening man to a sense of his moral responsibilities.—*Unpublished Testimonies*, January 11, 1897.

1138.   As religious aggression subverts the liberties of our nation, thosewho would stand for freedom of conscience will be placed in unfavorable positions. For their own sakes they should, while they have opportunity, become intelligent in regard to disease, its causes, prevention, and cure. Those who do this will find a field of labor anywhere. There will be suffering ones, plenty of them, who
will need help, not only among those of our own faith, but largely among those who know not the truth.—*The Medical Missionary*, 216.

AIM TO EDUCATE

1139.   They need an education in the science of how to treat the sick,for this will give them a welcome in any place.—*Unpublished Testimonies*, December 20, 1896.

1140.   If we would elevate the moral standard of any country where wemay be called to go, we must begin by correcting the physical habits of the people.—*The Medical Missionary*, 216.

1141.   The Lord has given special light concerning our hygienic principles, which should be given to others.... Those who are in ignorance are to be educated how to live in accordance with pure principles; to practise those things that will preserve the body in a healthy condition.—*Unpublished Testimonies*, July 5, 1892.

1142.   The medical missionary can do a great amount of good by educating the people as to how to live.—*The Review and Herald*, June 18, 1895.

1143.   Rally workers who possess true missionary zeal, and let themgo forth to diffuse light and knowledge far and near. Let them take the living principles of health reform into communities that to a large degree are ignorant of how they should live.—*Unpublished Testimonies*, July, 1895.

OPEN FIELDS

1144.   The South is a field where medical missionary work can be oneof the greatest blessings.—*Special Testimonies for Ministers and Workers* 6:49.

1145.   Those who love Christ will do the works of Christ. They will goforth to seek and to save that which was lost. They will not shun those who are despised, and turn aside from the colored race.
They will teach them how to read and how to perform manual labor, educating them to till the soil and to follow trades of various kinds.... The work pointed out is a most needful missionary enterprise.—*The Review and Herald*, January 14, 1896.

1146.   The field for medical missionary work is open before us. Weare now beginning to comprehend the light given years ago,—that health reform principles would form an entering wedge to the introduction of religious principles. To voice the words of John, "Behold the Lamb of God that taketh away the sins of the world." Would that all our workers might be enlightened, so that they could work intelligently as medical missionaries, for such knowledge would serve as credentials to them in finding access to homes and families wherein to sow the seeds of truth. We want to feel as Christ felt,—that we cannot abandon helpless, suffering ones to the evils of orphanage, and ignorance, and want, and sin, and crime.—*Unpublished Testimonies*, June 13, 1895.

CHAPTER XLI. - CHRISTIAN HELP WORK.

CHRIST'S AMBASSADORS

1147.　　　This is the special work now before us.—*Testimonies for the Church* 2:34.

1148.　　　Our own human affections and sympathies are not to wane awayand become extinct, but through living connection with God our love is to deepen, our interest to become more intense, our efforts more successful in promoting the happiness of those around us.... Souls about us are perishing for sympathy which is never expressed.—*The Signs of the Times*, July 3, 1893.

1149.　　　The Lord has set before you another work, the work of extendingthe truth by establishing centers of interest in cities, and sending workers into the highways and hedges.—*Special Testimonies for Ministers and Workers* 10:6.

1150.　　　Many individuals might be laboring in towns and cities, visitingfrom house to house, becoming acquainted with families, entering into their social life, dining at their tables, entering into conversation by their firesides, dropping the precious seed of truth all along the line. As they exercise their talents, Christ will give them wisdom, and many believers will be found rejoicing in the knowledge of the truth as a result of their labors.—*The Review and Herald*, July 9, 1895.

1151.　　　The standard of truth may be raised by humble men and women,and the youth, and even
children, may be a blessing to others, by revealing what the truth has done for them. God will use the most feeble instruments if they are wholly submitted to him. He can work through them to reach souls to whom the minister could not obtain access. There are the highways and byways to be searched. With your Bible in your hand, with your heart warm and glowing with the love of God, you may go out and tell others your experience; you may make known to them the truth that has impressed your heart, praying with faith that God will make your efforts successful in their salvation. Communicate light, and you will have more light to communicate. Thus you may become laborers together with God.—*The Review and Herald*, January 12, 1897.

1152.	No verbal description could reveal God to the world. Our Saviour employed human faculties, for only by adopting these could he be comprehended by humanity. Only humanity could reach humanity. He lived out the character of God through the human body which God had prepared for him.... If our people would administer to other souls who need their help, they would themselves be ministered unto by the chief Shepherd, and thousands would be rejoicing in the fold who are now wandering in the desert. Let every soul go to work to seek and to save the lost, ... visiting the dark places of the earth where there are no churches.—*The Review and Herald*, June 25, 1895.

1153.	In the path which the poor, the neglected, the suffering, and thesorrowing must tread, Christ walked while on earth, taking upon him all the woes
which the afflicted must bear. His home was among the poor. His family was not distinguished by learning, riches, or position. For many years he worked at his trade as a carpenter.—*Special Instruction Relating to the Review and Herald Office*, and The Work in Battle Creek, 13.

1154.	Union with Christ means the dispensing of his blessings.—*The Signs of the Times*, September 19, 1895.

1155.	The angels look upon the distressed of God's family upon theearth, and they are prepared to co-operate with the human agent in relieving oppression and suffering. They will co-operate with those who "break every yoke," who "bring the poor that are cast out to thy house."—*The Review and Herald*, July 23, 1895.

OUR DUTY TO THE POOR

1156.	There is no case of need for which some one is not responsible.—*The Signs of the Times*, September 19, 1895.

1157.	As long as there are hungry ones in God's world to be fed, nakedones to be clothed, souls perishing for the bread and water of salvation, every unnecessary indulgence, every overplus of capital, pleads for the poor and needy.

1158.	The poor and the needy were objects of his [Christ's] specialattention. He sought to inspire with hope the most rough and unpromising, setting before them the idea that they might become blameless and harmless, attaining such a character as would make them manifest as the children of God among a crooked and perverse generation, among whom they would shine as lights in the world.—*The Signs of the Times*, August 6, 1896.

1159.	What sacrifice are we ready to make that we may find the lostpearl, and place it in the hands of
our Saviour? The cities are teeming with iniquity; Satan suggests that it is impossible to do any good within their borders, and so they are sadly neglected. But there are lost pearls there, whose value you cannot realize until you earnestly seek to find them. There might be one hundred workers where there is but one seeking diligently, prayerfully, and with intense interest to find the pearls that are buried in the rubbish of these cities.—*The Review and Herald*, April 21, 1896.

1160.	When heavenly intelligences see those who claim to be sonsand daughters of God putting forth Christlike efforts to help the erring, manifesting a tender, sympathetic spirit for the repentant and the fallen, angels press close to them, and bring to their remembrance the very words that will soothe and uplift the soul.... Jesus has given his precious life, his personal attention, to the least of God's little ones; and the angels that excel in strength encamp round about them that fear God. Then let us be on our guard, and never permit one contemptuous thought to occupy the mind in regard to one of the little ones of God. We should look after the erring with solicitude, and speak encouraging words to the fallen, and fear lest by some unwise action we shall turn them away from the pitying Saviour.... There is a large, a very large number of straying and lost sheep that have perished in the wild deserts of sin, simply because no one went after them to search for them and to bring them back to the fold. Jesus uses the illustration of a lost sheep to show the need of seeking after those who have wandered from him; for a sheep once lost will
never find its way back to the fold without help. It must be sought for, it must be carried back to the fold.—*The Review and Herald*, June 30, 1896.

OUR DUTY TO THE SICK

1161.	We shall find the footprints of Jesus by the sick-bed, by the sideof suffering humanity, in the hovels of the poverty stricken and distressed. We may walk in these footsteps, comforting the suffering, speaking words of hope and comfort to the despondent. Doing as Jesus did when he was upon earth, we shall walk in his blessed steps.—*The Review and Herald*, June 9, 1896.

1162.　　　When the sick and wretched applied to the Saviour for help, hefirst relieved the poor, suffering body before he attempted to administer to the darkened mind. When the present misery of the supplicant was removed, his thoughts could better be directed into the channel of light and truth.—*The Spirit of Prophecy* 2:226.

1163.　　　When he sent out his disciples, he commissioned them to healthe sick as well as to preach the gospel. When he sent forth the seventy, he commanded them to heal the sick, and next to preach that the kingdom of God had come nigh unto them. Their physical health was to be first cared for, in order that the way might be prepared for their minds to be reached by those truths which the apostles were to preach. The Saviour of the world devoted more time and labor to healing the afflicted of their maladies than to preaching. His last injunction to his apostles, his representatives upon the earth, was to lay hands on the sick that they might recover. When the Master shall come, he will commend those who have visited the sick and relieved the necessities of the afflicted.—*Testimonies for the Church* 4:225.

OUR DUTY TO ORPHANS AND THE AGED

1164.　　　There are multitudes of poor children who need care and protection. There are multitudes of aged people who are dependent upon others for the necessities of life. The Lord has not designed that these sufferers should be neglected.—*The Review and Herald*, March 17, 1896.

1165.　　　Let the condition of helpless little ones appeal to every mother'sheart, that she may put into exercise a mother's love for homeless orphan children. Their helplessness appeals to every God-given attribute in human nature.—*The Medical Missionary*, 321.

1166.　　　Do we expect that those who are lost will be faultless? If youwould do something to be approved of Heaven, take a child who needs help, who needs forbearance, and the grace of Christ. We choose associates because we think they will benefit us; but Christ sought association with those whom he could benefit.—*The Signs of the Times*, April 1, 1889.

1167.   Our happiness will be proportionate to our unselfish works, prompted by divine love; for in the plan of salvation God has appointed the law of action and reaction, making the work of beneficence in all its branches twice blessed.—*The Signs of the Times*, November 25, 1886.

1168.   No one can give place in his own heart and life for the streamof God's blessing to flow to others, without receiving in himself a rich reward.—*Thoughts from the Mount of Blessing*, 112.

CHAPTER XLII. - LESSONS FROM THE EXPERIENCE OF THE CHILDREN OF ISRAEL.

The Modern Church Repeating the History of Ancient

ISRAEL

1169.   The trials of the children of Israel, and their attitude just beforethe first coming of Christ, illustrate the position of the people of God in their experience before the second coming of Christ.—*The Review and Herald*, February 18, 1890.

1170.   Satan's snares are laid for us as verily as they were laid for thechildren of Israel just prior to their entrance into the land of Canaan. We are repeating the history of that people.—*Testimonies for the Church* 5:160.

1171.   Their history should be a solemn warning to us. We need neverexpect that when the Lord has light for his people, Satan will stand calmly by and make no effort to prevent them from receiving it. Let us beware that we do not refuse the light God sends, because it does not come in a way to please us.... If there are any who do not see and accept the light themselves, let them not stand in the way of others.—*Testimonies for the Church* 5:728.

1172.   "I call heaven and earth to record this day against you, that I haveset before you life and death, blessing and cursing; therefore choose life, that both thou and thy seed may live; that thou mayest love the Lord thy God, and that thou mayest obey his voice, and that thou mayest cleave unto him; for he is thy life, and the length of thy days; that thou mayest dwell in the land which the Lord sware unto thy fathers, to Abraham, to Isaac, and to Jacob, to give them."

This song was not historical but prophetic. While it recounted the wonderful dealings of God with his people in the past, it also foreshadowed the great events of the future, the final victory of the faithful when Christ shall come the second time in power and glory.— *Patriarchs and Prophets*, 467.

1173.   The apostle Paul plainly states that the experience of the Israelitesin their travels has been recorded for the benefit of those living in this age of the world, those upon whom the ends of the world are come. We do not consider that our dangers are any less than those of the Hebrews, but greater.—*Testimonies for the Church* 3:358.

GOD'S DEALING WITH ISRAEL

1174. God in mercy called them out from the Egyptians, that they might worship him without hindrance or restraint. He wrought for them in the way by miracles, he proved and tried them by bringing them into strait places. After the wonderful dealings of God with them, and their deliverance so many times, they murmured when tried or proved by him. Their language was, "Would to God we had died by the hand of the Lord in the land of Egypt." They lusted for the leeks and onions there.... Said the angel, "Ye have done worse than they."—*Testimonies for the Church* 1:128.

THE INFLUENCE OF FLESH FOOD UPON MIND AND BODY

1175.   How frequently ancient Israel rebelled, and how often they werevisited with judgments, and thousands slain, because they would not heed the commands of God who had chosen them! The Israel of God in these last days are in constant danger of mingling with the world, and losing all signs of being the chosen people of God.... Shall we provoke him as did ancient Israel? Shall we bring his wrath upon us by departing from him, and mingling with the world and following the abominations of the nations around us? ... The same injunctions that rested upon ancient Israel rest upon God's people now, to be separate from the world. The great Head of the church has not changed. The experience of Christians in these days is much like the travels of ancient Israel. Please read 1 Corinthians 10, especially from the 6th to the 15th verse: "Now these things were our examples, to the intent we should not lust after evil things, as they also lusted. Neither be ye idolaters, as were some of them; as it is written, The people sat down to eat and drink, and rose up to play.... Neither let us tempt Christ, as some of them also tempted, and were destroyed of serpents. Neither murmur ye, as some of them also murmured, and were destroyed of the destroyer."—*Testimonies for the Church* 1:283.

1176.   The Lord intends to bring his people back to live upon simplefruits, vegetables, and grains. He led the children of Israel into the wilderness, where they could not get a flesh diet; and he gave them the bread of heaven. "Man did eat angels' food." But they craved the flesh pots of Egypt,
and mourned and cried for flesh, notwithstanding the promise of the Lord that if they would submit to his will, he would carry them into the land of Canaan, and establish them there, a pure holy, happy people, and there should not be a feeble one in all their tribes; for he would take away all sickness from among them. But although they had a plain "Thus saith the Lord," they mourned and wept, and murmured and complained, until the Lord was wroth with them. Because they were so determined to have the flesh of dead animals, he gave them the very diet that he had withheld from them. The Lord would have given them flesh from the first had it been essential to their health; but he had created and redeemed them, and led them the long journey in the wilderness, to educate, discipline and train them in correct habits. The Lord understood what influence flesh eating has upon the human system. He would have a people that would, in their physical appearance, bear the divine credentials, notwithstanding their long journey.—*Unpublished Testimonies*, November 5, 1896.

WARNINGS FROM THE EXPERIENCE OF ISRAEL

1177.   The religion of many among us will be the religion of apostate
Israel, because they love their own way, and forsake the way of the
Lord.—*The Signs of the Times*, November 3, 1890.

1178.   Because of Israel's disobedience and departure from
God, theywere allowed to be brought into close places, and to suffer
adversity; their enemies were permitted to make war with them, to
humble them and lead them to seek God in their trouble and distress.—
Testimonies for the Church 2:106.

1179.   "Moreover, brethren, I would not that ye should be
ignorant,how that all our fathers were under the cloud, and all passed
through the sea; and were all baptized unto Moses in the cloud and in
the sea; and did all eat the same spiritual meat; and did all drink the
same spiritual drink; for they drank of that spiritual Rock that followed
them: and that Rock was Christ. But with many of them God was not
well pleased: for they were overthrown in the wilderness." The
experience of Israel, referred to in the above words by the apostle, and
as recorded in the 105th and 106th psalms, contains lessons of warning
that the people of God in these last days especially need to study. I urge
that these chapters be read at least once every week.—*Special Testimony
to Ministers and Workers to Battle Creek Church*, 43.

1180.   With the history of the children of Israel before us, let us
takeheed, and not be found committing the same sins, following in the
same way of unbelief and rebellion.—*The Review and Herald*, April 18,
1893.

CHAPTER XLIII. - GOD IN NATURE.

THE SOURCE OF POWER

1181. Nature is a power, but the God of nature is unlimited in power. His works interpret his character. Those who judge him from his handiworks, and not from the suppositions of great men, will see his presence in everything. They behold his smile in the glad sunshine, and his love and care for man in the rich fields of autumn. Even the adornments of the earth, as seen in the grass of living green, the lovely flowers of every hue, and the lofty and varied trees of the forest, testify to the tender, fatherly care of our God, and to his desire to make his children happy.—*The Signs of the Times*, March 13, 1884.

OBJECT OF EDUCATION

1182.   The foundation of all right education is a knowledge of God....The first and most important lesson to be impressed upon young minds is the duty of regulating the life by the principles of the word of God.... The true object of education is to fit us for this service by developing and bringing into active exercise every faculty that we possess.—*The Signs of the Times*, March 20, 1884.

1183.   The only safety for the people now is to feel the importance ofcombining religious culture with general education, that we may escape the curse of unsanctified knowledge. Every effort should be made in the education of youth to impress their
minds with the loveliness and power of the truth as it is in Jesus. When the veil shall be removed which separates time from eternity, then will come to many minds the clear perception of the fallacy of human wisdom in comparison with the sure word of prophecy. All true science leads to harmony with and obedience to God.—*Unpublished Testimonies*.

RELATION OF SCIENCE AND REVELATION

1184. God is the foundation of everything. All true science is in harmony with his works, all true education leads to obedience to his government. Science opens new wonders to our view; she soars high and explores new depths; but she brings nothing from her research that conflicts with divine revelation. Ignorance may seek to support false views of God by appeals to science; but the book of nature and the written word do not disagree; each sheds light on the other. Rightly understood, they make us acquainted with God and his character by teaching us something of the wise and beneficent laws through which he works. We are thus led to adore his holy name, and to have an intelligent trust in his word.—*The Signs of the Times*, March 20, 1884.

THE BIBLE A TEST

1185.   Many, when they find themselves incapable of measuring theCreator and his works by their own imperfect knowledge of science, doubt the existence of God and attribute infinite power to nature. These persons have lost the simplicity of faith, and are removed far from God in mind and spirit. There should be a settled faith in the divinity of God's holy word. The Bible is not to be tested by men's ideas of science, but science is to be brought to the test of this unerring standard. When the Bible
makes statements of facts in nature, science may be compared with the written word, and a correct understanding of both will always prove them to be in harmony. One does not contradict the other. All truths, whether in nature or revelation, agree. Scientific research will open to the minds of the really wise, vast fields of thought and information. They will see God in his works, and will praise him. He will be to them first and best, and the mind will be centered upon him.—*The Signs of the Times*, March 13, 1884.

1186.   Nature is not God, nor ever was God. God is in nature, the voiceof nature testifies of God, but nature is not God. It only bears testimony to God's power as his created works. There is a personal God, the Father; there is a personal Christ, the Son.—*Unpublished Testimonies*, July 3, 1898.

1187.   God has permitted a flood of light to be poured upon the world indiscoveries in science and art; but when professedly scientific men lecture and write upon these subjects from a merely human standpoint, they will assuredly come to wrong conclusions. The greatest minds, if not guided by the word of God in their research, become bewildered in their attempts to investigate the relations of science and revelation. The Creator and his works are beyond their comprehension; and because they cannot explain these by natural laws, Bible history is considered unreliable. Those who doubt the reliability of the records of the Old and New Testaments will be led to go a step farther, and doubt the existence of God; and then, having let go their anchor, they are left to beat about upon the rocks of infidelity.

Moses wrote under the guidance of the Spirit of God,

and a correct theory of geology will never claim discoveries that cannot be reconciled with his statements. The idea that many stumble over, that God did not create matter when he brought the world into existence, limits the power of the Holy One of Israel.—*The Signs of the Times*, March 13, 1884.

1188.   Before the fall of Adam, not a cloud rested on the minds of our first parents to obscure their clear perception of the divine character of God. They were perfectly conformed to the will of God. A beautiful light, the light of God, surrounded them. Nature was their lesson book. The Lord instructed them in regard to the natural world, and then left with them this open book, that they might behold beauty in every object upon which their eyes should rest. The Lord visited the holy pair, and instructed them through the works of his hands.

The beauties of nature are an expression of the love of God for human intelligences, and in the garden of Eden the existence of God was demonstrated in the objects of nature that surrounded our first parents. Every tree planted in the garden spoke to them, saying that the invisible things of God were clearly seen, being understood by the things which were made, even his eternal power and Godhead.

But while thus God could be discerned in nature, this affords no solid argument in favor of a perfect knowledge of God being revealed in nature to Adam and his posterity after the fall. Nature could convey her lessons to man in his innocence; but sin and transgression brought a blight upon nature, and intervened between nature and nature's God. Had man never disobeyed his Creator, had he remained

in his state of perfect rectitude, he could have understood and known God. But when man disobeyed God, he gave evidence that he believed the words of an apostate rather than the words of God. He was told by the enemy to eat of the tree of knowledge. God had said, "Ye shall not eat of it, ... lest ye die." But Satan declared that by eating of it man would be exalted to an equality with God.

Adam and Eve listened to the voice of the tempter, and sinned against God. The light, the garments of heavenly innocence, departed from these tried, deceived souls, and in parting with the garments of innocence, they drew about them the dark robes of ignorance of God. The clear and perfect light of innocence which had hitherto surrounded them, had lightened everything which they had approached, but deprived of that heavenly light, the posterity of Adam could no longer trace the character of God in his created works. Therefore, after the fall, nature was not the only teacher of man. In order that the world might not remain in darkness, in eternal, spiritual night, the God of nature must meet man through Jesus Christ. The Son of God came to the world as a revelation of the Father. He was "that true light, which lighteth every man that cometh into the world."

The most difficult and humiliating lesson which man has to learn, if he is kept by the power of God, is his own inefficiency in depending upon human wisdom, and the sure failure of his own efforts to read nature correctly. Sin has obscured his vision, and he cannot interpret nature without placing it above God.—*Unpublished Testimonies*, July 3, 1898. 1189. Many teach that matter possesses vital power. They hold that certain properties are imparted to matter, and it is then left to act through its own inherent power; and that the operations of nature are carried on in harmony with fixed laws, that God himself cannot interfere with. This is false science, and is sustained by nothing in the word of God. Nature is not self-acting; she is the servant of her Creator. God does not annul his laws nor work contrary to them; but he is continually using them as his instruments. Nature testifies of an intelligence, a presence, an active agency, that works in, and through, and above her laws. There is in nature the continual working of the Father and the Son. Said Christ, "My Father worketh hitherto, and I work."

God has finished his creative work, but his energy is still exerted in upholding the objects of his creation. It is not because the mechanism that was once been set in motion continues its work by its own inherent energy that the pulse beats, and breath follows breath; but every breath, every pulsation of the heart, is an evidence of the all-pervading care of

Him in whom we live and have our being. It is not because of inherent power that year by year the earth produces her bounties, and continues her motion around the sun. The hand of God guides the planets, and keeps them in position in their orderly march through the heavens. It is through his power that vegetation flourishes, that the leaves appear and the flowers bloom. His word controls the elements, and by him the valleys are made fruitful. He covers

the heavens with clouds, and prepares rain for the earth; he "maketh grass to grow upon the mountains." "He giveth snow like wool; he scattereth the hoarfrost like ashes." "When he uttereth his voice, there is a multitude of waters in the heavens, and he causeth the vapors to ascend from the ends of the earth; he maketh lightnings with rain, and bringeth forth the wind out of his treasures."—*The Signs of the Times*, March 20, 1884.

OUR ONLY SECURITY

1190.   All the systems of philosophy devised by men have led to confusion and shame when God has not been recognized and honored. To lose faith in God is terrible. Prosperity cannot be a great blessing to nations or individuals, when once faith in his word is lost. Nothing is truly great but that which is eternal in its tendencies. Truth, justice, mercy, purity, and the love of God are imperishable. When men possess these qualities, they are brought into close relationship to God, and are candidates for the highest exaltation to which the race can aspire. They will disregard human praise, and will be superior to disappointment, weariness, the strife of tongues, and contentions for supremacy.

He whose soul is imbued with the Spirit of God will learn the lesson of confiding trust. Taking the written word as his counselor and guide, he will find in science an aid to understand God, but he will not become exalted till, in his blind self-conceit, he is a fool in his ideas of God.—*The Signs of the Times*, March 13, 1884.

1191.   God will not dwell with those who reject his truth; for all whodisregard truth dishonor its Author. Of every house that has not Jesus for an

abiding guest, he says when he withdraws his presence, "Your house is left unto you desolate." How can those who are destitute of divine enlightenment have correct ideas of God's plans and ways? They either deny him altogether, and ignore his existence, or they circumscribe his power by their own finite, worldly-wise views and opinions. Those who are connected with the infinite God are the only ones who can make a proper use of their knowledge or of the talents entrusted to them by the omniscient Creator. No man can ever truly excel in knowledge and influence unless he is connected with the God of wisdom and power.—*Unpublished*

Testimonies.

1192.   The real evidence of a living God is not merely a theory; it is the conviction that God has written in our hearts, illuminated and explained by his word. It is the living power in his created works, seen by a sanctified eye. The precious faith inspired of God gives strength and nobility of character. The natural powers are enlarged because of holy obedience. The life which we live by faith on the Son of God is a series of triumphs, not always seen and understood by the interested parties, but with results reaching far into the future, where we shall see and know as we are known.—*Unpublished Testimonies.*

SCIENCE FALSELY SO CALLED

1193.   Many are so intent upon excluding God from the exercise ofsovereign will and power in the established order of the universe, that they demean man, the noblest of his creatures. The theories and speculations of philosophy would make us believe that man has come by slow degrees, not merely from a savage state, but from the very lowest form of the
brute creation. They destroy man's dignity because they will not admit God's miraculous power.

God has illuminated the human intellect, and poured a flood of light on the world in the discoveries of art and science. But those who view these from a merely human standpoint will most assuredly come to wrong conclusions. The thorns of error, skepticism, and infidelity are disguised by being covered with the garments of philosophy and science. Satan has devised this ingenious manner of winning the soul away from the living God, away from the truth and religion. He exalts nature above nature's Creator.—*Unpublished Testimonies.*

1194.   Some may suppose that these grand things in the natural worldare God, but they are not God; they but show forth his glory. The ancient philosophers prided themselves upon their superior knowledge. But let us read the inspired apostle's understanding of the matter: "Professing themselves to be wise, they became fools, and changed the glory of the uncorruptible God into an image made like to corruptible man, and to birds, and fourfooted beasts, and creeping things.... Who changed the truth of God into a lie, and worshiped and served the creature more than the Creator, who is blessed forever."

In its human wisdom the world knows not God. Its wise men gather an imperfect knowledge of God through his created works, and then in their foolishness exalt nature and the laws of nature above nature's God. Nature is an open book which reveals God. All who are attracted to nature may behold

in it the God that created them. But those who have not a knowledge of God, in their acceptance of the revelation God has made of himself in Christ, will obtain only an imperfect knowledge of God in nature. This knowledge, so far from giving elevated conceptions of God, so far from elevating the mind, the soul, the heart, and bringing the whole being into conformity to the will of God, will make men idolaters. Professing to be wise, they become as fools.—*Unpublished Testimonies*, July 3, 1898.

THE INFINITE GOD

1195.   Men of the greatest intellect cannot understand the mysteriesof Jehovah as revealed in nature. Divine inspiration asks many questions which the most profound scholar cannot answer. These questions were not asked supposing that we could answer them, but to call our attention to the deep mysteries of God, and to make men know that their wisdom is limited, that in the common things of daily life there are mysteries past the comprehension of finite minds; that the judgment and purposes of God are past finding out, his wisdom unsearchable. If he reveals himself to man, it is by shrouding himself in the thick cloud of mystery. God's purpose is to conceal more of himself than he makes known to men. Could men fully understand the ways and works of God, they would not then believe him to be the infinite one. He is not to be comprehended by man in his wisdom, and reasons, and purposes. "His ways are past finding out." His love can never be explained upon natural principles. If this could be done, we would not feel that we could trust him with the interests of our souls. Skeptics refuse to believe

because with their finite minds they cannot comprehend the infinite power by which God reveals himself to men. Even the mechanism of the human body cannot be fully understood; it presents mysteries that baffle the most intelligent. Yet because human science cannot in its research explain the ways and works of the Creator, men will doubt the existence of God, and ascribe infinite power to nature. God's existence, his character, his law, are facts that all the reasoning of men of the highest attainments cannot controvert. They deny the claims of God and neglect the interests of their souls, because they cannot understand his ways and works. Yet God is ever seeking to instruct finite men, that they may exercise faith in him, and trust themselves wholly in his hands. Every drop of rain or flake of snow, every spear of grass, every leaf and flower and shrub, testifies of God. These little things, so common around us, teach the lesson that nothing is beneath the notice of the infinite God, nothing is too small for his attention.—*Unpublished Testimonies*.

1196.   "Consider the lilies of the field, how they grow." The gracefulforms and delicate hues of the plants and flowers may be copied by human skill; but what touch can impart life to even one flower or blade of grass? Every wayside blossom owes its being to the same power that set the starry worlds on high. Through all created things thrills one pulse of life from the great heart of God.... He who has given you life, knows your need of food to sustain it. He who created the body is not unmindful of your need of raiment. Will not he who

has bestowed the greater gift, bestow also what is needed to make it complete?—*Thoughts from the Mount of Blessing*, 136.

THE MYSTERY OF GOD

1197.   God is to be acknowledged more from what he does not reveal ofhimself than from that which is open to our limited comprehension. If men could comprehend the unsearchable wisdom of God, and could explain that which he has done or can do, they would no longer reverence him or fear his power. In divine revelation God has given to men mysteries that are incomprehensible, to command their faith. This must be so. If the ways and works of God could be explained by finite minds, he would not stand as supreme. Men may be ever searching, ever inquiring, ever learning, and yet there is an infinity beyond. The light is shining, ever shining with increasing brightness upon our pathway, if we but walk in its divine rays. But there is no darkness so dense, so impenetrable, as that which follows the rejection of Heaven's light, through whatever source it may come.

Can men comprehend God?—No. They may speculate in regard to his way and works, but only as finite beings can.—*Unpublished Testimonies.*

1198.　　Those who think they can obtain a knowledge of God aside from his Representative, whom the word declares is "the express image of his person," will need to become fools in their own estimation before they can be wise. Christ came as a personal Saviour to the world. He represented a personal God. He ascended on high as a personal Saviour, and will come again as he ascended into heaven, a personal Saviour. It is impossible to gain a perfect knowledge of God from nature, for nature itself is imperfect. A curse, a blight, is upon it. Yet the things of nature, marred as they are by the blight of sin, inculcate truths regarding the skilful Master Artist. One omnipotent Power, great in goodness in mercy, and in love, has created the earth, and even in its blighted state much that is beautiful remains. Nature's voice speaks, saying that there is a God back of nature, but it does not, in its imperfections, represent God. Nature cannot reveal the character of God in his moral perfection.—*Unpublished Testimonies*, July 3, 1898

BEACON LIGHTS

1199. The Bible is the most comprehensive and the most instructive history that men possess. It came fresh from the Fountain of eternal truth; and a divine hand has preserved its purity through all the ages. Its bright rays shine into the far-distant past, where human research seeks vainly to penetrate. In God's word only we find an authentic account of creation. Here we behold the power that laid the foundation of the earth, and that stretched out the heavens. In this word only can we find a history of our race unsullied by human prejudice or human pride....

In the varied scenes of nature also are lessons of divine wisdom for all who have learned to commune with God. The pages that opened in undimmed brightness to the gaze of the first pair in Eden, bear now a shadow. A blight has fallen upon the fair creation. And yet, wherever we turn are traces of primal loveliness. Wherever we may turn, we hear the voice of God, and behold his handiwork.

From the solemn roll of the deep-toned thunder and old ocean's ceaseless roll, to the glad songs that make the forests vocal with melody, nature's ten thousand voices speak his praise. In earth and air and sky, with their marvelous tint and color, varying in gorgeous contrast or softly blended in harmony, we behold his glory. The everlasting hills tell us of his power. The trees wave their green banners in the sunlight, and point us upward to their creator. The flowers that gem the earth with their beauty, whisper to us of Eden, and fill us with longings for its unfading loveliness. The living green that carpets the brown earth, tells us of God's care for the humblest of his creatures. The caves of the sea and the depths of the earth reveal his treasures. He who placed the pearls in the ocean, and the amethyst and chrysolite among the rocks, is a lover of the beautiful. The sun rising in the heavens is the representative of him who is the life and light of all that he has made. All the brightness and beauty that adorn the earth and light up the heavens, speak of God.

AN UNEXPLORED FIELD

Shall we, in the enjoyment of the gifts, forget the Giver? Let them rather lead us to contemplate his goodness and his love. Let all that is beautiful in our earthly home remind us of the crystal river and green fields, the waving trees and the living fountains, the shining city and the white-robed singers, of our heavenly home,—that world of beauty which no artist can picture, no mortal tongue describe. "Eye hath not seen, nor ear heard, neither have entered

into the heart of man, the things which God hath prepared for them that love him."

To dwell forever in this home of the blest, to bear in soul, body, and spirit, not the dark traces of sin and the curse, but the perfect likeness of our Creator, and through ceaseless ages to advance in wisdom, in knowledge and holiness, ever exploring new fields of thought, ever finding new wonders and new glories, ever increasing in capacity to know and to enjoy and to love, and knowing that there is still beyond us joy and love and wisdom infinite,—such is the object to which the Christian hope is pointing, for which Christian education is preparing. To secure this education, and to aid others to secure it, should be the object of the Christian's life.—*The Review and Herald*, July 11, 1882.

CHAPTER XLIV. - THE SPIRIT-FILLED LIFE.

THE OFFICE OF THE HOLY SPIRIT

1200.   The office of the Holy Spirit is to take the truth from the sacredpage, where God has placed it for the benefit of every soul whom he has created, and stamp that truth upon the mind.—*Unpublished Testimonies*, February 5, 1896.

1201.   The Spirit of God has unconfined range of the heavenly universe;and it is not in the province of finite human minds to limit its power or prescribe its operations.—*The Review and Herald*, August 25, 1896.

1202.   The juices of the vine, ascending from the root, are diffused tothe branches, sustaining growth and producing blossoms and fruit. So the life-giving power of the Holy Spirit, proceeding from Christ, and imparted to every disciple, pervades the soul, renews the motives and affections and even the most secret thoughts, and brings forth the precious fruit of holy deeds.—*Sketches from the Life of Paul*, 131.

1203.   Christ is our advocate, pleading in our behalf. The Spirit pleadswithin us. Then let us show perfect trust in our Leader, and not inquire of false guides.—*Unpublished Testimonies*, October 19, 1894.

1204.   The grace of God takes men as they are, and works as an educator, using every principle on which an all-sided education depends.

The steady influence of the grace of God trains the soul after

Christ's methods, and every fierce passion, every defective trait of character, is worked upon the molding influence of the Spirit of Christ, until the man has a new motive power, and becomes filled with the Holy Spirit of God, after the likeness of the divine similitude.—*Unpublished Testimonies*, March 16, 1896.

1205.   The Holy Spirit is the source of all power, and works as a living,active agent in the new life created in the soul. The Holy Spirit is to be in us a divine indweller.—*The Review and Herald*, June 29, 1897.

1206.   Jesus conveys the circulating vitality of a pure and sanctifiedChrist-like love through every part of our human nature. When this love is expressed in the character, it reveals to all those with whom we associate that it is possible for God to be formed within, the hope of glory.—*Unpublished Testimonies*, June 21, 1897.

1207.   Christ is to live in his human agents, and work through theirfaculties, and act through their capabilities. Their will must be submitted to his will, they must act with his Spirit, that it may be no more they that live, but Christ that liveth in them.—*The Signs of the Times*, October 3, 1892.

1208.   Wherever we go, we bear the abiding presence of the One so dearto us; for we abide in Christ by a living faith. He is abiding in our hearts by our individual, appropriating faith. We have the companionship of the divine Jesus, and as we realize his presence, our thoughts are brought into captivity to him. Our experience in divine things will be in proportion to the vividness of our sense of his companionship.—*The Signs of the Times*, September 3, 1896.

1209.   It is not you that work the Holy Spirit, but the Holy Spirit must work you. There is a winning, compelling power in the gospel of Jesus Christ. It is the Holy Spirit that makes the truth impressive.—*Special Testimony to Ministers and Workers*, No. 03, 14.

1210.   To those who truly love God the Holy Spirit will reveal truthsthat have faded from the mind, and will also reveal truths that are entirely new.—*The Review and Herald*, August 17, 1897.

1211.   Each one must fight his own battle against self. Heed the teachings of the Holy Spirit. If this is done, they will be repeated again and again, until the impressions are, as it were, "lead in the rock forever."—*Special Testimonies for Ministers and Workers* 7:39.

1212.   As we give ourselves wholly to Christ, our countenances willreflect his image. They will be purified, sanctified, and ennobled by his grace.—*Unpublished Testimonies*, June 27, 1897.

1213.   There is no limit to the usefulness of those who put self to oneside, make room for the working of the Holy Spirit upon their hearts, and live lives wholly sanctified to the service of God, enduring the necessary discipline imposed by the Lord without complaining or fainting by the way.—*Special Testimonies On Education*, 120.

CHARACTERISTICS OF A SURRENDERED LIFE

1214.   The whole person is privileged to bear a decided testimony inevery line, in feature, in temper, in words, in character, that the service of God is good.—*Unpublished Testimonies*, November 6, 1897.

1215.   As you surrender to the truth, you will reproduce the truth, a living epistle, known and read of all men.—*Unpublished Testimonies*, October 27, 1897.

1216.   As God works in the heart, and man surrenders his will to God,and co-operates with God, he works out in the life what God works in by the Holy Spirit, and there is harmony between the purpose of the heart and the practise of the life.—*The Signs of the Times*, March 20, 1893.

1217.   When Christ comes into the soul, he brings the calmness of heaven.—*Unpublished Testimonies*, October 27, 1897..

1218.   The Holy Spirit is his representative, and it works to effect transformations so wonderful that angels look upon them with astonishment and joy. *The Signs of the Times*, May 20, 1896.

1219.   When self is merged in Christ, there will be such a display of hispower as will melt and subdue hearts.—*Unpublished Testimonies*, April 27, 1898.

1220.   It is the Spirit of God that quickens the lifeless faculties of thesoul to appreciate heavenly things, and attracts the affections toward God and the truth. Without the presence of Jesus in the heart, religious service is only dead, cold formalism. The longing desire for communion with God soon ceases when the Spirit of God is grieved from us; but when Christ is within us the hope of glory, we are constantly directed to think and act in reference to the glory of God. The question will arise, "Will this do honor to Jesus? Will this be approved by him?"—*The Review and Herald*, April 17, 1888.

1221. The Bible is full of knowledge, and all who come to its studywith a heart to understand will find the mind enlarged and the faculties strengthened to comprehend these precious, far-reaching truths. The Holy Spirit will impress them upon the mind and soul.—*Special Testimonies On Education*, 153.

1222. As the works of God are studied, the Holy Spirit flashes conviction into the mind. It is not the conviction which logical reasoning produces; but unless the mind has become too dark to know God, the eye too dim to see him, the ear too dull to hear his voice, a deeper meaning is grasped, and the sublime, spiritual truths of the written word are impressed on the heart.—*Special Testimonies On Education*, 59.

1223. If we consent, He can and will so identify himself with our thoughts and aims, so blend our hearts and minds into conformity with his will, that when obeying him, we shall but carry out our own impulses. The will, refined and sanctified, will find its highest delight in doing his service.—*The Signs of the Times*, November 19, 1896.

CONDITIONS FAVORABLE TO GROWTH

1224. Real piety begins when all compromise with sin is at an end.—*Thoughts from the Mount of Blessing*, 125.

1225. He who yields himself most unreservedly to the influence of theHoly Spirit is best qualified to do acceptable service for the Master.—*The Review and Herald*, July 9, 1895.

1226. Your energies are required to co-operate with God. Without this,if it were possible to force upon you with a hundredfold greater intensity the influences of the Spirit of God, it would not make you a Christian, a fit subject for heaven. The stronghold of Satan would not be broken. There must be the willing and the doing on the part of the receiver. There must be an action, represented as coming out from the world and being separate. There must be a doing of the words of Christ. The soul must be emptied of self, that Christ may pour his Spirit into the vacuum. Christ must be chosen as the heavenly guest. The will must be placed on the side of God's will. Then there is a new heart, and new, holy resolves. It is Jesus enthroned in the soul that makes every action easy in his service.—*The Signs of the Times*, December 28, 1891.

1227.   Christians must practise temperance in all things. We have noright to neglect the body and strength and soul and mind, which are to be given to the Lord in consecrated service. We are made up of body and senses, as well as of conscience and affections. Our impulses and passions have their seat in the body; therefore there must be no abuse of any of our organs.—*Unpublished Testimonies*, September 27, 1896.

1228.   God desires that we shall have a care, a regard, and an appreciation for our bodies,—the temple of the Holy Spirit. He desires that the body shall be kept in the most healthy condition possible, and under the most spiritual influence, that the talents he has given us may be used to render perfect service to him.—*Unpublished Testimonies*, September 27, 1896.

1229.   He shall shine through their minds as the light of the world. "Toas many as received him, to them gave he power to become the sons of God, even to them that believed on his name." But in order that this may be, God demands that every intellectual and physical capability be offered as a consecrated oblation to him.—*Unpublished Testimonies*, July 6, 1896.

1230.   We are to keep advancing heavenward, developing a solid religious character. The measure of the Holy Spirit we receive will be proportionate to the measure of our desire and faith exercised to get it, and the use we shall make of the light and knowledge that shall be given us. We shall be entrusted with the Holy Spirit according to our capacity to receive it and our ability to impart it to others.—*The Review and Herald*, May 5, 1896.

1231.   The more studiously the intellect is cultivated, the more effectively it can be used in the service of God, if it is placed under the control of his Spirit.—*Special Testimonies On Education*, 57.

1232.   If men will receive the ministration of his Holy Spirit, the richestgift God can bestow, they will impart blessings to all who are connected with them.—*Unpublished Testimonies*, July 6, 1896.

HINDRANCES TO SPIRITUAL GROWTH

1233.　　　The wilful commission of a known sin silences the witnessingvoice of the Spirit, and separates the soul from God. Jesus cannot abide in the heart that disregards the divine law. God will honor those only who honor him.—*The Signs of the Times*, June 19, 1884.

1234.　　　No one need look upon the sin against the Holy Ghost as something mysterious and indefinable The sin against the Holy Ghost is the sin of persistent refusal to respond to the invitations to repent.—*The Review and Herald*, June 29, 1897.

1235.　　　Let all examine their own hearts, to see if they are not cherishingthat which is a positive injury to them, and in the place of opening the door of the heart to let Jesus, the Sun of Righteousness, in, are complaining of the dearth of the Spirit of God. Let these search for their idols, and cast them out. Let them cut away from every unhealthful indulgence in eating and drinking. Let them bring their daily practise into harmony with nature's laws. By
doing, as well as believing, an atmosphere will be created about the soul that will be a savor of life unto life.—*Unpublished Testimonies*, August 25, 1897.

1236.　　　God cannot let his Holy Spirit rest upon those who are enfeeblingthemselves by gluttony.—*The Review and Herald*, May 8, 1883.

1237.　　　The brain nerves which communicate with the entire system are the only medium through which Heaven can communicate with man, and affect his inmost life. Whatever disturbs the circulation of the electric currents in the nervous system, lessens the strength of the vital powers, and the result is a deadening of the sensibilities of the mind.—*Testimonies for the Church* 2:347.

1238.　　　Why should we not show the attractive part of our faith? Whyshould we go like a crippled band of mourners, groaning all the way along our journey to our Father's house?—*Unpublished Testimonies*, January 12, 1898.

Made in the USA
Middletown, DE
23 August 2024

59633190R00126